A Kayaker's Guide to
Lake Champlain

Exploring the New York, Vermont & Quebec Shores

Catherine Frank & Margaret Holden

BLACK·DOME

Published by

Black Dome Press Corp.
1011 Route 296, Hensonville, New York 12439
www.blackdomepress.com
Tel: (518) 734–6357

First Edition Paperback 2009

Library of Congress Cataloging-in-Publication Data

Frank, Catherine L.

A kayaker's guide to Lake Champlain : exploring the New York, Vermont & Quebec shores /
Catherine L. Frank and Margaret D. Holden.— 1st ed. paperback.

p. cm.

Includes bibliographical references and index.

ISBN 978-1-883789-65-7 (trade pbk.)

1. Kayaking—Champlain, Lake, Region—Guidebooks. 2. Champlain, Lake, Region—Guidebooks. I. Holden, Margaret Dodge, 1938- II. Title.

GV776.C45F73 2009

797.122'40974754--dc22

2009024959

Outdoor recreational activities are by their very nature potentially hazardous and contain risk. Small craft on Lake Champlain must exercise extreme caution. See "Caution and
Safety Tips: Pause before Jumping In," beginning on page 3.

Front cover: Photograph by Douglas Hyde.

Paddle maps and chapter maps by Cathy Frank. (The maps are based on a reproduction of
U.S. Government NOAA charts and have been reduced in size for the purposes of this book.
They are not meant to be a substitute for the full-sized charts.)

Illustrations and Lake Champlain map by Elayne Sears © 2009.

Design: Toelke Associates, www.toelkeassociates.com

Printed in the USA

10 9 8 7 6 5 4 3 2 1

Dedication

To our grandchildren Georgia, Mattie and Eliza,

and Eli and Amara

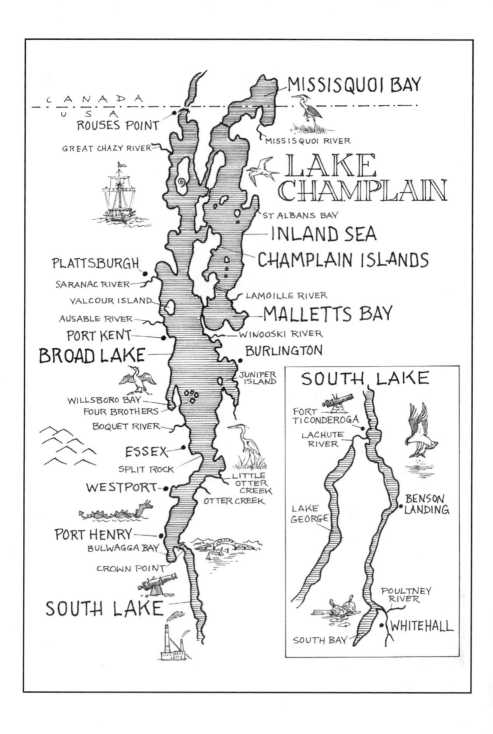

Contents

Foreword

Cathy Frank and Margy Holden have not been completely honest with us. They claim to have written a kayaker's guide to Lake Champlain, but after reviewing their manuscript to prepare this foreword I'm afraid I must cry "foul."

The manuscript I have been reviewing is much more than just a kayaker's guide and is certainly not just a guide for paddlers. This is one of the best all-around, multifaceted orientations to the lake I have ever read, and it will be of benefit to any lake student, boater, shoreline explorer, bird watcher, diver, hiker, or anyone with an interest in gaining a better understanding of this wonderful place we call Lake Champlain. The fact that it is being released during the Quad-ricentennial of Samuel de Champlain's brief, profound and only journey to this place adds to its importance.

I immediately got caught up in Cathy's and Margy's narrative, partly because it put me in mind of my own experiences and career on the lake. I can easily understand how the project almost spontaneously germinated and then grew. The writers began their journey modestly and somewhat by accident. While looking for a way to exercise and take advantage of their seasonal living on Grand Isle, one of the beautiful Champlain Islands that the explorer described in his 1609 travel writings, the authors resolved that they would paddle around their home island. But as they began to log paddling events and experience the beauty, character and nature of this special place, they realized they were involved in a much more comprehensive and dynamic experience than they first realized. As they paddled, the project kept expanding until, by the end, they had circumnavigated not just their entire island but the entire lake. Encouraged by family and friends, they became determined to write about it. My own experience with the lake was somewhat similar.

In 1974 I came to Lake Champlain a newly minted scuba diving instructor and law school graduate. I needed a work opportunity that would pay the bills and yet provide me with enough free time to study for the bar exam. This was the era when oil barges and tugs still came to Burlington via the Hudson River and Champlain Canal to bring fuel oil to the numerous storage tanks that lined the waterfront. I was hired as an all-purpose diver and to help deploy booms around the barges as they pumped out their contents. I also began to teach scuba diving classes at Camp Kill Kare State Park at the end of Hatha-way Point on beautiful St. Albans Bay. Like Cathy and Margy, it didn't take long before I was drawn into the special nature of the lake and determined to expand my relationship with it.

My diving work took me to new areas of the lake, and my fascination began to expand with the growing revelation that this incredibly beautiful place also contained a long, rich and important record of human events. During the summer of 1974, I was deployed to spend an extended period assisting with an underwater inspection of the Crown Point Bridge. I decided to set up camp at the New York State campground right next to the site. After spending the day under the water, at night I would walk over the ruins of Fort St. Frederic and Crown Point simply amazed that French and British forces had expended such world-changing efforts right here in this mountain lake.

Having been drawn into the story, I read Ralph Nading Hill's *Lake Champlain: Key to Liberty*, which revealed in chapter after chapter the long, continuous sequence of rich human events that helped define the New World. I remember being totally blown away by the growing realization that so many incredible and world-altering events had occurred here. The more I learned, the more I wanted to know. The more I knew, the more I wanted to explore and now, some thirty-plus years later, I also have had the extraordinary experience of traveling, diving and exploring all the places on and under Lake Champlain.

It is through my own personal and expanding experience with Lake Champlain that I felt a kinship and connection as I made my way through Cathy's and Margy's story. I could completely understand how they could have begun their project to paddle their island and not have been able to stop until they had paddled the entire lake.

I loved the way the book begins and provides an orientation to so many different aspects of lake history, geology, geography, water quality and wildlife. I particularly enjoyed their thoughtful, authoritative and instructive safety briefings about the lake's wind and weather and rapidly changing conditions, the ever-present hazard of slimy rocks, the need to be aware of the seasonally changing water temperature and the common-sense approach to using the lake.

From this broad and informative introduction the authors then get down to the meat of their story, the area-by-area description of places to paddle and the things the paddler needs to know about each place. But beyond the launch sites and takeouts, the places to stop, the routes and the highlights and their own logbook reports of their paddles, I love the digressions to the special historical significance of each place, the legends of Champ and the military bombardment of Carleton Prize. It's this mix of technical guidebook information and historical and human interest that provides the special insight for paddler and non-paddler alike.

Special anniversaries offer an opportunity to focus on particular events and reflect on their place in the scheme of things. So it is that in this year we have an opportunity to reexamine the events surrounding the travels of French explorer Samuel de Champlain to *"a large lake with beautiful islands and surrounded by a great deal of beautiful country ..."*. This was how the lake was described to Champlain by his Native allies and how he came to become the first European to travel here. This he did, in July 1609, as part of a war party of Northern Alliance Native Peoples who had told Champlain he would be able to travel the entire way to the lake in his *chalupa*, a vessel that could sail and explore the region and physically support his crew. It was with profound disappointment that Champlain arrived at the rapids at Chambly and realized this was not the case and that his support vessel, his mobile fortification, could not make the passage.

The fate of the expedition hung in the balance as Champlain contemplated what to do about this unexpected disappointment. He describes in his writing how *"after thinking things over by myself, I resolved to go there ..."*. The rest is history. Sending the *chalupa* back to Tadoussac, Champlain, two French volunteers and sixty warriors entered this lake and began to explore it in twenty-four birch-bark canoes. Champlain's visit was powered by paddle and, in essence, it can be said that his writings produced the first written paddler's guide to Lake Champlain. I can't help but feel that Champlain himself would have reviewed a copy of Cathy's and Margy's wonderful, informative and well-written new book, *A Kayaker's Guide to Lake Champlain*, and smiled at the effort, commitment and results.

Arthur B. Cohn
Executive Director
Lake Champlain Maritime Museum
June 2009

Acknowledgments

We are indebted to our families, friends and acquaintances who encouraged us with their enthusiasm for this project. When they began to ask, "When is the book coming out?" we realized there was no way out but to actually get it done.

First and foremost we thank Peter Espenshade, former director of the Lake Champlain Land Trust. He not only suggested we create a blog of our Lake Champlain journeys on the Land Trust Web site, he then challenged us to write this book and was even willing and enthusiastic about reading the manuscript for accuracy and inclusiveness. We were inspired on our own to paddle, but Peter inspired us to share the experience with others.

Susan Williamson motivated us to sit down and get to work with schedule and structure, told us to cut the first version at least in half, and patiently brought her formidable editing skills to bear on our writing. Holly Crawford offered us useful suggestions and insight.

Dick Heilman shared his love and knowledge of Lake Champlain, particularly its naval history, and made suggestions about our writing on that subject. His careful reading of the book and his insightful suggestions were invaluable.

We are indebted to Art Cohn for writing the foreword to this book. We have great respect and admiration for the vast amount of work that he has done in researching, preserving, and bringing to life so much of the history and lore of Lake Champlain. We appreciate Katie Dolan and Chris Boget taking time from their important work to read and comment. Additionally, Chris enthusiastically answered many questions about the flora and fauna we saw in our travels.

Debby Bergh, Barbara Heilman, and Pat Boyd were courageous enough to be our very first readers. Bern Collins not only offered encouragement, but helped us in our search for a publisher. Gordon and Carol Perlmutter generously offered their time, boat, and computer resources when needed. We owe a big hug of thanks to our friend Elle Berger for picking us up from the floor when we were at a low point and giving us her hard-earned wisdom about the process of writing and publishing a book.

Many people willingly shared their expertise. David Capen and Mark LaBarr not only told their stories of research and stewardship on the bird islands, but allowed us to accompany them on a monitoring trip. George Starbuck patiently explained the intricacies of the internal seiche. Linda Fitch shared her knowledge of the fossil preserves on Isle La Motte as well as other island history. Marjorie Gale, Vermont State Geologist, generously took the time to read the geology section and make valuable suggestions. Others to whom we are indebted include: Mark Sweeny, Refuge Manager for the Missisquoi National Wildlife Refuge; Nathalie Zinger, Quebec Region Vice President of the Nature Conservancy of Canada; Jack Drake, retired Professor of Geology at the University of Vermont;

Robert Jones, author of many books on Vermont's railroads; Chris Boget, Executive Director of the Lake Champlain Land Trust; and Chris Gordon, former Associate Director of the South Hero Land Trust.

The team from Black Dome Press earned our endless thanks: copyeditor Matina Billias for her attention to detail; Ron Toelke for his designer's eye and implementation; and editor Steve Hoare and publisher Debbie Allen. With good humor and seemingly endless patience, Steve and Debbie accepted our submission, provided constant encouragement, a keen eye for what was missing, and unrelenting skill at making a better book. They proved to be the kind of partners that these writers dreamed about.

Special thanks go to our wonderful daughters: Martha, whose publishing experience led her to ask, "And what shelf is this book going to sit on in the bookstore?"; Jane, author of several books, whose many summers on the deck with her computer set an example for us; and Becky and Cheryl, whose abilities to distil the essence of an idea or paragraph were continuously helpful. All four willingly answered our many questions and, most importantly, gave us ongoing encouragement.

Husbands Doug and Joe made more contributions than we can possibly list here. They were early editors, drove and dropped us off, took pictures, but most of all supported us throughout and good-naturedly accepted the fact that even when we were setting off for a day of kayaking, we were really going to work.

(Cathy) Additionally I want to acknowledge and thank my wonderful husband for his infinite patience, his turning a blind eye to my surreptitiously removing most of his enormous collection of Vermont history books from his office one by one as I needed to look up yet one more aspect of Lake Champlain's past, for always agreeing to read and edit, and for waiting four years before ever asking when the book was going to be done.

(Margy) When I traded trips to the office for my kayak, Doug was the one who understood that this was only the beginning. Always happy to share his fine editing and photography skills when the light was good, even on cold, calm and not so calm mornings, he generously gave real and moral support while putting up with attention focused on the book instead of on closer-to-home pursuits. Always thoughtful, his gift of an exceptional paddle made the trip more fun and symbolized his support.

Preface

Seen from the Water

We began paddling on Lake Champlain for the exercise, the sheer fun of discovery, and the camaraderie. We began for the joy of paddling, but very quickly the beauty and diversity we found on this amazing lake and its shores enveloped us. With each trip we became more awed, curious, and respectful. We discovered that this body of water, like most things examined closely, is far more complex than we ever imagined.

In the summers, we live within six miles of each other in the Lake Champlain Islands halfway between New York and Vermont. Acquainted through community activities, a chance encounter in the local grocery store resulted in a "project" of circumnavigating Grand Isle by kayak, which Cathy had begun and Margy invited herself to join. Well, one island led to the next, and by the time we had finished the last of the Champlain Islands, we certainly weren't going to quit this adventure. We decided to paddle all the rest of Lake Champlain.

Leaving behind the everyday paddling routes near home, we headed out to cover every inch of shoreline. Lake Champlain, at more than 120 miles long, divides New York from Vermont, reaches into Canada, and has an astonishing 650-mile (1,046-kilometer) perimeter and 70 islands. What an excuse this gave us to keep paddling! We did so in bits and pieces, interrupted by work, family events, foul weather, and other life exigencies. Our trips ranged from 5 to 22 miles (8 to 35 kilometers) long, each a day trip taken between May and October over the course of several years. We paddled some sections of the lake two or even three times. As a result, this journey has taken us close to 700 miles (1,127 kilometers), powered only by our own energy and the siren song of Lake Champlain.

We thought we knew Lake Champlain. After all, we'd lived near its shores most of our adult years. What we found out, however, was that we knew quite a bit about a very small area of a large and fascinating lake system. As we paddled, questions arose. Why are the rocks in this part of the lake different from those with which we were familiar? Why would someone have built that lighthouse there? What kind of water plant is that? What was the story of that battle? Being curious types, we wanted answers to the questions that arose. We were surprised by undeveloped shoreline, overdeveloped shoreline, the clarity or lack of clarity of the water, the sometimes overwhelming weed growth, the cliffs, and the unique personalities of the different parts of the lake. We learned that Lake Champlain has many different faces.

Initially, we just paddled. Then, encouraged by Peter Espenshade, at that time the Executive Director of the Lake Champlain Land Trust, we began a blog of our trips on the trust's Web site. The idea of a book emerged gradually. Each day that we paddled, our bond with the lake became stronger. At some point it became "our" lake, not just to explore, experience, and learn about, but to protect, explain, and advocate for. If we could get some of this information out there, maybe it would increase knowledge and support for the lake and encourage others to leave familiar shores behind to experience other parts of Lake Champlain.

What we saw differed with each trip; location, season, and weather dictated what we experienced. We were intrigued by wildlife, water conditions, natural beauty, geology, people, and shoreline development, and we came to understand the lake's geography and historical significance. Nor did we view the lake or each trip with the same eyes or sensibility. There were so many things to look at (and we each had our favorites) that having two sets of eyes helped us to see things that we might have otherwise missed on our own.

We are somewhat fit, somewhat cautious, lake lovers who can pace ourselves for up to six hours at a time. We make our trips as short or long as we want and as launch sites will allow and, with few exceptions, we are never far from shore. In fact, traveling close to shore is what allowed us to see so much.

We also revel in what we call the Zen of paddling. The continuous rhythm of paddling relaxes the body and leaves the senses and mind free to roam. Thoughts arise, often more creative than when trying to force them. Surrounding details like the sheen on the water, the sound of water lapping on a rock, or the scent of the lake, become vivid. Time is irrelevant.

We are mindful that many have traveled the waters of Lake Champlain before us in far less seaworthy or maneuverable craft. Most ventured out onto this powerful and unpredictable lake without benefit of Internet weather radar, lightweight paddles, spray skirts, and cell phones. We admire their accomplishments.

Today, in fair weather when the water is above a certain temperature, people enjoy parts of the lake aboard all sorts of recreational craft, though it still amazes us how deserted the lake can be on many beautiful weekdays. Lake Champlain provides each of us the opportunity for unique experiences to enjoy in our own way. We hope this book will encourage others to try places they have never before visited and to let curiosity be their guide to the wonders the lake offers.

Another day, another paddle.

Caution and Safety Tips

Pause before Jumping In

Outdoor recreational activities are by their very nature potentially hazardous and contain risk. All participants in such activities must assume responsibility for their own actions and safety. No book can be a substitute for good judgment. The outdoors is forever changing. The authors and the publisher cannot be held responsible for inaccuracies, errors, or omissions, or for any changes in the details of this publication, or for the consequences of any reliance on the information contained herein, or for the safety of people in the outdoors.

The weather, wind, and waves on Lake Champlain change abruptly, often with little warning and in spite of the weather forecast. Getting caught on the water in a storm or high winds can quickly become life-threatening. Always check the forecast, watch the weather, and do not leave shore if storms and/or high winds are predicted or the wind and weather appear at all questionable.

Competency (ours that is): We don't challenge gale force winds, do Eskimo rolls to right our capsized kayaks, or venture out in December's freezing waters. We are pretty good at paddling in a straight line—when we want to. Some of our paddles are as short as an hour, and others up to six hours. We learned that we could go as far as we wanted or needed to with adequate amounts of sports drinks, snacks, rest and relief stops, curiosity, and a sense of humor.

Safety, Comfort and Equipment

Lake Champlain weather is unpredictable. We check the weather forecast, and check it again. We look online at NOAA recreational weather forecast for Burlington, which predicts wind speed on Lake Champlain, and Weather Underground. We listen to Vermont Public Radio forecasts from the Fairbanks Museum and follow weatherman Chris Bouchard's recommendation to add 50 percent to the forecasted land wind speed. Additionally, we note places where we can get off the water quickly if the weather turns bad, which it can do unexpectedly. If there are no such places on our route, we do not paddle there on a questionable weather day.

Wind and Waves. The wind speed over water is often 50 percent more than that over land. Wind creates waves, and waves command respect. Waves have peaks and troughs, and just after a wave has passed, it can bounce off a cliff to attack from the other side. The size of waves is affected by the force of the wind, the depth of the water, and the *fetch*—the uninterrupted distance of water over which the wind has blown. Waves build and crash when they reach a shallow shore. The longer the *fetch*, the more time the waves have to grow in size. A thoughtful check of a chart to note how long the stretch of open water is to windward can provide warning of potentially wavy areas. Because of its north-south orientation and prevailing winds of the same orientation, there are places on Lake Champlain where the fetch creates predictably larger waves than can be expected elsewhere under the same wind conditions.

We began paddling with the idea that on a windy day we could always find a protected shore. Wrong! On a windy day, when the waves have built, there may be lee moments, but waves have the ability to wrap around almost every shore and pile up on shallow shores.

We always check the wind conditions before setting out, mindful of the fact that what we see can be deceptive. The contours of the shoreline affect the force of the wind and the size of the waves, and when looking downwind, the size of the waves is not evident. We are always prepared to leave the water if conditions become more than we feel safe handling. If we are going to paddle away from the shore, we choose a calm day. There is no substitute for using good judgment.

Facilities are few and far between. We found restrooms at launch sites, public beaches, marinas, and food purveyors. The remaining 99 percent of the lakeshore does not have these conveniences. To compound the issue, there are stretches of shoreline that are private property for miles. When making a water-based rest stop, we eventually learned to select water significantly shallower than our legs are long, underwater surfaces that support our body weight so that we don't sink into adhesive clay, and rocks absent of the slime that guarantees a slip. Our lessons were learned the hard way through performing unanticipated and sometimes painful acrobatics and by cleaning clay from the inside of our kayaks.

Almost all underwater rocks are slippery. Step carefully.

There are many bigger and faster boats on the lake. Kayaks and canoes are hard to see, especially in wavy conditions. We stay alert to the boats around us, wear bright colors to increase our visibility, and stay together so that we are more visible in high-traffic areas. Four ferries cross Lake Champlain, and sizable tour boats operate out of Burlington and Plattsburgh. They have the right of way and should be given a wide berth.

Wildlife. As curious paddlers who are interested in wildlife, we did not think of ourselves as threats. Wrong. As paddlers, we are more of a disturbance to turtles than are powerboats. Paddlers can, and do, invade their territory, while power-boats speed by, usually at a distance. We also found out that paddling too close to the bird-nesting islands stresses the birds, which may fly away and leave the young temporarily unprotected. Take binoculars to enjoy wildlife, and stay far out from their nesting areas.

Private Property. While there are a significant number of state parks, municipal beaches, public boat accesses, conserved land, and state and national wildlife refuges along Lake Champlain, a large part of the lakeshore is privately owned. We took great care not to stop on private land. All stopping places listed in this book are open to the public. Similarly, we have listed only public launch sites except where they are scarce, in which case we note convenient private marinas where one can launch, usually for a small fee. Note that signage is minimal from the lake side of the shore. What is private and what is public is not always obvious.

If you carry it in, carry it out. Leave no trace.

Do leave what belongs there for the next person to appreciate. There may be a lot of fossils and other relics on the lakeshore, but if each of us took some home, that historical record would disappear.

Safety Equipment and Practices

1. Wear life preservers when on the water. We are both strong swimmers, but we would rather float than sink if we happen to go over and hit our heads or fall into water that is cold enough to take our breath away. It is important to try on life preservers and to test them while sitting in a kayak before you buy. They should be comfortable, brightly colored, and have reflective tape. Most kayakers wear Coast Guard-approved Type 3 vests, which will keep you afloat, but not necessarily face up in the water.

A note about tipping over: it happens in kayaks, most often in shallow water when trying to get in and out of the kayak. The same applies to canoes. Unexpected weather, wind, and waves can play havoc with a boat's stability as well. At the beginning of the season, we actually paddle our kayaks out in water above our heads and tip over, just for practice. Righting a kayak and reentering in deep water is tricky, but it's a lot easier with another kayaker to help. When paddling alone away from shore, it is best to carry paddle floats or sponsons. They, too, however, take practice to be able to use effectively. Righting an overturned canoe also takes practice, but it is easier to get back into than a kayak. Sloshing and bailing the water out of the canoe still offers a challenge. Like almost everything else, it gets easier with practice.

2. Wear spray skirts. We do, even when they are not attached to our boats. We may look funny on shore, but they are easier to attach if we are already in them and unexpectedly find waves washing over the gunnels.

3. Wear wetsuits in spring and fall, when water temperatures are cold and an unexpected swim can rapidly result in hypothermia. Is there a beginning and end to the paddling season? That depends on the level of risk that the paddler is willing to undertake. As the temperature lowers, we are very careful to stay within easy wading distance from shore. Hypothermia can also occur in warm weather when the water is still cold or the air temperature drops quickly.

The Effects of Hypothermia in Cold Water

Water Temperature (F)	Exhaustion or Unconsciousness	Expected time of survival
32.5	Under 15 min.	Under 15–45 min.
32.5–40	15–30 min	30–90 min.
40–50	30–60 min.	1–3 hrs.
50–60	1–2 hrs.	1–6 hrs.
60–70	2–7 hrs.	2–40 hrs.
70–80	2–12 hrs.	3 hrs–indefinite

Lake Champlain Paddlers' Trail, 2008 Guidebook & Stewardship Manual, 10th edition (Lake Champlain Committee), p.16.

4. Use a paddle leash. We do, so we won't have to paddle with our hands if our paddle should happen to get away from us. Always carry at least one spare paddle.

5. Tell someone where you are going and when you expect to return. Even though we paddled together, someone always knew where we were headed and when we expected to get back.

6. Paddle with someone, especially if leaving shore.

7. Other safety equipment we take includes:
    a. **Raingear,** or at least a **windbreaker.** If we get chilled, a warm layer helps ward off hypothermia. We also take **dry clothes** with us, or at least leave a set in the car.
    b. **Tow rope.**
    c. **Bilge pump and sponge.**
    d. **A cell phone** in a waterproof container—turned off. We don't want to run the battery down or ruin a good day on the lake with a ringing phone.
    e. A **loud whistle** attached to the pocket of our life vests to attract attention in case we need help.
    f. **First-aid kit.**

Creature Comforts

1. Sunglasses and hat (might also be considered health/safety equipment).

2. Ample sunscreen and SPF-rated lip balm.

3. Water shoes or sandals. Zebra mussel shells and sharp rocks cut.

4. Road map to find launch sites. (It's not as easy as it looks. *Vermont County Road Atlas* provides essential Vermont details; New York and Quebec access areas are often on main roads, and a road map works.)

5. Navigational Chart. Maybe you can't get lost paddling along the shore, but it is helpful as well as interesting to know where along the shore you are.

6. Money.

7. Snacks, lunch, and chocolate. We learned the hard way to keep these essentials on the deck within easy access. If there is no handy place to land, retrieving from a sealed hatch is difficult.

8. Plenty of water and sports drink. (Lake water is best treated before drinking.)

9. One of us wears paddling gloves to prevent blisters; the other does not.

10. Through trial and error we learned to dress for the inevitable wet bottoms by wearing lightweight **running shorts.** Both lining and shorts dry quickly and look presentable on shore.

11. Oh yes. If we have spotted a second car at the end of the paddle, we make sure to take THAT set of **car keys** with us. (We enjoyed the paddle, but that doesn't mean that our bodies are ready to immediately repeat it.)

12. A waterproof waist pouch to keep sensitive items such as cell phones, cameras, binoculars, and car keys dry. Paddling is basically a wet sport; even on calm days, water makes its way into the boat.

Equipment. This book is about paddling Lake Champlain and is not meant to be used as a book on how to paddle and what equipment to buy. There are many good books on the market for that purpose. Below we offer some very general thoughts on what sort of craft is needed for Lake Champlain.

Kayaks (and other paddle craft). Lake Champlain paddling requires a craft that will track well, is stable in rough water, and is light enough to lift onto the top of a car and maneuver in and out of the water. Margy started out with an eight-foot-long peapod-shaped kayak. It was great to lift onto the car, but she bobbed around like a cork in any kind of waves. Cathy had an old, sixty-pound, sixteen-foot sea kayak with rudder. We cursed it every time we lifted it onto the van, but it was stable in rough seas. Two years into our paddling, Margy upgraded to a hip-width, fourteen-foot Current Designs, and Cathy to a smaller and lighter Necky. Balancing length (stability), weight, and comfort takes trial and error. What makes women well-designed to give birth (wide hips) means we have trouble fitting into kayaks designed for men. Men come in all shapes and sizes, too. A kayak has to be tried on. While it may feel silly to sit in kayaks on the floor of a store, we did it. A demonstration day on the water, which most kayak stores offer, is an even better option. Cockpit size is important. The smaller the cockpit, the harder it is to get in and out of.

Canoes. There are as many options for canoe designs as there are for kayaks. For paddling on Lake Champlain, tracking, stability, comfort, and weight are all important. For some, the way a canoe looks is important. Depending on how it will be used, some qualities may be more important than others.

We've been asked whether a kayak or canoe is a better choice for use on Lake Champlain. The choice is a personal one and should be based on how the paddler will use the craft. A canoeist has a greater range of paddling positions, can switch sides on which to paddle, and sits higher above the water. In rough water the canoeist must position the canoe to minimize shipping water, while the kayaker can attach a spray skirt to seal out water. An upset canoe in deep water may be easier to reenter than a kayak. The important thing is to take the opportunity to try different craft before making a choice.

Paddles. A paddle is a paddle, but it takes less energy to use a lightweight one than a heavy one. Inversely, the lighter they are, the more they cost.

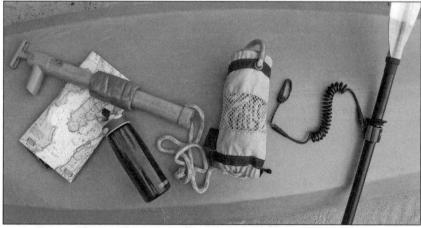

Gear: bilge pump, tow rope, paddle leash, water bottle, map.

Users' Guide to this Book

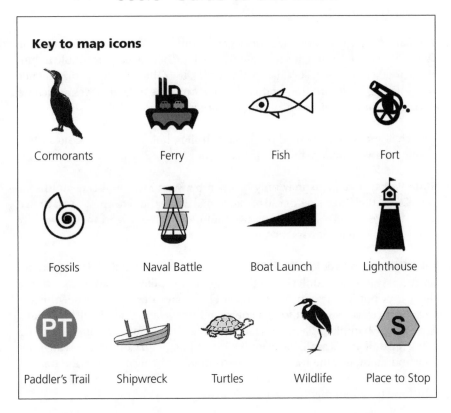

Key to map icons

Cormorants	Ferry	Fish	Fort
Fossils	Naval Battle	Boat Launch	Lighthouse
Paddler's Trail	Shipwreck	Turtles	Wildlife	Place to Stop

Our Trips: We set out to paddle the entire shoreline of Lake Champlain. The particular trips we took reflect that effort. Many of those trips north of Crown Point required the use of two cars. However, every paddle can be done as an out-and-back trip of whatever length one chooses. The trip matrix at the end of the book and the maps associated with each trip identify points of interest along every shoreline. The direction we paddled almost always depended on which way the wind was blowing that day. All trips may be paddled in the reverse direction.

Paddle Boxes: A paddle box at the beginning of each trip description summarizes the details and highlights.

Distances: Distances reflect the ins and outs of the shoreline, and so are often longer than a point-to-point measurement listed in many boating guides. The shoreline route from Button Bay to Converse Bay, which includes paddling in and out of numerous bays as opposed to a direct route, would be one example of this. Our distances, measured using our high-tech method—a piece of string on a chart—take into account a convoluted shoreline; thus, distances in the book are subject to the vagaries of our method.

Trip Ratings: We have not rated the degree of difficulty of each trip, because the factors that would define it vary from day to day. There is no perceivable uphill, steep or otherwise, on Lake Champlain. Rather, the difficulty of any trip depends on its length, how hard the wind is blowing, exposure to large waves, which we have noted in the paddle boxes, and the air temperature.

Launch Sites: We mostly used public launch sites, but we list private sites when public sites were unavailable or inconvenient.

State Parks: State parks may only be open between Memorial Day and Labor Day. Check their Web sites or call ahead to make sure they are open. Most charge a fee, but Vermont residents sixty-two and older can apply to their town/city clerks for a permanent pass for a much smaller fee.

Lake Champlain Paddlers Trail (PT): This series of overnight and day-use shoreline access sites for paddlers runs the length of the lake. We have indicated the thirty-four public sites on our charts (PT). Private sites have not been listed, because their use is subject to renegotiation from year to year. Published yearly, "The Lake Champlain Paddlers Trail Guide" is an essential resource for those using the trail and is available from the Lake Champlain Committee, which created and maintains the trail. Stops are continually being added to the trail, so it is important to have the most up-to-date guide. A few sites are day use only, which we have indicated in the paddle boxes.

Changes: The shoreline is a dynamic, evolving scene. Heron rookeries, which disappear from a particular location only to sometimes reappear at a later date, are but one example. We wrote this book using the most current available information. As you paddle the shore of Lake Champlain, you will inevitably find changes. Please report changes to our Web site: www.kayakinglakechamplain.com.

Chapter I

About Lake Champlain

A General Physical Description of Lake Champlain

For those who have fallen under its spell, it is impossible to reduce Lake Champlain to a description of its physical properties. This 435-square-mile (1,119-square-kilometer) lake, 120 miles (193 kilometers) long, and 12 miles (19 kilometers) wide at its broadest point, is so much more than the sum of its parts.

Lake Champlain flows from south to north between two mountain ranges, the Green Mountains of Vermont on the east and the Adirondack Mountains of New York on the west. The lake's northern end extends into the Province of Quebec, Canada. With an average elevation of 95 feet (29 meters) above sea level, Lake Champlain plunges to 400 feet (122 meters) in depth just off the New York shore at Split Rock Point, but is as little as 5–15 feet (1.5 to 4.6 meters) deep at the north and south ends. From the time that man first navigated on water, Lake Champlain has been a transportation highway connecting the Atlantic Ocean at the mouth of the Hudson River to the Gulf of St. Lawrence in Quebec, and giving access to the Mohawk River to the west. These routes became easier when canals were built to replace portages in the nineteenth century.

Some of Lake Champlain's shores are densely populated; others are virtually deserted. Seventy islands range in size from a protruding rock to land large enough to support farms. Lake Champlain is often called the sixth great lake, especially when Congress is voting on funds for lake restoration, but it is only one-fourteenth the size of Lake Ontario, the smallest of the Great Lakes. To us, there is no question of status. It is the greatest of lakes.

Beginning in the north, Lake Champlain can be divided into five distinctly different sections:

Missisquoi Bay. Missisquoi Bay balloons out at the northeast end of the lake, on top of the Inland Sea. Much of the bay is in Quebec. It is a shallow saucer of water, about 5 miles (8 kilometers) across, and 14 feet (4.6 meters) at the deepest part.

The Inland Sea. The Inland Sea is bound to the south by the Sandbar Causeway, to the west by the Champlain Islands and Alburgh, and to the east by the mainland of Vermont. It is about 25 miles (40 kilometers) long, varying in width from 3–5 miles (4.8–8 kilometers) across, and is dotted with islands.

Malletts Bay. The former Rutland Railroad Causeway to the west, now a recreation path, and the Sandbar Causeway to the north separate inner and outer Malletts bays from the rest of the lake. These deepwater bays are home to a large number of recreational watercraft.

The Broad Lake. What most people envision when they think of Lake Champlain is the 90 mile area south from the Richelieu River to Crown Point. The southern half has the deepest water and the highest mountains. To the north, shorelines flatten and the water becomes shallower. Because this section is so large, we have divided it into north, east, and west when describing our trips.

The South Lake. Between Crown Point and Whitehall, 30 miles (48.3 kilometers) to the south, Lake Champlain looks more like a river than a lake. The water is shallow, murky, and filled with Eurasian milfoil and water chestnut along the shore. Wildlife abounds.

Wildlife

Champ. Lake Champlain is home to the legendary monster affectionately known as Champ. The Algonquin Indians reportedly told Samuel De Champlain about an 8–10-foot-long (2.4–3-meter) monster, which the Iroquois called *Chaousarou* and the Abenaki named *Tatoskok*. Champ sightings continue today, and her existence is the source of great debate. Alas, we did not see Champ in our travels. (This should not be viewed as adding useful evidence on either side of the debate.) We choose to believe she exists until proven otherwise and are happy to have her serve as a lively reminder that there is much yet to learn about Lake Champlain.

Other Lake Residents. According to the Lake Champlain Basin Program Web site (www.lcbp.org) and the 2000 Census, about 571,000 people live in the Champlain Basin and over 200,000 depend on it for their drinking water. (There are a remarkable 99 public water systems and almost 4,150 individuals who draw their water directly from the lake.) Approximately 81 species of fish, 318 species of birds,

Approaching storm.

56 species of mammals, and several dozen species of amphibians and reptiles also rely on Lake Champlain for their drinking water. Additionally, Lake Champlain provides resting and feeding sites for 20,000 to 40,000 ducks and geese during their fall and spring migrations along the Atlantic flyway. The human residents have concentrated themselves most densely on the Vermont shore in and around greater Burlington and on the New York shore in the Plattsburgh area.

Place Names

Because of the rich tapestry of peoples and events that make up the long history of Lake Champlain, place names on the Lake are a mixture of Native American (Iroquois and Abenaki), French, English, and American English. In many cases, place names changed as control and ownership of land changed, but not always.

The Abenaki named the *Winooski River* for the wild onions that grew alongside it, causing the French to call it the *Ouinoustick*. Vermont's first big land developers, Ethan and Ira Allen, bought most of the land along the river in the 1790s and anglicized the name to Onion River. According to Ester Swift, in *Vermont Place-Names*, that name survived for 100 years until Montpelier, Vermont, residents reputedly upset that their community, the capital of Vermont, was known as Montpelier-on-the-Onion started a campaign to have the name changed back to the original Abenaki name *Winooski*.

With the exception of naming a few significant islands for gods, the Native Americans had a uniquely succinct and descriptive way of identifying places to reflect their nature and geography. For example, *Mississiak* or *Missisquoi*, meaning "People of the Marshy Grassy Place," describes this incredible, sandy, marshy, river delta so well.

Weather

Lake Champlain has justly earned its reputation for fierce storms that blow up suddenly. Everyone who ventures out onto the water needs to heed the weather forecast, but while a forecast is an essential piece of information, the relationship between it and the actual weather events of the day can be tenuous. Keeping a wary eye on the western sky, where much of the weather comes from, is just as important as checking the forecast before leaving shore. Happily, the weather can also be delightfully sunny with moderate wind or mirror-like calm.

Water Quality

While the eighteenth- and nineteenth-century battles on Lake Champlain were military, the most important battles today are over ways to improve water quality. The significance of this effort cannot be overstated. Thousands of people depend on the lake for water, income, visual enjoyment, and recreation. It is estimated that lake-related activities generate more than $4 billion in annual tourist expenditures. Water quality determines which animal, plant, and fish species will thrive and survive, as well as the safety of pets and people.

Phosphorus. Phosphorus supports the growth of algae, which in turn decreases water clarity, causes excessive aquatic plant growth, and will eventually impact organisms living in the lake. Several areas of Lake Champlain—Missisquoi Bay, St. Albans Bay, and the South Lake—contain such high levels of phosphorus that they are considered eutrophic (rich in mineral and organic nutrients that promote proliferation of plant life and reduce oxygen content). Malletts Bay contains the least amount of phosphorus, and other sections of the lake fall in between. New York and Vermont have agreed to a phosphorus reduction plan in which a total minimum daily load (TMDL) standard for phosphorus has been set for each section of the lake, and funds have been allocated for remediation efforts. Both states are aiming to meet the standards. Some areas often meet or exceed the standards, while most others have yet to achieve them. Scientists and lay people alike have come to realize that any lake cleanup is a complicated and long-term effort that must be relentless to be successful.

Phosphorus comes from identifiable point sources such as wastewater treatment plants, and non-point sources including farms, parking lots, and even the individual use of phosphorus-rich fertilizer on lawns. Phosphorus can enter the water directly, such as through a pipe from an industrial plant, or it can flow into Lake Champlain through streams and storm runoff. While point-source pollution has been dramatically reduced by such means as upgrading wastewater treatment facilities, non-point sources, because they are so numerous and varied, are more difficult to remediate. Currently, more than half of non-point pollution comes from agriculture, more than a third from developed land, and the rest from diverse sources. Sadly, the effect may be cumulative, because phosphorous settles into the bottom sediments of the lake only to be slowly released back into the water. Research, monitoring, and remediation work to reduce phosphorus levels for the whole lake is ongoing. This body of water must be considered when we make personal, business, community, and statewide decisions. Each of us can make a difference and needs to be an advocate for the health of Lake Champlain.

Toxic substances. Toxic substances, which include PCB's (polychlorinated biphenyls) and metals such as lead, mercury, arsenic, and nickel, are invisible components of Lake Champlain's water. When toxins are present above the prescribed, acceptable levels, they can harm vegetation, animals, and humans. Cumberland Bay, Burlington Bay, and outer Malletts Bay have been remediated or are undergoing remediation and follow-up monitoring for specific toxins. Some substances like mercury are found in bottom sediments throughout the lake. Fish consumption advisories exist for most species of game and large fish taken from Lake Champlain.

Nuisance Invasive Species

While a decline in water quality challenges some native species, many nuisance invasive species have a much higher tolerance. This direct relationship between nuisance invasive species and water quality is but one of the ways that the unwanted can take over Lake Champlain. The bilge water in boats carries fragments of milfoil, water chestnut, and zebra mussels into Lake Champlain from other lakes and from one bay to another. Alien species of fish swim or are brought here. The arrival of the zebra mussel caused a crisis for individual and community water systems, practically eradicated the native mussel species, and resulted in swimmers having to wear protective water shoes. Most nuisance invasive species pose a significant threat not only to the quality of the water, but to Lake Champlain as we know it.

The habits of invasive nuisance species further challenge fish and plants that may have thrived here for centuries. Rock snot smothers the native plants in tributaries. Invasive alewife and white perch, whose number are continually increasing, are not only more aggressive feeders at the same table as native species, but also eat the larvae of native species. Significant die-offs of alewife not only signify the extent of their numbers, but pose shoreline cleanup challenges. In an ironic twist, the invasive zebra mussel feeds on and reduces the zooplankton concentration in the water, thus making the water clearer. Lest you think this is a good thing, however, by removing the zooplankton it removes an essential food for native (and other species) from the bottom of the food chain. Other examples abound. The quality of our water is key to what swims and grows in it.

Lake Champlain's Internal Seiche

The internal seiche is the mechanism that moves and mixes the water in Lake Champlain. Swimmers may unknowingly experience the internal seiche when they find a sharp difference in water temperature in the same location from one day to the next.

Temperature and wind set up the internal seiche. Water is most dense at 40 degrees. When summer air warms Lake Champlain, it creates a layer of higher-temperature, less dense water on the surface, while the water 40 to 80 feet below forms a fairly cohesive, cooler, thermocline layer (the region in a thermally stratified body of water that separates warmer surface water from cold deep water and in which temperature decreases rapidly with depth, dropping one degree per foot). In summer and fall, strong southerly winds actually push the warmer, less dense surface water to the north end of the lake. Since the surface of the lake remains level, the weight of this piled-up warm water depresses the denser, cooler thermocline down, sending it south. In a north wind the reverse happens. This sets up a huge underwater rocking motion, called the internal seiche, which reverses itself roughly every four days.

The resulting underwater currents have been measured at over 100 feet (30.5 meters) deep and are strong enough to resuspend bottom sediments. The internal seiche is good news in the deeper main lake and bays, which benefit from the continual exchange of water. In an enclosed place like Shelburne Bay, which has three wastewater treatment plants plus an intake for Champlain Water District, the internal seiche constitutes an essential ingredient in the bay's ability to refresh itself. The internal seiche can be bad news when it disburses contaminated suspended solids to other parts of the lake. Shallow bays are not deep enough to benefit from the action of the internal seiche.

Warning.

Dr. George Starbuck, who identified the phenomenon in Lake Champlain, questioned us as to whether we noticed internal seiche currents while paddling. He believes that the velocity of the internal seiche could create surface currents that might be most noticeable where Lake Champlain funnels into narrows between Split Rock and Thompsons Point or Cumberland Head and Grand Isle.

The dramatic movement of the internal seiche continues to be the subject of ongoing study because of its potential to impact the water quality of Lake Champlain.

Human Impact

Like the Joni Mitchell song, Lake Champlain goes round and round in the circle game. The more we love it, the more we use it, building homes and parking lots on shores, which speed phosphorus and other contaminants into the lake. We use our boats, which invisibly transport invasive species. Still, more of us arrive to experience the Champlain Valley, to farm its fields, to swim in its waters. When we become alarmed by the sight of algae-filled water, we try to control pollution and improve water quality. The issues are huge and the needs are great. The key

Milfoil.

Water chestnut.

is to remember the interconnectedness of our Champlain Basin, and to recognize that our individual and corporate actions directly impact this lake and the flora and fauna we share it with.

Lake Champlain's Geologic History

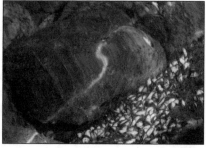

Zebra mussels.

To fully understand how Lake Champlain arrived at its present configuration and to appreciate the evidence of the diversity of past life found along its current shores, we need to go back to the Paleozoic Era, 250–500 million years ago.

Plate Tectonics. Over billions of years, the independent plates that make up the Earth's surface have collided, merged, and separated, as if in a giant global game of bumper cars. Mountain ranges have been thrust up and destroyed, oceans created and closed, and continents joined together and split. This plate shuffle continues today, literally beneath our feet. Not surprisingly, then, the land upon which Lake Champlain sits has not always been located where it is today, at about 45° north of the equator, 95 feet (29 meters) above sea level, and hundreds of miles from the nearest ocean.

The Rocks of Lake Champlain. The rock that lines the shore of the New York side of the lake from Port Kent south formed over a billion years ago from igneous and metamorphic rock buried deep within the Earth. This same ancient rock, forced up into a large dome, formed the Adirondack Mountains roughly 500 million years ago.

The rock along the Vermont and northern part of the New York shores is young by comparison, 450–500 million years old. When these rocks were formed, what became the Champlain Valley was about 25° south of the equator on the edge of a shallow sea. Fish and plants had not yet evolved, but microscopic single-celled algae and bacteria, plus various multicellular organisms such as trilobites filled the shallow coastal waters. As organisms died, they dropped to the muddy sea floor, which over time was compressed into limestone and shale. The fossils encased in this limestone are visible along Lake Champlain's shore today.

Ice Ages. At least four successive glaciers have covered the Champlain Valley. Ice sheets over one mile (1.6 kilometers) thick have expanded and contracted rhythmically about every 100,000 years. The last glacier began to recede from the northeast about 15,000 years ago and had left the Champlain Valley around 13,000 years ago.

Lake Vermont. As the last glacier's receding edge moved slowly northward and exposed the land that is now the Lake Champlain basin, a huge ice dam formed at its northern end, trapping all of the melting water and creating Lake Vermont, which drained south. This lake was 600 feet (183 meters) above sea level, three times wider than the present Lake Champlain, and reached almost to the base of the Green Mountains. If Burlington and Plattsburgh had existed then, they would have been 500 feet (152 meters) underwater. Lake Vermont lasted for approximately 2,000 years.

The Champlain Sea. When the glacier receded farther and the ice dam melted, much of the water in Lake Vermont flowed out into the ocean via the St. Lawrence River. The weight of the huge ice sheet over thousands of years had depressed the land, however, so after the fresh water from Lake Vermont poured out, saltwater flowed in. Lake Vermont became the Champlain Sea, an arm of the St. Lawrence River, which was then a large ocean estuary. The Champlain Sea was significantly smaller than Lake Vermont, but much larger than today's Lake Champlain. Beluga whales (railway workers found the skeleton of a Beluga whale in Charlotte, Vermont, in 1849), seals, Atlantic cod, mussels, and other sea creatures thrived, and beach grass, beach heather, and beach pea took root along the shores. These plants, although rare, can still be found today in sandy places along the shore.

Lake Champlain. As the land slowly continued to rebound from the weight of the glacier (it continues to do so today), the northern end of the lake rose above sea level. Once again, water flowed out to the ocean, rather than from the ocean into the lake. Eventually, Lake Champlain became a freshwater lake, fed only by the rains and rivers of its huge drainage basin. According to the Lake Champlain Basin Atlas, it is estimated that Lake Champlain, with its present physical borders, has existed for about 9,000 years.

Sand and Sand Dunes. When the glaciers receded, debris-filled glacier melt, rock, and gravel flowed down the rivers. As the rivers widened and their current slowed, they dropped large particles first, then smaller ones, into the riverbed, leaving the lighter sand particles to be deposited last, usually at the river's mouth. The sandy river deltas and sand beaches that we find today were created from particles from Lake Vermont and the Champlain Sea. It is believed that sand from the Lamoille and Winooski rivers is responsible for most of the sand on the beaches in the northern lake.

Sand creation continues today. Winds and waves erode rock along the shore, making still more sand. The prevailing south wind and waves continually move sand from the river mouths to the north, depositing it on south-facing shores. On some of these shores, which face a long fetch to the south, wind and waves create constantly moving dunes. Although a product of the

Common Fossils of Lake Champlain

Below are pictures of the most commonly found fossils on the shores of Lake Champlain, along with a sketch of what the whole living organism once looked like. Sometimes it is possible to find a complete fossil, but a fragment, slice, or angled view of part of an organism is more common. The fragments are more difficult to identify, but can usually at least be recognized as being part of a fossil. Almost all fossils found on Lake Champlain are 460–480 million years old.

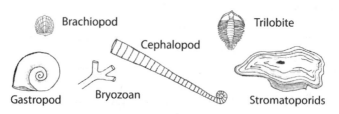

Bryozoans— tiny, soft–bodied, simple branching organisms that lived in colonies.

Lake Champlain's fossils often look like tiny twigs and can be as small as one-quarter of an inch long. They are usually found in layers.

Brachiopods— look like small clamshells and are usually found in groups, often packed together.

They have a ridge running down the center that is not always obvious.

Stromatoporoids—cabbage-like structures that are the ancestors to the sponge.

Cephalopods— related to gastropods, and similar to a chambered nautilus of today.

Gastropods— snails, these organisms are prevalent on Lake Champlain and

some can be quite large.

Trilobites—lobster-like creatures that became extinct 400 million years ago and,

like lobsters, they shed their shells in order to grow.

Fossil finding.

same forces that create ocean sand dunes, Lake Champlain's dunes are much smaller versions and unfortunately, are often diminished or destroyed by human development.

The Lake Champlain we know today may not exist 100,000 years from now, when glaciers could well return again. It is humbling to realize that we are only one species in a long line that has come and gone over the past 400 million years, living on the latest but not last configuration of the continents and oceans that produced Lake Champlain.

A Brief History of the Inhabitants and Their Conflicts

According to Jan Albers, in *Hands on the Land*, humans first came into the Champlain Valley about 11,000 years ago (about 9,000 B.C.) as the last glacier was retreating. These first inhabitants of the Champlain Valley, the Early Paleo-Indian peoples, wandered the shores of the Champlain Sea. It is believed that they lived in a tundra environment, probably drawn by an abundance of wildlife including caribou, mammoth, ocean fish, whales, and seals, with the water moderating the air temperature.

Long before Samuel de Champlain visited in 1609, Native Americans roamed the Champlain basin. The richest archeological sites of these peoples have been found at East Creek (on the Vermont side, east of Ticonderoga) and the mouths of the Winooski and Missisquoi rivers. From Champlain's visit in 1609 until after the War of 1812, first the French and British, and then the British and Americans contested ownership of the land and waterway.

With a few exceptions, most of the towns along the lake were not permanently settled until after the hostilities of the American Revolution ended.

A Time Frame of Major Events on Lake Champlain

French and Indian War (also called the *Seven Years' War*, 1754–1763). From 1609 until 1760, working from a foothold in Canada, the French were the controlling (but contested) presence on the lake. In 1760 the British defeated the French and took control not only of Lake Champlain, but also of all the French settlements to the north and east, holding these lands until the American Revolution.

The American Revolution. From the American capture of the British forts at Crown Point and Fort Ticonderoga in 1775, to the Battle of Saratoga in the summer of 1777, Lake Champlain was a major battleground of the American war for independence because of its strategic location, partially separating New England from the rest of the colonies, and because of its role as a natural transportation route. The Battle of Valcour in 1776 is particularly noteworthy because of the crucial role Benedict Arnold's small fleet, despite losing the battle, played in stalling the British advance south for one year. This gave the American army time to strengthen its forces and defeat the British the following year at Saratoga.

The War of 1812. Between the Revolution and the War of 1812, Great Britain and its Canadian colonies harassed the new country by impressing its seamen, restricting its trade with France, and by other means. Lake Champlain again became a center of action, particularly since the British, who maintained a presence on Point au Fer, continued to target American shipping in that area. A decisive battle fought in Plattsburgh Bay helped the American cause, but the boundary with Canada was not officially affirmed until the Treaty of Ghent, which ended the war.

Commerce

The use of Lake Champlain as a trade route by canoe began long before the days of Samuel de Champlain. After the arrival of Europeans in the 1600s, sail, then steam, and then gas engines powered the vehicles of commerce. Until the railroads were built, Lake Champlain united the two states of New York and Vermont, bringing them closer together as commercial boat traffic crisscrossed the water up and down the length of the lake. With the advent of the railroads and the improvement of roads, cross-lake commerce all but disappeared and the lake became a water barrier separating the two states. Today, two bridges, as well as two seasonal and two year-round ferries, carry cars and trucks across the water bearing an increasing number of commuters as well as cargo bound for distant destinations.

Lake Champlain Time Line

- 500 million years ago—Adirondack Mountains formed from rock 1.3 billion years old; coral and marine life in Iapetus Ocean form fossils.
- 2 million years ago—the most recent ice age began.
- 13,000–12,000 B.C.—Lake Vermont formed as the glaciers melted and then blocked the outflow of water from the Champlain Valley to the north.
- 13,000 to 11,000 B.C.—first human inhabitants of the Champlain Valley.
- 11,000 B.C.—Champlain Sea replaced Lake Vermont.
- 1609—Samuel de Champlain, first European to visit Lake Champlain.
- 1609–1759—French settlement of the Champlain Valley.
- 1759–1777—English occupation of Champlain Valley.
- 1775–1783—American Revolution.
- 1812–1814—War of 1812.
- 1823—Champlain Canal opened.
- 1840–1870s—railroads built.
- 21st century—Margy and Cathy paddle Lake Champlain.

Feeling small.

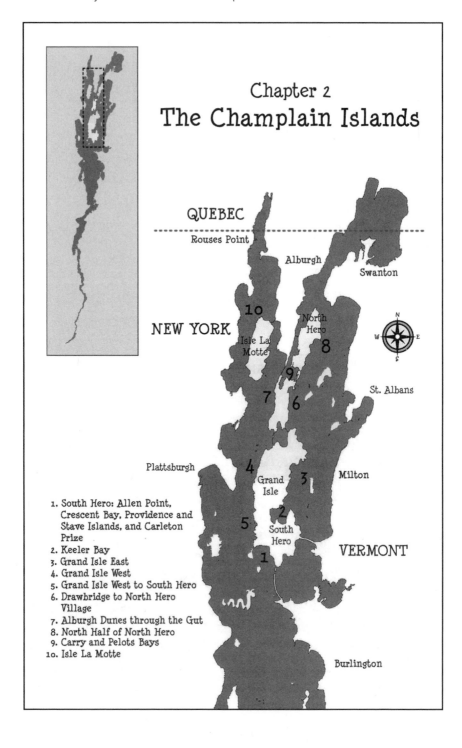

Chapter 2
The Champlain Islands

QUEBEC

Rouses Point

Alburgh

Swanton

NEW YORK

10

North Hero

8

Isle La Motte

9

7

6

St. Albans

Plattsburgh

4

Grand Isle

3

Milton

1. South Hero: Allen Point, Crescent Bay, Providence and Stave Islands, and Carleton Prize
2. Keeler Bay
3. Grand Isle East
4. Grand Isle West
5. Grand Isle West to South Hero
6. Drawbridge to North Hero Village
7. Alburgh Dunes through the Gut
8. North Half of North Hero
9. Carry and Pelots Bays
10. Isle La Motte

2

5

South Hero

1

VERMONT

Burlington

Chapter II

The Champlain Islands

A Paddler's Treasure Trove

Grand Isle, North Hero, and Isle La Motte, plus the Vermont town of Alburgh—collectively referred to as the Champlain Islands—sit in the middle of the northern third of the lake. The "Alburgh Tongue" drops down between North Hero and Isle La Motte, giving Alburgh the appearance of a fourth island, although it is actually a peninsula with its northern and only land border attached to Quebec.

These islands dwarf the other 67-plus islands on the lake. At 14 miles by 3 miles (22.5 by 4.8 kilometers), Grand Isle is the largest of the three. Today, they are connected to Vermont and New York and to each other by a combination of causeways, bridges, and a ferry. From the time the islands were settled in the early 1780s until the middle of the nineteenth century, however, crossing to this area was a challenge. As a result they have a personality all their own.

A Toll Bridge

The first bridge to the islands at the Sandbar was completed in December 1850, after fifty-five years of effort on the part of the islanders to alleviate their physical isolation from the rest of Vermont. Single wagons drawn by one horse crossed for 20¢, and a lone footman or woman for 5¢. Ironically, the bridge's grand opening occurred when the winter ice had formed. True to Vermonters' reputation for frugality, instead of paying to use the long-awaited new bridge, everyone drove across the ice until the spring thaw, by which time the ice and heavy winds had done considerable damage to the new bridge and it had to be repaired before it had ever been used.

Even today this area is not easily tamed. In the spring of 1994, wind and ice combined to topple into the water just south of the Sandbar the main electrical transmission line from Quebec that supplies Vermont and much of New England. That line is now buried under the south shoulder of the causeway. It was as if nature had spoken—one of the most spectacular views on Lake Champlain no longer has a transmission line running through it.

▶ **South Hero**

South Hero: Allen Point, Crescent Bay, Providence and Stave Islands, and Carleton Prize — *The Scenic Route*

1

by Cathy Frank

- ■ **Launch site/Take out:** Allen Point F&W Area (cartop launch only), off Martin Rd., South Hero, Vermont
- ■ **Distance:** 10.5 miles (17 kilometers)
- ■ **Alternative launch sites:** Whites Beach (West Shore Rd., South Hero, Vermont)
- ■ **Places to stop:** Above launch sites and Carleton Prize, Malletts Bay Causeway
- ■ **Highlights:** Carleton Prize, Malletts Bay Causeway, interesting rock formations, fossils, exceptional views to the Adirondacks and Green Mountains
- ■ **Route:** This circle route closely follows the shallow shoreline until Phelps Point, where it crosses open water between each island and back to the South Hero shore. Stopping points are evenly spaced. Possible alternative routes include starting at either launch site and paddling directly to any one or combination of islands, or paddling only the shore of Crescent Bay. Carleton Prize loop (4 miles/6.4 kilometers); all three islands loop (7.5 miles/12 kilometers); Crescent Bay shore round-trip (7 miles/11.3 kilometers).
- ■ **Comments:** Strong south winds produce large waves in this bay, and a strong NW wind increases in strength as it funnels through the Narrows. On weekends there is significant fast-moving boat traffic from the causeway cut through the Narrows and also in the channel between Stave Island and Carleton Prize.

The Paddle:

Hoping to keep her feet warm and dry from the cold water of early June, Margy arrives wearing orange Wellies with red flowers given to her by her granddaughters. She looks more like Mary Poppins with a paddle than my kayaking partner.

After putting in, we head north past rock of thin, gray shale layers, drizzled with calcite—what we have come to call "paint-can rock," because it looks as if someone has dribbled white paint on the rocks. Calcite-decorated pebbles cover the shore and lake bottom as well. Just before turning west we pass an erratic boulder at the base of the shale embankment. Textured by cracks and crevices, it is almost perfectly round, teasing us to imagine it rolling into place on a powerful wave. At the top of the cliff, tall evergreens look as if they could fall into the water below with the slightest provocation.

South Hero's Whites Beach, the only public access on this shore, appears empty as we pass. This area, locally referred to as Crescent Bay, but unmarked on the chart, is dotted with summer camps west to Phelps Point. On the western half of the bay, you have to look carefully to see the natural sand dunes behind the beach. The dunes have been significantly diminished by development since late 1940.

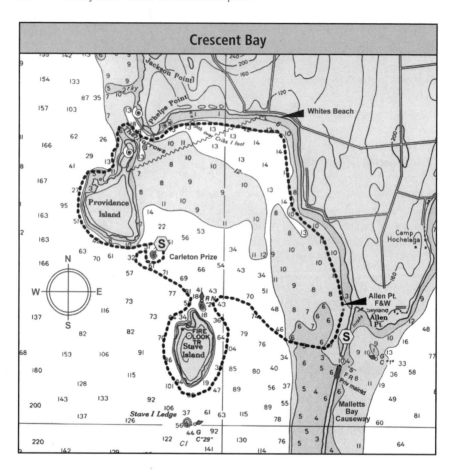

At rocky Phelps Point at the western end of the bay, we pull closer to shore to look for fossils. We spot one beautiful specimen of the 460-million-year-old cabbage-type fossils (stromatoporoid) that are similar to those found at Good-sell Ridge in Isle La Motte.

Just through the Narrows, we encounter a huge stone duck blind that looks like a WWII coastal fortress, made from rocks cut long ago from an old quarry near the point. Even these rocks contain fossils. We turn and head south, cross-ing the Narrows to Providence Island.

Providence Island, Stave Island, Carleton Prize

Paddling south along the western side of Providence Island, no more than 4 feet (1.2 meters) from shore, we hear the distant call of a loon and, shortly after, spy a doe and two fawns drinking at the water's edge. It is not uncommon to find deer on the islands, yet they are rarely seen once the summer residents return.

▶ **South Hero**

Providence (138 acres/55.8 hectares) and Stave (77 acres/31 hectares) islands are owned privately, so there are no places to land on either. The west sides of both islands have wonderful cliffs and rock formations, some as high as 30 feet (9.1 meters).The rock layers closest to the water are arranged like layers of a cake with frosting oozing out between them. An occasional large trapezoid of rock has slipped several feet or fallen off completely. White cedars with their bare roots exposed look as if they are doing a death-defying dance to stay upright on the thin soil above. Small clumps of wildflowers grow on the tiniest of ledges.

The rocky south shore of Providence reminds us of a well-built fortress that has stood the assault of wind, waves, and ice for millennia. The higher cliffs of the southeastern corner suddenly give way to the less dramatic, rock-cobble beaches of the eastern shore, where we leave Providence and head southeast to tiny Carleton Prize.

Carleton Prize. This small rocky jewel, conserved by the Lake Champlain Land Trust in 1978, has stood silent witness not only to the many merchant vessels, warships, smugglers, and pleasure boats that have come and gone from Malletts Bay, but also to those that have passed to the west headed up or down the lake.

Its name derives from an incident in October 1776, when Carleton Prize was more than just a witness to history. The morning after the famous Battle of Valcour, British General Guy Carleton sailed to this island in pursuit of the escaping American fleet. In the heavy fog he mistook the island for a fleeing American ship, but no matter how many cannonballs he fired, the ship would

Carleton Prize.

not sink. Only after the fog lifted did he realize that he had been firing on an island. We paddle around the island slowly, as if meeting an old friend after a long winter. It appears much like a large rock with a thin veneer of soil; a stand of cedar trees sits atop its 20-foot-high (6-meter) cliffs. It is possible to land on the north end of the island where a primitive trail climbs sharply up a dirt embankment to the top of the ledge and over to the south side.

Stave Island. The west shore of Stave resembles Providence, but with more of everything—higher cliffs, more defined bands of rock, more determined cedars, and more enticing caves. Like Providence, its shoreline must be viewed from no more than several feet away to be fully appreciated. Rounding the south side, we are careful not to block a mother merganser with her brood of chicks swimming near shore. As with Providence Island, the east side of Stave consists of a gently sloping, rock-pebble beach. The northeast corner of the island has a submerged shoal that is well marked by both navigation buoys and an ongoing visiting contingent of ducks, gulls, and cormorants.

Having spooked all the birds as we cross the shoal, we turn east and head home across the bay, completing one of the nicest circuits on Lake Champlain.

Layer cake rock.

▶ **South Hero**

Keeler Bay — *A Quiet Place*   **2**

by Cathy Frank

- **Launch site/Take out:** Keeler Bay F&W Area, Rt. 2, South Hero, Vermont
- **Distance**: 7 miles (11.2 kilometers)
- **Alternative launch sites**: None
- **Places to stop:** None aside from the launch site
- **Highlights:** Abundant wildlife in marshes adjacent to Rt. 2
- **Route:** This protected circle route closely follows the shoreline through a large marsh and then along a camp-lined shore, except for crossing the opening to the bay and circling Kellogg Island. There are no places to stop.
- **Comments:** This is one of the most protected routes on the lake, and boat traffic is limited.

The Paddle:

This well-protected bay opening to the northeast, almost 2 miles (3.2 kilometers) long and 1.5 miles (2.4 kilometers) at its mouth, is the perfect paddle for what is left of a "partly sunny with chance of thunderstorms" afternoon. And what a delightful surprise it turns out to be.

We paddle south from the fishing access past a few camps, a trailer park, and then into the marsh. This little arm close to Route 2 is incredibly rich in wildlife, both native and invasive. The sounds of cars passing mingle with the gentle lapping of waves and the squawk of a heron. The southern end of the bay is lined with cattails, thick with reeds and blooming yellow water lilies. The water is opaque.

When we venture out of the open channel in the middle of the marsh, we find ourselves locked in thick Eurasian milfoil, akin to paddling in spaghetti. We start involuntarily each time a fish jumps near our kayaks. A fisherman explains that bowfin, a large prehistoric fish, are prevalent here. It does make us think about how thin the layer of plastic is that separates us from what lies beneath the water's surface. This is clearly not water we are anxious to swim in, but it is a wonderful place to sit quietly and observe the wildlife for which this plant-crowded bay is home.

A great blue heron keeps its distance from us as it fishes the rich waters. Margy spots a black-crowned night heron blending beautifully into the vegetation, and then, quite by accident, we get too close to three tiny black and white duck chicks. With mom nowhere in sight, their camouflage protects them. We paddle away in one direction as they paddle off in the other. It's amazing how many little dramas of survival play out in these waters.

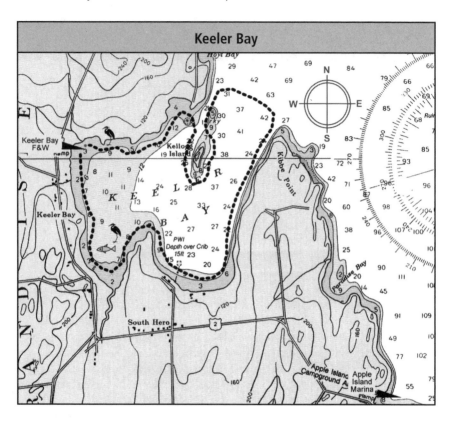

Kibbe Point. On the outer part of the bay, the shore is lined with older camps of small to moderate size. A wonderful, large, weathered, wooden swimming raft is anchored near the base of Kibbe Point. It has the look of a neighborhood project. A 5-foot (1.5-meter) pole sticks up in the middle with a solar landscaping light on top. Windsocks fly from all four corners, and mesh netting is draped from the pole out to the corners. We see no evidence that gulls have successfully landed. On the other hand we don't see any people, either.

Kellog Island. We turn north to Kellog Island, a small, private island (4 acres/1.6 hectares) with a camp on its north end. Two fishermen on the far side report no luck. On the north side of the bay, we watch a heron in the shallow water. It takes long, graceful steps, slowly moving away from the shore as it follows something our eyes cannot see. It stands perfectly still for what seems many minutes and then, in an instant, its neck shoots down into the water and retracts with a fish tightly speared on its mouth, perpendicular to its beak. It flies back to shore, lands, flips the fish 90° and (gulp) swallows it whole, its neck bulging as the fish slides slowly down. It almost hurts to watch. We paddle back to the fishing access just as thunderheads start to build in the west.

▶ **Keeler Bay**

Grand Isle East: Drawbridge to Sandbar
Pastoral Pleasures

3

by Cathy Frank

- ▪ **Launch site:** East side of Rt. 2 just north of drawbridge (unmarked), North Hero, Vermont
- ▪ **Distance:** 15 miles (24 kilometers)
- ▪ **Take out:** Apple Island Marina ($, Rt. 2, South Hero, Vermont)
- ▪ **Alternative launch sites:** Knight Point State Park ($, PT, Rt. 2, North Hero, Vermont), Grand Isle Town Beach (cartop launch only, E. Shore Rd., North in Pearl Bay, Vermont), Grand Isle State Park ($, PT, State Park Rd., off Rt. 2, Grand Isle, Vermont), Keeler Bay F&W Area (Rt. 2, Keeler Bay, Vermont), Sandbar F&W Area (Rt. 2, Milton, Vermont)
- ▪ **Places to stop:** Grand Isle State Park
- ▪ **Highlights:** Drawbridge, scenic view of Eagle Mountain, Green Mountains and islands of Inland Sea
- ▪ **Route:** This route closely follows the shoreline past homes, camps and farms except for a half mile where it crosses the opening to Keeler Bay. Alternate route involves launching or ending at Keeler Bay F&W (½ mile shorter) or adding a loop of Keeler Bay to the route (6.5 miles/10.4 kilometers additional distance).
- ▪ **Comments:** If you launch from Knight State Park, avoid large gears on the sides of the drawbridge when raised and watch currents and boat traffic under the bridge. This eastern shoreline does not give protection from strong north and south winds and waves.

The Paddle:

After leaving a car at the Apple Island Marina, we drive the length of Grand Isle to the small pebble beach on the east side of Route 2, just north of the drawbridge. In no time we are on the water, headed south. A line of weekend boaters slowly progresses under the open drawbridge. We watch them pass and then dart to Ladd Point on the northeastern tip of Grand Isle. The low and gently rolling countryside is green and lush. The shoreline is a mixture of open farmland with areas of camps and year-round homes set back from the water. Savage Island and a faint suggestion of the Sandbar Causeway come into view to the south. To the southeast, beyond Savage, we can see 574-foot-high (175-meter) Eagle Mountain on the Milton shoreline, rising steeply from the water's edge.

The historic Island Villa Hotel (the Grand Isle Lake House today) commands the view on the bluff just east of Pearl Bay. When built in 1903, it was considered a luxury hotel. Local history tells of people arriving in "city clothes" and fancy cars and being expected to wear "formal attire" at dinner. Fishing clothes, however, were acceptable at lunch. After a forty-year interlude as a sum-

Grand Isle East

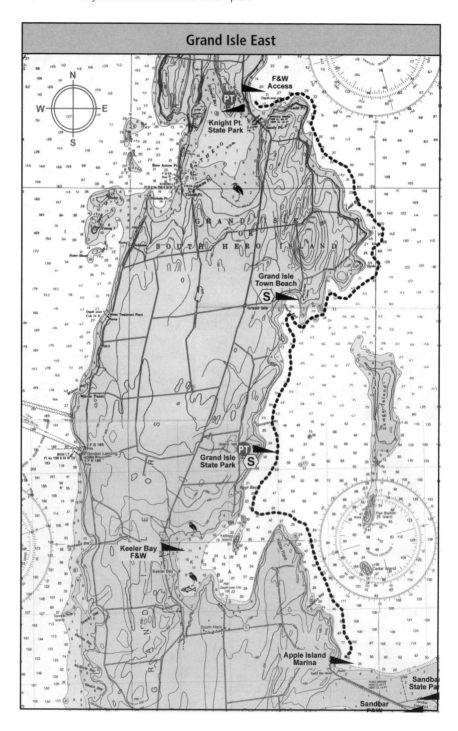

▶ **Grand Isle East: Drawbridge to Sandbar**

mer camp for girls run by the Sisters of Mercy, today it is a meeting and event facility conserved by the Preservation Trust of Vermont.

With the Grand Isle Town Beach behind us and Grand Isle State Park not yet in sight, we stop for lunch by rafting up, which creates our own, two-kayak-wide, picnic table. We forget time and worldly responsibilities as we lazily drift southward on the gentle north wind.

Savage Island slips by to the east. The laughter and yells of swimmers on the State Park beach interrupt the silence. In no time we find ourselves paddling by the mouth of Keeler Bay across to Kibbe Point. Colonies of old camps set close together remind us of summer life on the lake at the turn of the twentieth century. Near the causeway a row of ice-battered cottonwood trees prove their strength. As we turn into Apple Island Marina, a heron prances along the dock, headed out as we head in.

Island drawbridge.

by Margy Holden

- **Launch site:** Knight Point State Park ($, PT), Rt. 2, North Hero, Vermont
- **Distance:** 8 miles (13 kilometers)
- **Take out**: Vantines F&W Area (West Shore Rd., Grand Isle, VT)
- **Alternative launch sites:** East side of Rt. 2 just north of drawbridge (unmarked), North Hero, Vermont
- **Places to stop:** None aside from launch sites
- **Highlights**: Knight Point State Park, Island Line Railroad bed, Young Island (to prevent disturbing nesting sites, do not land), wildlife, cobble beach, views of the Adirondacks and the convoluted shore of The Gut
- **Route:** This route follows the shallow north shore of The Gut before crossing the narrow opening in the old railroad bed between Bow Arrow Point and the north shore of Grand Isle. It then follows the marshy north shore and shallow west shore of Grand Isle. Alternative routes include combining this trip with Grand Isle West to South Hero for a 16-mile (26-kilometer) trip or making a circle trip following the shoreline of The Gut.
- **Comments:** Avoid large gears on the sides of the drawbridge when raised. Watch currents and boat traffic under the bridge and in the narrow opening in the railroad bed. Waves will build along the west shore of Grand Isle, which is open to south, west, and north winds. The Gut is protected.

The Paddle:

Options abound for trips on this stretch of water. We choose to paddle 8 miles (13 kilometers) from Knight Point State Park to the Vantines Fish and Wildlife Access on West Shore Road in Grand Isle. We later go an equal distance from Vantines to Whites Beach in South Hero. The entire trip can also be done at one time. Circumnavigating The Gut between Grand Isle and North Hero makes a good, short, 4-mile (6-kilometer) trip.

At its broadest north-south reach, The Gut is over 2 miles (3 kilometers) long, bordered on the east by a drawbridge that connects North Hero and Grand Isle, and on the west by a causeway that once supported the Island Line rail bed, an extension of the one found between South Hero and Colchester.

Knight Point. The beach at Knight Point State Park is almost deserted, even on this warm summer day. I wonder how many of the people who crowd Sandbar State Park realize that Knight Point State Park is just fifteen minutes farther up Route 2. Fifty-four-acre (22-hectare) Knight Point State Park has a picnic area, a shelter, and is the home of the Island Center for the Arts, where numerous summer performances are held.

▶ **Grand Isle West**

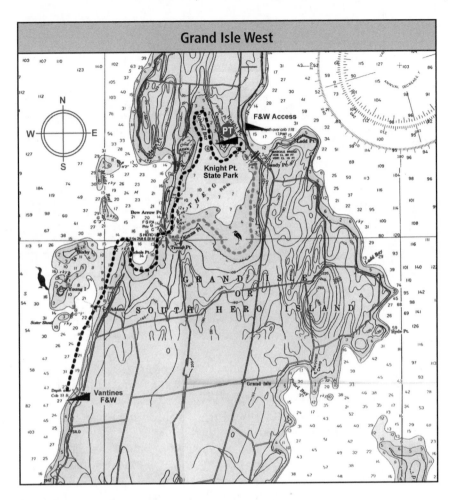

The land just west of the park has been designated Campmeeting Point Natural Area by the State of Vermont. As we paddle toward the point, evenly rounded stones, golf ball to softball size, replace the sand beach. This is geologically defined as a cobble beach, the longest stretch of this phenomenon to be found on Lake Champlain. The stones may have been carried into this protected area by the glaciers or worn down by wave action in the prehistoric sea. Windswept oaks and maples rise majestically above the cobbles on the shore. Hop hornbeam and hickory grow farther inland. Birds and other wildlife find protection in the adjacent cedar grove. The trail system on the point is easily accessible.

From Campmeeting Point, the shoreline curves north into Hibbard Bay, forming a long inlet between Campmeeting and Bow Arrow points. Camp Abenaki, founded in 1901 and run by the YMCA of Burlington, occupies the picturesque shore on the west side of Hibbard Bay. I can almost hear the echoes

Spanning the Gap

Knight Point. What was The Gut like before the drawbridge? Communication between the early settlers of Grand Isle and North Hero was challenging until John Knight, after whom the state park is named, began a ferry service in 1785. His family operated it until 1892, when a swing bridge was built. The bridge could be rotated ninety degrees from the center to accommodate passing boats. In windy conditions the bridge could be so difficult to operate that the tender's wife or a fisherman had to be recruited to lend a helping hand. A drawbridge replaced the swing bridge in 1955. It lifts every half hour on demand during the boating season, temporarily halting the summer tourists and year-round commuters who keep Route 2 busy.

The Gut is an unusual name. Unable to find its origin, we appreciate the humor of the individual who began using the moniker. This stomach-shaped body of water takes in boat traffic at either end and spills it out the other. We have resisted using a number of puns.

of more than a hundred years of happy campers including my husband, who taught sailing, and Cathy's husband, who was a camper. The tradition of summers at Camp Abenaki continues to this day.

Bow Arrow Point resembles a long icicle hanging south from North Hero. From 1901 to 1961, it supported the rail bed of the Island Line, one link on its route from Burlington to Alburgh. A swing bridge built 40 feet (12 meters) above the water connected the tip of Bow Arrow Point in North Hero to the tip of Tromp Point, a finger reaching northward from Grand Isle. Two swinging bridges in less than two miles must have been quite a sight. The small building at the southern tip of Bow Arrow Point is the old tender's house. Now owned privately, it has been refurbished as a seasonal cottage. Below the cottage we see the underwater ruins of a rock crib that must have supported a bridge pier.

We can almost cross from Bow Arrow Point in North Hero to Tromp Point in Grand Isle with one stroke of our paddles. But beware of the current. At its deepest point The Gut reaches almost 12 feet (4 meters), but off the north shore of Grand Isle the water shrinks to a depth of 3 feet (less than 1 meter) and under.

The British fleet under General Carleton is reputed to have hidden near here on October 10, 1776, the night before they encountered the American fleet in the Battle of Valcour.

Leaving The Gut, we paddle silently from Tromp Point to Nichols Point hoping to see waterfowl and then pausing to give a merganser mother time to

▶ **Grand Isle West**

lead her train of chicks away from us. The shallowness of this bay limits boat traffic, while the marshy land prohibits development. It makes an ideal nesting and resting spot for waterfowl. In the high water, one can paddle inside the marsh to appreciate the frogs and spawning fish. We think snow when the seed fuzz from the cottonwoods drifts down on us, and it is magical when dragonflies land to inspect the bows of our kayaks. Much of the time the tip of Nichols Point becomes an island, and today we paddle between it and Grand Isle, not disturbing the cormorants and ring-bill gulls that perch on the rocks.

The Sister Islands. Young and Bixby islands lie off the northwestern end of Grand Isle. Bixby, the northernmost of the two, is owned privately, but Young Island is owned by the State of Vermont. They don't look much like sisters. Bixby wins the beauty contest with its woods and cottages. Young is almost bald, has one forlorn building and a few remnants of bare tree trunks. Yet appearances can be deceiving, as Young Island is far from unoccupied. Along with the Four Brothers Islands off the New York shore near Willsboro, Young has provided a nesting site for the infamous double-crested cormorant, ring billed gulls, and other colonial species. Over time the cormorants have denuded the island with their intense nesting and guano. Young is at the center of a controversy about how to manage the double-crested cormorant population. In 2008, the Vermont Department of Fish and Wildlife was successful in eliminating the cormorants and planned to do the same to much of the rest of the bird population in order to create a park. Environmental groups vigorously protest the plan. Young and Bixby Islands make good destinations to paddle around, as long as we don't try to land and we stay far enough away to not disturb the birds.

The Cormorant Quandary

The presence of the double-crested cormorant and its impact on Lake Champlain are environmental and political issues. Their sheer numbers and aggressive nesting habit drive out other species. When cormorants inhabit an island, they eventually denude it, leaving it barren of its original vegetation. Fishermen worry that cormorants take more than their share of fish. Young Island, off the Grand Isle shore, and the Four Brothers Islands, off Willsboro Point, are dramatic examples of what these birds can do and have become the focus of concern and research.

The statistics are impressive. A single cormorant nest was found on Young Island in 1981. Eleven years later there were thirty-four, and by 1998 the population had exploded exponentially to 2,597.

By 2004, David Capen, an ornithologist and professor at the University of Vermont, estimated the cormorant population on Lake Champlain to be close to 20,000 birds, nesting predominantly on Young Island and the Four Brothers. Why such a large increase? Professor Capen points out that the cormorants are wintering at huge fish farms in the southern United States, where food is unlimited, allowing them to return north in the spring dramatically healthier and therefore more productive.

In reaction to the explosive increase in the cormorant population, Professor Capen and his graduate students began a series of experiments in 2001. The goal was to limit the cormorant population without disturbing the birds and possibly causing them to move to, nest on, and denude additional islands. The solution that evolved was to coat eggs in some nests at night with corn oil. Oiling prevents the eggs from hatching; doing it at night is less disturbing to the birds. As long as some eggs hatch, the cormorants' instincts are fulfilled, making them unlikely to re-nest elsewhere. Can you imagine gingerly stepping through sleeping cormorants on their nests of delicate eggs in the dark? These committed scientists and students see the impact these birds have on an island's vegetation and believe in what they are doing. This successful experiment did cause a gradual decrease in the cormorant population without dispersing them to other islands.

In 2004 the Vermont Department of Fish and Wildlife, which owns Young Island, applied for and received a permit to shoot 20 percent of the nesting cormorants there. This action reduced the cormorant population on Young, but after the first year of shooting, 20 percent of the cormorants moved to nest on the Four Brothers, a dramatic example of how an action in one part of an ecosystem inevitably impacts another part. Some cormorants have since tried to return to Young Island, which is more convenient to their favorite fishing spots for yellow perch on the northern part of the lake. By 2008, however, the State of Vermont had eliminated the entire population of nesting cormorants on Young Island, causing many of the birds to disperse to other islands in the lake and some sites along the lakeshore, such as Porter's Bay and Crown Point.

The Nature Conservancy, which owns the Four Brothers Islands, in 2008 for the first time began active management of the cormorant population there by using the proven egg-oiling method. It is hoped that this procedure will gradually decrease the population of cormorants without dispersing them to other locations around the lake.

▶ **Grand Isle West**

As the cormorant population increases, so do their human enemies. The first controlled study of social attitudes about the cormorants among people who use Lake Champlain is a step in demonstrating how attitudes, not just science, influence decision-making.

Adams Landing. Adams Landing, on the Grand Isle shore, is less than a mile from Young and Bixby. What a bustling place this was for those traveling Lake Champlain in the 1700s and 1800s using man, wind, and then steam power. As the name implies, landings like Adams, Wilcox Cove, and Chazy were centers of commerce, providing goods and shelter for travelers up and down the lake. The small frame building on the point at Adams Landing was once a general store. The gracious, large, brick and wood frame homes nearby served as inns in former lives. A huge cottonwood grows on the vestiges of rock cribs that once formed the basis for piers.

The views ahead on Lake Champlain of the high peaks of the Adirondacks become more spectacular as we paddle south from the landing. In contrast, the view directly across from us is completely flat. From Adams Landing south to the fishing access on West Shore Road, cliffs alternate with shale beaches, seasonal cottages, year-round homes, and one farm. We see a good example of eroding lakeshore in a number of old homes that sit much too close to the cliff edge.

The Fish & Wildlife Access can be a busy place, but today there is no competition for the ramp. The Gut and the islands make a brief but full paddle.

Young Island.

5 **Grand Isle West to South Hero**
A Sunset Shore

by Margy Holden

- ■ **Launch site:** Vantines F&W Area, West Shore Rd., Grand Isle, Vermont
- ■ **Distance:** 8 miles (13 kilometers)
- ■ **Take out:** Whites Beach (West Shore Rd., South Hero, Vermont)
- ■ **Places to stop:** Above launch sites and Grand Isle Ferry Dock and restaurant (pebble beach on south side of ferry slips), Ed Weed Fish Hatchery, Lake Champlain Basin Program (within walking distance)
- ■ **Highlights:** Ed Weed Fish Hatchery, Lake Champlain Basin Program Information, ferry, islands, views of the Adirondacks
- ■ **Route:** This route hugs the shallow, settled west shore of Grand Isle, passing cliffs and shale beaches, in and out of numerous bays. The proximity of Providence Island provides the opportunity for an additional loop (3 miles/ 5 kilometers).
- ■ **Comments:** Give wide berth to the ferry and currents it creates. Waves build up along the west shore of Grand Isle in winds from the south, west, and north. Heavy, fast-moving boat traffic is possible through the narrows between Phelps Point and Providence Island.

The Paddle:

We push off for a relaxing paddle passing cottages and year-round homes where an increasing number of residents commute to Burlington. Shale cliffs and beaches line the shore and in some places harbor trilobite fossils. We admire another historic brick inn and find modern cultural artifacts—golf balls sit in the sandy shallows just below the Wilcox Cove Golf Course and Cottages. Nearby, we check out the busy waterfront to the Lake Champlain Adult Campground.

Gordons Landing. Gordons Landing has been a center of activity from the time Grand Isle was settled. Beginning in winters in the 1700s, sleighs, carriages, and eventually cars crossed the frozen lake on the ice between here and Cumberland Head. The first summer ferry service started in 1796. It's hard to believe that there was enough traffic. Times haven't changed. The Lake Champlain Transportation Company's ferries carry close to 3,000 commuters a day around the clock, along with cars, camper trailers, and tractor trailers. Now home to the Ed Weed Fish Culture Station, the Lake Champlain Basin Project, and the Grand Isle Ferry, Gordons Landing has become a hub of lake-related work.

The Lake Champlain Basin Program and a Fish and Wildlife office occupy the historic Gordon House on the grounds of the fish hatchery. The Basin Program receives federal, state, provincial, and local funds, channeling them into research and programs to support the well-being of Lake Champlain. It is a cooperative

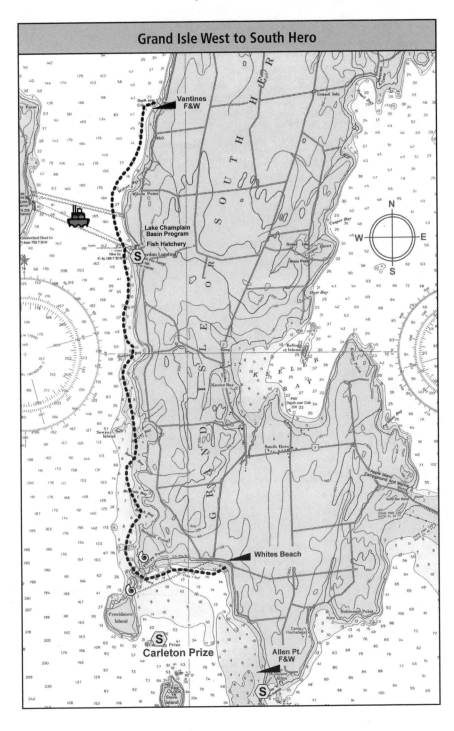

Grand Isle West to South Hero

The Hatchery

The Ed Weed Fish Culture Station, a fish hatchery built in 1991 by the State of Vermont, looks down on Gordons Landing in Grand Isle. This hatchery produces 130,000 pounds of trout and salmon in 18-month cycles, plus 350,000 brown and rainbow trout trophy fish. The output stocks Vermont streams and lakes as well as fresh water in other states. Paddlers can visit the huge tanks to watch fish of all sizes feed in the continuously moving water, the polishing pond, the exit stream, and an educational center with live exhibits and videos.

Uneaten fish food and feces, rich in phosphorus, flow to a treatment facility and through a settling pond before entering the weed-choked bay below the hatchery. The settling pond is a haven for migrating waterfowl. A strong sport-fishing lobby supports the hatchery on Lake Champlain. It was originally proposed for Fields Bay in Addison County, Vermont, a shallow bay near Otter Creek, but a homeowner protest ensued. Grand Isle was chosen because one of the intake pipes providing cold water, essential for fish culture, could be located in deep, frigid water. Grand Isle residents welcomed the hatchery as an employer and tourist destination. But what is the impact of this phosphorus on the lake? Studies carried out during the permitting process for the hatchery showed that the phosphorus-loaded effluent could be carried north and out of the lake by the strong current. We hope that it does not increase phosphorus levels here or elsewhere.

venture that includes Vermont, New York, and Quebec, and is one of the major programs advocating for and providing information about Lake Champlain.

We leave Gordons Landing, skirt the approaching ferry, and head south along a well-settled shoreline. At Eagle Camp, where families have been spending their vacations since the 1800s, the waterfront is a busy place. We pass privately owned Sawyer Island and enjoy four more bays before reaching Phelps Point. We paddle through The Narrows between Providence and South Hero, along the sandy beach, and take out at Whites Beach. This paddle has given us much to see and much to contemplate.

▶ **Grand Isle West to South Hero**

Drawbridge to North Hero Village and Back
Lake Weather—A Lesson Learned

6

by Cathy Frank

- ■ **Launch site/Take out:** East side of Rt. 2 just north of drawbridge (unmarked), North Hero, Vermont
- ■ **Distance:** 7.5 miles (12 kilometers)
- ■ **Alternative launch sites:** Knight Point State Park ($, PT, Rt. 2, North Hero, Vermont), Hero's Welcome ($, Rt. 2, in North Hero village, Vermont)
- ■ **Places to stop:** None aside from launch sites
- ■ **Highlights:** Wildlife in marsh at south end of City Bay, scenic views of Green Mountains and islands of the Inland Sea
- ■ **Route:** This loop route hugs the shallow eastern shoreline of North Hero, but also offers the option to paddle across open water to Knight (public access) and Dameas (privately owned) islands. There are no public stopping places along the shore between the put-in north of the drawbridge and City Bay.
- ■ **Comments:** If you launch from Knight State Park, avoid large gears on the sides of the drawbridge when raised and watch currents and boat traffic under the bridge. This eastern shoreline does not give protection from strong north and south winds and waves.

The Paddle:

The weather report is for a warm, sunny day without significant winds. We park at the pull-off on the east side of Rt. 2 just north of the bridge.

North Hero is basically a farming community. The gently sloping shoreline dotted with a scattering of camps, homes, and farms looks east to Burton Island and St. Albans Bay and the Green Mountains beyond.

Enjoying the tranquility of the day and place, and the view of Mt. Mansfield and Jay Peak to the east, we note with surprise the faint rumble of thunder in the distance and discover some dark clouds well to the north and east of us. Most storms on the lake travel from west to east, so we are not too worried, but find it a little disconcerting. It is not the preferred background music of kayaking. We continue paddling, observing an occasional kingfisher hovering above the water searching for dinner. We follow another storm cloud's progress attentively as it, too, passes well to the north of us. So much for the weather forecast!

As we approach North Hero village nestled into shallow and protected City Bay, the dark clouds in the west appear more numerous and the distant thunder becomes an almost steady, dull, background rumble. I have my heart set on sipping a cold iced tea on the deck at Hero's Welcome while watching the shore birds and ducks congregated in the marshland in the south part of the bay, but the thunder is persuasive and we are starting to feel vulnerable. So, forgoing the pleasures of Hero's Welcome and the allure of the bay, we reluctantly turn

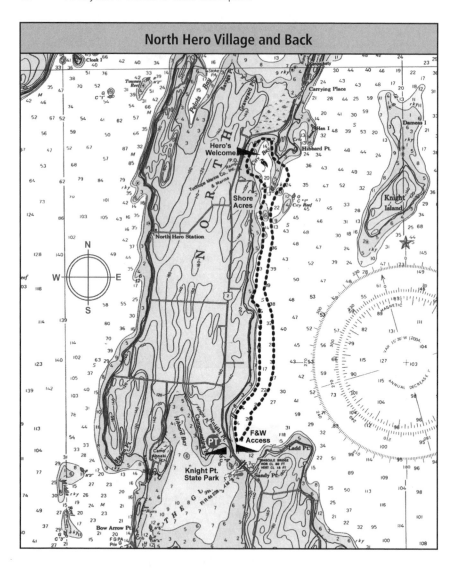

North Hero Village and Back

around and paddle south, being careful to stay close to the gently sloping shore should we need to exit the water instantly.

Just as we approach the large, manicured lawns of Shore Acres, a small resort with a restaurant and inn about a mile south of City Bay, it is clear that a storm is coming directly at us. The thunder is frequent and loud, and my eye catches a glimpse of lightning. I look back at Margy and point to the west. She nods, and simultaneously we turn toward shore, paddling as hard as we can. We pull our boats out of the water quickly, turn them over, secure our paddles underneath, and run up to the Shore Acres Restaurant as the skies open up.

▶ **Drawbridge to North Hero Village and Back**

Once we are safely inside and our adrenalin levels start to return to normal, the smell of food hits our nostrils and our thoughts turn to lunch. Somewhat concerned about our wet, bedraggled appearance, we sheepishly ask the woman at the desk if we might have lunch. She responds in the affirmative. We quickly do an inventory of our pockets and discover that we have one $10 bill and no credit cards between us. Lunch will be small. So, attired in wet sandals, shorts, and T-shirts, we follow the waitress to our table.

We are led to a table next to two couples who are looking at us rather strangely. As we try to sit down, we realize we still have our life jackets on. Ah, yes. Trying to be as nonchalant as we can, we nod politely, take off our life jackets, hang them on the back of our chairs, sit down, and proceed to look at the menu, as if wearing life jackets to lunch were something we did every day.

By the time we leave, the storm has passed and the sun is shining. We slip our kayaks back in the water and push off from shore with a great deal more respect for Lake Champlain's changeable weather than we had when we began this paddle. Relaxed, we start to notice the camps along the shore, the islands of the Inland Sea, and the mountains beyond. Life is good.

One thing is certain—neither of us will ever kayak without cash and a credit card again. And, regardless of the forecast, we will always make a mental note of places to pull out. We were lucky North Hero has a gently sloping shoreline. Lessons well-learned. Lastly, we will always have warm thoughts in our hearts for Shore Acres—our refuge in the storm.

Gathering storm.

Alburgh Dunes State Park through The Gut
Paddling the Island Line

by Margy Holden

- **Launch site:** Alburgh Dunes State Park ($), Coon Point Rd. off Rt. 129, Alburgh, Vermont
- **Distance:** 13 miles (21 kilometers)
- **Take out:** Vermont Boat Launch (east of Rt. 2, just north of drawbridge, North Hero, Vermont)
- **Alternative launch sites:** North Hero Marina ($, Pelots Point Rd., North Hero, Vermont), Knight Point State Park ($, PT, Rt. 2, North Hero, Vermont), Holcomb Bay–LaBombard F&W Access (Access Rd., off Quarry Rd., Isle la Motte, Vermont)
- **Places to stop:** Pelots Point F&W Fishing Access (unmarked from the water)
- **Highlights:** Sand dunes, beach pea, and cedar forest of Alburgh Dunes State Park (trails accessible from beach), Island Line Railroad bed, drawbridge, views of the distant Adirondacks, Isle la Motte, and Carry Bay
- **Route:** This route follows the settled North Hero western shoreline with its cliffs and shale beaches. Between The Gut and the drawbridge, the choice is to paddle either the south shore of North Hero or the north shore of Grand Isle, depending on wind and waves.
- **Comments:** Avoid large gears on the sides of the drawbridge when raised and watch currents and boat traffic under the bridge and in the openings in the Island Line Railroad bed. Waves can build on the west side of North Hero in south, west, and north winds. Routes in The Gut are protected from high winds and the fetch.

The Paddle:
We begin at Alburgh Dunes State Park, travel the length of Alburgh's Point of Tongue, cross the outlet to Carry Bay, follow the west shore of North Hero, pass through The Gut, under the drawbridge, and take out along Route 2. The scenery on this dead calm, early fall day swarms our senses with one delight after another before the wind picks up a bit.

We push off from the beach looking south, enchanted by the still water that mirrors back an incredible vista. Wow! On the shore we have just left to the north, the tiny sand dunes and beach pea backed by cedar forest reminds us that this ever-evolving landscape once held saltwater. Just ahead, the shale cliffs of Point of Tongue, named by the French, support homes ranging from huge to most modest. We've hardly begun and we have already witnessed the evidence of geologic drama and French settlement, and experienced striking scenery.

Paddling south along Point of Tongue, we spot a familiar site. The huge marble blocks that support the bed of the Rutland Island Line separate Carry Bay from the rest of Lake Champlain. Many of these enormous blocks show the long, parallel gouges made for the dynamite charges used to cleave them from

▶ **Alburgh Dunes State Park through The Gut**

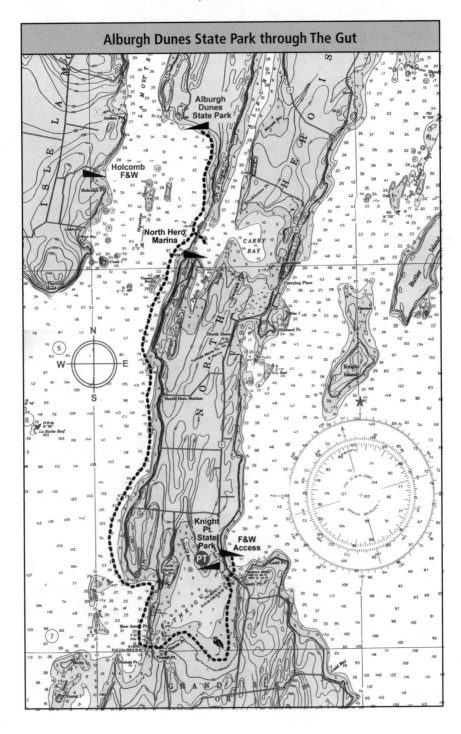

Alburgh Dunes State Park through The Gut

Vermont quarries. Were these ends and pieces, rejected for the facades of urban buildings? They sure have weathered lots of storms here.

Unable to resist, we paddle briefly into Carry Bay. The kind of algae we see in the water today led to a successful movement to have the north end of the railroad bed removed. To the south, the North Hero Marina employees lift a huge powerboat out of the water. On a day like this, would the owners wish they had chosen a later date? Maybe not, because tomorrow the temperature could be in the forties with a strong NW wind. Such is the nature of fall on the lake.

A current strong enough to dimple the calm water propels us back through the opening into the broad lake. Dead ahead, Isle la Motte and Cloak Island beckon from less than a mile away to the west, suggesting a circle trip back to the State Park. So many routes, so little time. Committed to our planned route, we turn south. Tall masts of boats in the marina protrude behind the railroad causeway. We land briefly at the fishing access to explore a beach mounded high with tiny Lake Champlain-crafted pebbles.

In this completely still water, we must be able to see down twenty feet. What look like edible-sized yellow perch dart into the weeds, probably scared by the shadows of our approaching kayaks. Zebra mussels fill grooves highlighting the north-south glacial striations in the flat rock slabs on the bottom. The occasional tire appears to be another favorite zebra mussel habitat. Improbably tall weeds occasionally reach all the way to the surface.

Twenty-foot cliffs dominate the scenery south of the causeway. Cedars cling to the top, hiding the dwellings and the road. A few have succumbed to

North Hero reflections.

▶ Alburgh Dunes State Park through The Gut

recent high winds and lie fully leaved in the shallow water. A moored boat floats upside-down in the deeper water. We think that we can see examples of gastropod fossils in the cliffs, which is not surprising given our proximity to the Isle la Motte fossil preserve.

We continue south for three miles along a straight, settled, North Hero western shore, broken only occasionally by open fields. To the south, the view of the high peaks of the Adirondacks comes closer and ever more dramatic. To the west, the marina at Mooney Bay bristles with the masts of sailboats, but the land behind has leveled out into lake plain. Homeowners, appreciating the day, seem to have found projects to do along the shore and wave as we pass. Flocks of geese create a constant chorus overhead. We inhale the beauty around us, savoring near and distant views, the fall scents of water, earth, cedar, drying turtle grass from the shore, and the sights beneath the surface of the water.

All too soon, boat traffic picks up as we approach The Gut. We pass under the cliffs of Hazen Point beneath its imposing old home, circle a small bay, and continue along skinny Bow Arrow Point into an increasing breeze from the south. For the second time today we paddle along the Island Line Railroad bed that extends the tip of the point. Reaching the end, we scoot through the current to the tip of the railroad bed that reaches out from Grand Isle. The trains used to cross this opening on a swing bridge forty feet above the water. The bridge is gone, but fishermen favor this spot with its fast-moving water.

Should we follow the north or south shore of The Gut? With the wind increasing from the south, we vote for the protected shore and continue along the east side of the railroad bed in Grand Isle.

We paddle along Simms Point out of the wind, passing a shore unmarked by buildings except for one modern dwelling and a boarded-up, stately, brick home that resembles the architecture of historic inns along this shore. We see cornfields in the distance. I absentmindedly stare at what I think is a weed floating on the surface, but come to attention when it opens its mouth and flicks its tongue. It disappears before I can get a closer look. We haven't seen many water snakes on Lake Champlain.

East of Simms Point, reeds, and then cattails fill the water while the sounds of unseen harvesters penetrate the tall trees along the shore. With almost a mile to the drawbridge and the wind behind us, we practically fly northeast across the shallow, weed-filled bay past houses and camps tucked between the shore and Route 2. An elderly couple fishing beneath the drawbridge waves to us. They seem unperturbed when we jump at the thunderous sound of a truck hitting the metal decking on the bridge high above us. On the east side of the bridge, in the short distance to the access, someone has built a rock monolith, hidden from the road, but right here for us to appreciate. It is an unexpected present at the end of a beautiful day.

It's been our first three-town day: we began in Alburgh, covered much of the west shore of North Hero, and ended along the north shore of Grand Isle.

| 8 | **Paddling the North Half of North Hero**
South Wind—Another Lesson Learned |

by Cathy Frank

- ■ **Launch site:** Hero's Welcome ($), Rt. 2, in center of North Hero village, Vermont
- ■ **Distance:** 16 miles (25.7 kilometers)
- ■ **Take out:** North Hero Marina ($, Pelots Point Rd., North Hero, Vermont)
- ■ **Alternative launch sites:** King Bay F&W Area (Lake View Dr., North Hero, Vermont), Stoney Point (also called Stephenson's) F&W Area (Lakeview Drive to North End Rd. East, North Hero, Vermont), North Hero State Park ($, PT, 9 Lakeview Dr. to north Hero State Park Rd., North Hero, Vermont)
- ■ **Places to stop:** None aside from launch sites
- ■ **Highlights:** North Hero State Park and its abundant wildlife, scenic views of islands of the Inland Sea, wildlife in Carry Bay, scenic views of Isle La Motte and the Adirondacks through opening of old Island Line railway causeway
- ■ **Route:** This "almost" loop route in mostly shallow water offers pastoral shoreline on the east side, a picnic and swimming area at North Hero State Park and marshy, undeveloped areas on the east side of the Alburgh Passage. The narrow Alburgh Passage offers smooth water even in a moderate wind.
- ■ **Comments:** Many launch sites make infinite trip variations possible. There is no way to cross Rt. 2 at the historic carry on public property except when the water is neither too high nor too low, when one can paddle under Rt. 2 through the culvert that connects Carry Bay to the Inland Sea. The eastern shore of North Hero does not give protection from strong north and south winds and waves. A strong south wind affects the Alburgh Passage, but produces no significant waves. Carry Bay can be quite rough in strong north and south winds.

The Paddle:

The northern part of North Hero is almost an island unto itself, save for the fifty-foot-wide Carrying Place at its southern end that connects it to the southern part of North Hero. It is tempting to paddle around it as if it were an island. However, because there is no public access on either side of Carrying Place, the only way over or under this barrier is through a roughly six-foot-diameter culvert that is only passable by kayak when the water level is neither too high nor too low. (It is sad and ironic that this historic portage, used throughout history as a shortcut between the broad lake and the Inland Sea, is today so inaccessible to the public.)

The first time we circumnavigated the northern part of North Hero, Birdland, a funky little restaurant at the southern end of Carrying Place and that had property on both sides of Carrying Place, was still open (it is now closed), and they allowed us to start from there. The second time, we started at Hero's Welcome in City Bay and ended our trip at the North Hero Marina at Pelots Bay.

▶ **Paddling the North Half of North Hero**

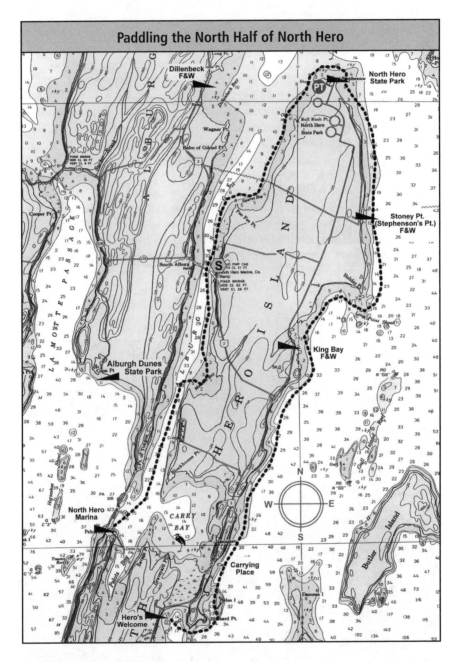

Paddling the North Half of North Hero

Additionally, there are four public access ramps on this north part of the island, all of which can be used as starting points for out-and-back trips of whatever length you choose.

The South Wind. We are both free and desperate to paddle on this otherwise beautiful day. We are convinced that if we hug the east shore, we will avoid the full brunt of today's 10–20-MPH south wind. (This was early in our journey around Lake Champlain, and we had a lot to learn about the lake's south wind— mainly, that there are days one should just stay home.)

We wade out a few yards into the shallow water and try to get ourselves in our kayaks while they bob up and down in the 3-foot (.9-meter) waves. We were sure we would not encounter waves this close to shore. I immediately tip my kayak over before I ever get in it. (Underwater rocks, innocent as they may look, are almost always slippery. Unfortunately, knowing this does not help.) I get up, dust myself off, so to speak, and finally make it into the kayak on the third try. (Have we mentioned that it is impossible to go kayaking without getting wet?) With some difficulty we attach our spray skirts, turn northeast and, propelled both by wind and waves, take off like rockets up the 8-mile (12.9-kilometer) length of the eastern shore. Like the southern part of North Hero, farms, homes and camps dot the gently rolling landscape on this part of the island.

We quickly find that staying in the shallow water close to shore is a big problem as we encounter bigger waves and an unorganized sort of chop that brings waves breaking over our bow and stern from almost every direction. This effect is

Find the Carry Bay culvert (viewed from the west side).

▶ Paddling the North Half of North Hero

most pronounced near Long Point Shoal, where we are forced even farther from shore. On a calmer day it would be fun to stop at one of the public launch sites along this section of shoreline for a swim or snack.

With all this unharnessed power behind us, we should be enjoying a free ride. Instead, we are straining to keep our kayaks on top of the waves, heading northeast, and avoiding underwater hazards. Margy is particularly vocal about her little 8-foot (2.4-meter) peapod-shaped kayak. She is constantly thrown from wave to wave and finding it difficult to stay on course. Her boat was not meant for these waves. *We* were not meant for these waves. There is no way to stop until we round Stephenson Point and find ourselves in the lee in front of North Hero State Park. What a relief! We are exhausted and exhilarated—and famished. From this delightful spot, Hog Island and the Maquam shore of mainland Vermont are only a mile away. We watch cars and trucks crossing the Missisquoi Bay Bridge about 3 miles (4.8 kilometers) northeast.

Most of this 399-acre (161.5-hectare) state park was once farmed. A third has an elevation of less than 100 feet (30.5 meters) above sea level. This flood-prone area is a rich and diverse wildlife habitat. Several migratory bird species—mallards, blacks, and wood ducks, among others—nest here, as do map turtles. Fish spawn in the flooded areas.

We are not anxious to leave this calm cocoon, but there is only one way home. So, after a quick swim and lunch, we get back in our kayaks and paddle west for only a short distance before we round the northwest corner of the island and feel the full brunt of the south wind, this time in our faces as we head up the Alburgh Passage. A little more than 5 miles long (8 kilometers), it is less than a third of a mile wide in places, a fact that minimizes the size of the waves, but not the wind itself. I find it amazing that a glacier can carve such a narrow channel when the land on either side is not particularly rocky or elevated. I have the urge to grab North Hero and give it a shove west, closing the gap and attaching it to Alburgh. Then we could walk. Once we pass beyond the state park boundary, the undeveloped forested shoreline becomes dotted with homes, camps and farms.

It is a long, slow, energy-consuming paddle south. We stop only once, behind a small anchorage and marina at the South Alburgh bridge, to have a snack and rest. It is incredibly peaceful. "Margy, can we stay here forever? Was this your idea or mine?"

Shallow and protected Macomb Bay looks inviting, promising abundant wildlife viewing, but our energy level is rapidly diminishing. Unfortunately, the wind is not. So we continue south. When we reach Carry Bay, much to our dismay, the waves return. Our arms have just enough energy left to paddle a wobbly line back to the Marina. Before we are off the water Margy blurts out, "I'm buying a new kayak. Tomorrow!"

On our first trip we stumbled ashore, straightened our fingers from their claw-like grip on the paddles, and triumphantly marched into Birdland, where Margy ordered a hot fudge sundae and I, a huge vanilla milkshake. We sat there for about 45 minutes savoring every bite and sip. Comfort food? No way. Pure and simple, this was conquest food.

Lessons learned: we agree that we should have postponed this trip, but having completed it without major mishaps (just total exhaustion), we are glad we did it. It has boosted our confidence, both in ourselves and in each other. Spending a windy day on Lake Champlain in a kayak is a learning experience with its own set of unique observations. Some lessons must be learned the hard way.

Outing.

▶ Paddling the North Half of North Hero

Carry and Pelots Bays
Marsh and More

9

by Cathy Frank

- **Launch site/Take out:** North Hero Marina ($), Pelots Point Rd., North Hero, Vermont
- **Distance:** 8 miles (12.9 kilometers)
- **Alternative launch sites:** none
- **Places to stop:** None aside from launch site
- **Highlights:** Abundant wildlife in both bays, scenic views of Isle La Motte and the Adirondacks through opening of old Island Line railway causeway
- **Route:** This relatively protected loop route through shallow water is rich in wildlife and scenic beauty, thanks to abundant marsh areas. There are no places to stop, but there are plenty of places to stop paddling and rest. When the lake level is high, the area accessible by kayak in the shallow marsh areas expands considerably. The lack of large boat traffic gives this place a serene atmosphere.
- **Comments:** Watch for poison ivy at Pelots Point F&W Fishing Area. Carry Bay can be quite rough in strong north and south winds.

The Paddle:

These two shallow protected bays are rich in wildlife and short on heavy boat traffic—a perfect place for paddlers. The old Island Line causeway running across the western opening augments this natural configuration, providing an added layer of protection or interference, depending on your point of view. This is the third railroad causeway we have encountered in the islands, and we cannot help but be somewhat horrified (and at the same time impressed) by the impact these causeways have had on three significant areas in the Champlain Islands—Malletts Bay, The Gut, and Carry Bay. In all three areas the causeways enclose bays. They also seem to restrict water flow to and from the broad lake. The shallow water in Carry and Pelots bays is prone to algae growth in the summer.

This early July day, the water clarity is excellent. As we head north along the railway causeway, we linger for a moment at the opening to the broad lake. Like the Malletts Bay opening, there used to be a swing bridge back in the days of the railroad. From here there is a clear view to Isle La Motte, the New York shore, and the Adirondacks. From any point on the lake, it is rare to see just one body of water or point of land. There are almost always layers for the eye to peel away.

At camp-lined Point of the Tongue, an unusual name with French origins, we turn east, crossing the Alburgh Passage, and head for Blockhouse Point, named after a British blockhouse that guarded the entrance to Carry Bay up until 1794, well after the British had lost the American Revolution (1783). By far the most interesting parts of Carry Bay are the marshy east and south sides. The high

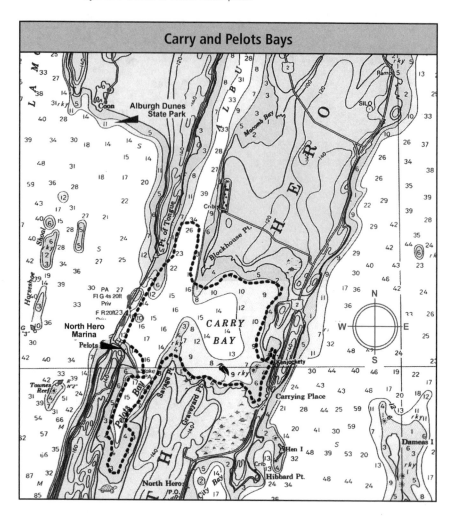

Carry and Pelots Bays

water level, more characteristic of spring than early July, allows us to paddle in between bushes and trees, by a large beaver lodge, and over fallen logs. Sharply bent rushes, together with their watery mirror images, create perfectly symmetrical geometric shapes. The cloud-dotted blue sky adds another dimension.

A stand of cottonwoods, some growing at a disconcerting angle to vertical, and others dead but still standing, lines the eastern shore. Their fluffy cotton-like seeds dot the water. These large, water-loving trees, common along the shores of Lake Champlain, always command attention.

We almost miss the culvert that runs under the road to the Inland Sea, because only the top fourth of it is above water today. We stop and watch the methodical fishing technique of a lone heron before moving on. This rich natural world is broken by some well-kept, year-round homes around the point in

▶ **Carry and Pelots Bays**

Bryozoan.

Pelots Bay, but once past those we are again into unspoiled wetland. Yellow water lilies abound, as do tall stands of cattails. Attached to reeds about 6–8 inches below the water are some freshwater bryozoans—huge, ball-shaped blobs that look like a mass of frogs' eggs but are actually marine invertebrate animals that form permanently attached colonies. Turtles of all sizes sun themselves on partially submerged logs. This wonderful wetland needs to be passed through slowly in order to take in all that is going on here.

We drive home with thoughts of paddling this biologically rich area again—perhaps in another season.

Cottonwoods—how stable are these trees, anyway?

10   Isle La Motte — *Paddling through Time*

by Cathy Frank

- **Launch site/Take out:** Holcomb Bay–Labombard F&W Area, Access Rd. off Quarry Rd., Isle La Motte, Vermont. It looks like a driveway; take a sharp right at the house and proceed to the end.
- **Distance:** 15 miles (24 kilometers)
- **Alternative launch sites:** Stoney Point F&W Area (West Shore Rd., Isle La Motte, Vermont), Horicon F&W Area (West Shore Rd., Alburgh, Vermont, one-half mile north of Isle La Motte Bridge)
- **Places to stop:** Above launch sites and St. Anne's Shrine
- **Highlights:** St. Anne's Shrine and swimming beach, shoreline fossils, Goodsell Ridge Fossil Preserve, Fisk Quarry, scenic views of both the Green Mountains and Adirondacks
- **Route:** This lengthy loop route is done in shallow water along gently rolling land dotted with camps, homes and farms, except for around the Head on the south end of the island, where water depth drops to 40 feet very close to shore. The distance between stopping places on the east shore is almost 5 miles (8 kilometers). Privately owned Cloak Island sits an eighth of a mile offshore and offers a delightful additional option. Boat traffic is limited on the eastern side of Isle La Motte, but the main boating route to Canada lies off the western shore.
- **Comments:** Don't miss a visit to the Goodsell Ridge Fossil Preserve (Quarry Road) and Fisk Quarry (West Shore Rd.) before or after your trip. Fossils can be found along the south and southeast shores of the island. Falcons have been sighted on Cloak Island. Neither the east nor west sides of the island offers protection from a strong south wind and waves; however, the eastern shore is somewhat protected in a strong northwest wind if one stays close to shore.

If ever there were an underappreciated location on Lake Champlain, Isle La Motte is it. This most northerly island on the lake, 7 miles long (11.2 kilometers) by less than 3 miles wide (4.8 kilometers), is approximately ten miles (16 kilometers) from the Canadian border, with a year-round population of only 488 (per the 2000 census). It is the site of the first permanent European settlement in Vermont and the home of 480-million-year-old fossils.

While off the beaten path today, Isle La Motte was a key location when this country was first settled by Europeans and the primary means of transportation was by water. For the French and eventually the English who occupied the land to the north, it bordered the main route to the south. Representing French interests in the partially settled area north of Vermont, Samuel de Champlain first viewed Lake Champlain with a group of Algonquin Indians in 1609, just two years after Jamestown was settled and thirteen years before the *Mayflower* landed

Isle La Motte

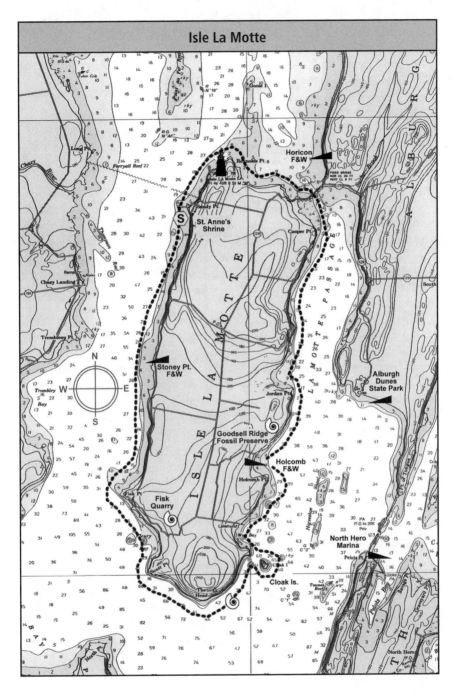

at Plymouth Rock. Fort Ste. Anne on the northwest end of Isle La Motte was built by the French in 1666 to protect themselves from Mohawk invasions from the south and to stage their own counter-invasions. The island is named for Pierre de St. Paul, Sieur de la Motte, who supervised the construction of the fort.

An Incredible Fossil Treasury

That is all recent history compared to this island's incredible fossil record (see "Geology" in Introduction). Fossils almost a half billion years old, created when ancient North America was situated just south of the equator and awash in the warm waters of a shallow tropical sea, can be found on the southern third of the island. It is believed to be the world's oldest biologically diverse reef. Thanks to the foresight of the people of this small community, the Isle La Motte Preservation Trust in partnership with the Preservation Trust of Vermont has conserved Fisk Quarry (1998) and, with the help of Lake Champlain Land Trust, created the Goodsell Ridge Preserve (2005), two exceptional places to view these fossils. (See "Fossils" in Introduction). These sites, as well as some on Valcour Island in New York, have recently been designated National Natural Landmarks.

There is a progression in the complexity of the fossilized organisms found on the island from south to north. The oldest and simplest fossils are on the southern tip of the island, and the most complex are at Goodsell Ridge, farther north. The span of geologic time between is believed to be several million years, although it is not known for sure. Many of these same fossils appear elsewhere on the lake (Valcour, South Hero, Garden Island, Button Bay), but none of these sites contain the diversity found here. Thanks to active quarries on the island throughout the nineteenth century, before it was understood what these "blemishes" in the rock were, these fossils can also be found in the stone buildings on the island (the Historical Society Building is a good place to look), as well as in the floor of the Vermont State House, Radio City Music Hall in New York City, and the National Gallery of Art in Washington, D.C.

Goodsell Ridge Fossil Preserve

The Goodsell Ridge Fossil Preserve, (http://www.ilmpt.org/) an 80-acre (32.4-hectare) outdoor park, is a great place to visit, even if paddling is not your thing. Kids and adults seem to all end up on their hands and knees looking at and feeling the fossils embedded in the large slabs of exposed rock found in this former cow pasture. This is not a place where you have to worry about breaking the displays. They clearly have stood the test of time. It is the ultimate hands-on museum.

▶ **Isle La Motte**

Looking at fossils, Goodsell Ridge Fossil Preserve.

This is a wonderful paddlers' route. You can circumnavigate an island without having to paddle out into the middle of the lake to get to it. The best place to start is the Holcomb Bay–Labombard Fish and Wildlife Access, because you have to drive down Quarry Road right past Goodsell Ridge Fossil Preserve to get there, and a stop at the preserve allows you to familiarize yourself with fossils on Isle la Motte before you start looking for them embedded in shoreline rock.

The Paddle:

Even with a gentle tail wind, it feels like a long paddle from our launch site north to the causeway bridge that connects Isle La Motte to the Alburgh Tongue, perhaps because this is the longest paddle we have yet undertaken and we are just a little unsure of our ability to handle it. The Isle La Motte lighthouse, just to the west of Reynolds Point on the northwestern corner of the island, is a welcome sight. Like many lighthouses on Lake Champlain, it has a long history culminating in recent restoration. Three cheers for refurbished lighthouses and the people who work to save them!

We stop for lunch and a swim at St. Anne's Shrine and beach. This is the site of the original 1666 fort. The first Bishop of Burlington bought this property in the late 1800s, built a small chapel, and in 1893 dedicated it to St. Anne de Beaupre, for whom the first fort was named. Run today by the Edmundite Fathers, it is still an active destination for Catholics and other tourists during the warmer months of the year.

Back in our kayaks and headed south, we feel like we could reach out and touch New York, no more than a mile away. A short distance beyond Fisk Point, we lose the shoreline road and become enthralled with the south end of the island that appears to be, with the exception of two or three houses, undeveloped and covered with tall cedars. None of the land is conserved or state-owned, but the few owners of this large area account for its natural state. Cedars, some almost 2 feet (.6 meters) in diameter, are larger than almost any we have seen elsewhere on the lake. They sit atop ragged walls in some places, and in others, on slabs of rock flat and low enough to land on. This cedar forest is dense. Some trees have spread their roots like a spider web on the top of the cliff. Others grow out along the rock walls. These trees are long-lived, some being 200 years old.

Rounding the south end of the Head of Isle La Motte, we paddle by a large sailboat anchored offshore just as its owner decides to descend, stark naked, down the ladder for a swim—or is it a bath? I can't decide whether to turn my head, change course, or just keep going. In the end I smile, wave *bonjour*, and just keep going. Without looking, I know Margy is doing the same. It adds a good laugh to our day.

As we approach the southeast end of the Head, reported to have the most primitive fossils—small creatures that are no more than a fraction of an inch long—we move as close as possible to shore to see if we can spot any evidence of them. Unfortunately, there are lots of rocks sitting half-submerged or hiding just below the water's surface, so getting within a foot or two of the vertical rocks is a little tricky, especially since the wind has picked up. I tune out those painful kayak scraping noises.

And find fossils we do, lots of them. These densely packed little rods, some slightly curved and others appearing as small, hollow circles, usually appear in a 6-inch (15-centimeter) layer or in clumps. We would have missed them altogether had we not been paddling very close to shore. As I urge Margy in closer to the rocks to get a really good look at them, she teases me about my somewhat fanatical fossil fascination. Clearly these little rock-bound worms lack the grace and power of an osprey flying overhead. Why am I so excited about them? I find it hard to believe that these most ancient of fossils can be found right here on Isle La Motte, in our own backyard so to speak, rather than anywhere else in the world. Their age challenges my sense of time and place. We humans are still just newcomers to the scene, small players in the overall scheme of things. I like being humbled that way.

Having had our fossil fill (at least for the moment), we head for small Cloak Island just a quarter of a mile off the southeast corner of Isle La Motte. There have been reports of peregrine falcons nesting on this island in the past. Margy spots what looks like a peregrine falcon's nest, vertical streaks of white guano dripping from a ledge halfway up the side of the 50-foot (12.2-meter) cliff. We see no sign of birds, but the guano looks white and fresh. We also see no fossils.

▶ **Isle La Motte**

This 5-acre (2-hectare) island is owned privately. The origin of its name is somewhat unclear, but legend has it that Isle La Motte resident Eleanor Roberts, wife of Ichabod Ebenezer Fisk, a man reportedly quick to anger, ran off one stormy night to escape her husband's wrath. Her sons told their father that she had drowned. She never appeared again, but the next spring, when the ice went out, her cloak was found on the shore of the island and it has been called Cloak Island ever since.

Back at our launch site, we stop to examine one large, lone rock in the water just to the north of the actual launch. It, too, has a good display of the tiny rod-like fossils we saw on the south end of the island. Before today we would never have noticed them.

It has been what you might call an historic day. And, despite no improved conditioning on our part, 15 miles (24 kilometers) has become our new gold standard for trip length. What power the mind has!

Tenacious roots.

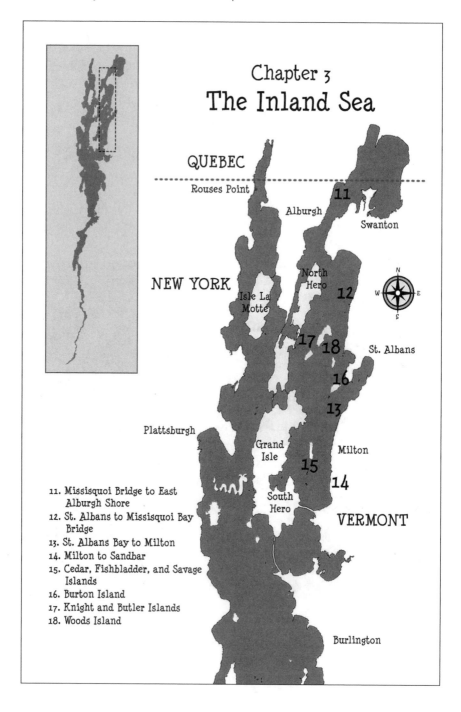

Chapter 3
The Inland Sea

QUEBEC

Rouses Point

Alburgh

11

Swanton

NEW YORK

North Hero

Isle La Motte

12

St. Albans

17 18

16

13

Plattsburgh

Grand Isle

Milton

15

South Hero

14

VERMONT

11. Missisquoi Bridge to East Alburgh Shore
12. St. Albans to Missisquoi Bay Bridge
13. St. Albans Bay to Milton
14. Milton to Sandbar
15. Cedar, Fishbladder, and Savage Islands
16. Burton Island
17. Knight and Butler Islands
18. Woods Island

Burlington

Chapter III

The
Inland Sea

Bound by the Sandbar Causeway on the south, the Missisquoi Bay Bridge on the north, Vermont on the east, and the Champlain Islands and Alburgh on the west, the Inland Sea is separated from the main north/south route on Lake Champlain and thus has a personality all of its own. The rolling land in the south half of the Inland Sea flattens out toward the north. It is a relatively peaceful arm of Lake Champlain, studded with islands, and a favorite destination for boaters. Much of it feels more like the last century. Even in this smaller section of Lake Champlain, the wind can tease the water into challenging waves, but on a calmer day, this area is hard to beat.

Common terns.

Missisquoi Bridge to East Alburgh Shore
Battling the Bloom

11

by Cathy Frank

- **Launch site:** West Swanton F&W Area, Rt. 78 adjacent to Missisquoi Bridge, West Swanton, Vermont
- **Distance:** 7 miles (11.2 kilometers)
- **Take out:** Dillenbeck F&W Area (Rt. 2, Alburgh, Vermont, east shore)
- **Alternative launch sites:** Alburgh Lakeshore Park, Trestle Rd., Alburgh, Vermont
- **Places to stop:** None aside from launch sites
- **Highlights:** Railroad swing bridge, wildlife (particularly in Ransom Bay)
- **Route:** This short route runs under the Missisquoi auto and railroad bridges and along the shallow east shore of Alburgh. It is relatively protected from all but a strong south wind. It can be made into a loop route by crossing open water from Dillenbeck F&W Access to the north end of North Hero State Park, where there is a nice picnic and swimming area, and then across open water to the shallow water of the West Swanton shore (13.5 miles/21.7 kilometers). This return route would not be protected from strong north and south winds and waves.
- **Comments:** There is the potential for algae-rich green water (and possible toxic algae blooms) near the mouth of Missisquoi Bay in warm weather. There is a raspberry stand at the west end of the Missisquoi Bridge.

Missisquoi bridges.

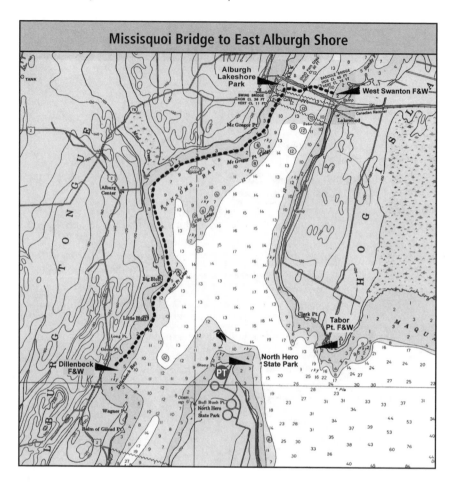

The Paddle:

This is a good paddle to do in the cooler weather of early summer or fall when the water is clear. In the hot summer months, Missisquoi Bay to the north is noted for its potential for green-tinged, algae-filled water and occasional toxic algae blooms. When those blooms occur, there is always the chance that these conditions have spilled out into the northern part of the Inland Sea, so we approach this mid-July paddle with a little apprehension. An overly rich, somewhat unpleasant organic odor greets us as we get out of the car. From a distance, the lake is a perfect mirror of the white puffy clouds and blue sky above, but close up the water is a brownish green, although clear enough to see the rocks and pebbles beneath the water close to the shore. It is not until we get on the water that we notice small olive-green blobs floating by. Yuck!

We head south under the Missisquoi Bay Bridge and Canadian National railroad trestle. Bridges are never meant to be looked at from below, and these are no exception. Surely this trestle cannot be as rickety as it appears if it is still in use. Just the same, I'm glad we are going under and not passing over it. Unfortunately, the curd-like blobs are with us even after we pass under the bridges.

We find it disconcerting to see the lake look like this and hope that it is an anomaly that will disappear when the temperature cools or the wind picks up. On the other hand, wishing the algae away just doesn't cut it unless we each take responsibility for the current state of the lake and participate in the huge effort it will take to restore it to a healthy state.

Once on the Alburgh side, we swing by the relatively new Alburgh Lakeshore Park with public beach, cartop boat access, and a day stop on the Paddlers Trail. A group of small, closely spaced, older camps line the Alburgh shore beyond the beach. Unlike the water quality, they look as if they haven't changed much through the decades. As we pass Mud Creek, turtles poke their heads up through the algae in this green-tinged bay, almost daring us to come closer. When we do, they disappear back into the hidden world below. Willows and cottonwoods grow along the sandy shore.

The water becomes clearer the farther south we paddle until we arrive at Dillenbeck Bay and our take-out point, where the green curd-like lumps are again prevalent. We cannot distinguish a toxic from a nontoxic algae bloom, but even tiny amounts of a toxic bloom can be deadly to pets and small children, and we don't want to take any home with us. Unfortunately, we have to wade through it to get to shore. Getting out of a kayak without getting ones feet wet is like trying to mail a letter in a mailbox with one hand. It just can't be done.

This short, midsummer paddle has been a bittersweet trip, forcing us to come face-to-face with the reality of human-accelerated eutrophication* of the shallower areas of our lake.

---

*The process by which a body of water becomes enriched in dissolved nutrients (as phosphates) that stimulate the growth of aquatic plant life, usually resulting in the depletion of dissolved oxygen. This is an early stage in the creation of a marsh or bog.

12   St. Albans to Missisquoi Bay Bridge
A Long Shore

by Cathy Frank

- ◼ **Launch site**: Kill Kare State Park ($, PT), Hathaway Rd., off Rt. 36, St. Albans, Vermont
- ◼ **Distance:** 18.5 miles (29.8 kilometers)
- ◼ **Take out:** West Swanton F&W Area (Rt. 78 adjacent to Missisquoi Bridge, West Swanton, Vermont)
- ◼ **Alternative launch sites:** Swanton Beach (Rt. 36, corner of Lake Street, Maquam Shore Rd., Swanton, Vermont), St. Albans Bay F&W Area (Hathaway Point Rd. off VT Rt. 36, St. Albans, Vermont), Tabor Point F&W Area (Tabor Rd. off Rt. 78, Swanton, Vermont), Alburgh Lakeshore Park (Trestle Rd., Alburgh, Vermont)
- ◼ **Places to stop:** Above launch sites and Burton Island (PT), Woods Island (PT)
- ◼ **Highlights:** Scenic views of islands of the Inland Sea, Missisquoi National Wildlife Refuge, Maquam Wildlife Management Area, birds galore
- ◼ **Route:** The southern end of this route passes close to Burton and Woods islands, both exceptional stopping places. Then, there is a long straight stretch (7.5 miles/12 kilometers) with no place to stop until Swanton Beach. From there northward, the route passes close to the wildlife management areas with opportunities for wildlife sightings, particularly birds.
- ◼ **Comments:** Missisquoi National Wildlife Refuge Visitors Center (Tabor Rd. off Rt. 87) offers walking trails and wildlife displays. Keep a safe distance from Popasquash Island to avoid disturbing nesting birds. There is a ramp marked on the chart just opposite Butler Island, and another just north of Cheney Point, that we were not able to find. This route does not offer protection from strong north and south winds and waves.

The Paddle:

Kill Kare, a former boys' camp north of St. Albans and one of the most beautiful of the Vermont State Parks, features grand old trees that provide shade on hot days, nearly deserted beaches, and a lovely old homestead with historic pictures hanging in its lobby. Taking advantage of its cartop boat launch at the north end of the park, we push off and head north, crossing the one-mile opening of Lapans Bay.

Thanks to this rare relatively straight shoreline, our destination is visible far off in the distance. Are we really going to paddle that far? Just before Cheney Point, 6.5 miles (10.5 kilometers) into our trip, we pass Popasquash Island, only a quarter of an acre in size. The endangered common tern has been nesting here since at least the 1890s, according to Audubon Vermont. We keep our distance, staying well outside the conservation buoys so as not to frighten or disturb any nesting birds.

▶ **St. Albans to Missisquoi Bay Bridge**

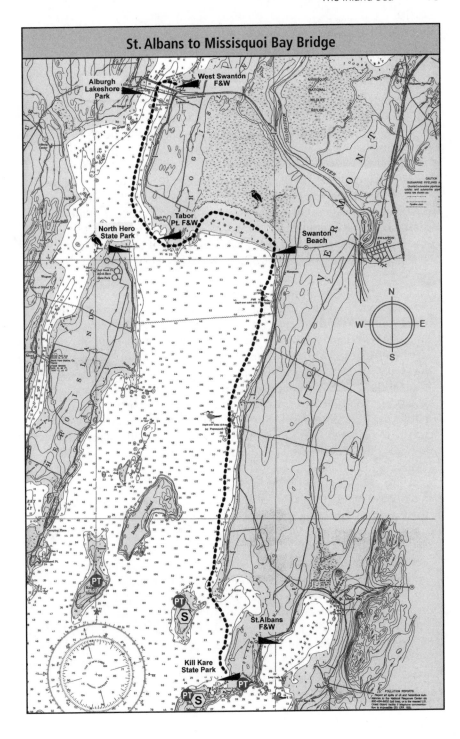

St. Albans to Missisquoi Bay Bridge

Smuggling on Lake Champlain

From the end of the American Revolution (Treaty of Paris, 1783), when significant numbers of Americans started to resettle the land around Lake Champlain, until the completion of the Champlain Canal at Whitehall in 1823, which opened a trade route between Vermont and southern New York, trade with Canada to the north was both commonplace and essential, if not always legal. Lumber, iron, potash, paper, cattle, sheep, grain, and maple sugar flowed north. European goods, including such essentials as cloth, rum, coffee, and chocolate flowed south via Canada, together with a large number of furs as well. This trade continued despite a Canadian embargo on exporting furs to the United States, which was not lifted until 1796, and a general U.S. embargo on trade with Canada declared by Thomas Jefferson in 1808.

Lake Champlain was a smugglers dream where small boats could be navigated through narrow passages. One of the most popular smuggling routes along the east shore of the lake from St. Albans Bay to Maquam Creek ran through what are now the Maquam Wildlife Management Area and the Missisquoi Wildlife Refuge. (Maquam Creek has since changed course and would not make a good smuggling route today.) Creative techniques included anchoring boats laden with goods just south of the border, and then cutting the anchor line and letting the prevailing south wind deliver them to Canada with only nature to blame or prosecute. After the War of 1812, British Canada became a legal trade partner and smuggling became unnecessary. But that didn't last forever.

During Prohibition (1920–1933), Lake Champlain again became a haven for smugglers when "Rum Runners" once again used these tried and proven routes to import alcoholic products.

The *Black Snake* Affair

Perhaps the most infamous smuggling affair in the lake's history involved the fourteen-oared *Black Snake*, which regularly smuggled up to 100 barrels of potash* per trip between Burlington and Quebec just prior to the War of 1812. In August of 1808, the U.S. revenue cutter *Fly* finally caught the *Black Snake* while it was tied up near the mouth of the Winooski River. A deadly encounter ensued. When it was over, the captain of the *Fly* and two of his men were dead, and all the smugglers captured and taken into custody. Eight men were indicted, but in the end only one was sentenced to be hanged while the others received less severe punishments and some were eventually pardoned.

*Potash, the common name for potassium carbonate, used in making glass, soap, and fertilizer, was made by early settlers from ashes produced when they cut and burned trees to clear their land.

With the exception of Woods Island, just north of Burton Island, there are no public places to stop along this shore until the Swanton Town Park at the beginning of Maquam Bay (the Algonquin name for Beaver Bay), 10 miles (16.1 kilometers) into our paddle.

Both the Maquam Wildlife Management Area and the large Missisquoi National Wildlife Refuge, which abut this bay, have been created by the meandering delta of the Missisquoi River. Together they comprise the largest wetland complex on Lake Champlain. With large areas of wetland and two creeks (First and Maquam), wildlife abounds. Besides shore and wading birds and waterfowl, harriers, hawks, owls, osprey, bald eagles and heron can be seen. Additionally, First and Maquam creeks are sunning locations for the endangered spiny softshell turtle, which nests in Missisquoi Wildlife Refuge.

At the west end of Maquam Bay, Hog Island looks more like an extension of the land than an island in its own right. Only the chart tells us otherwise. We are close enough to the northern end of North Hero to reach out and touch the state park. As we round Hog Island, the Missisquoi Bridge, almost 3 miles (4.8 kilometers) away, is a welcome sight.

Without doubt the most interesting parts of this trip are Maquam Bay, Maquam Wildlife Management Area, and the Missisquoi National Wildlife Refuge, which can be reached from the Swanton Town Beach. The Missisquoi National Wildlife Refuge Visitor Center, just off Route 78 about a mile east of the Missisquoi Bridge, has scenic trails and informative displays and is worth a visit.

No one is going to steal this sign.

13 | St. Albans Bay to Milton
Colorful and Varied Shoreline

by Cathy Frank

- **Launch site:** Kill Kare State Park ($, PT day-use only), Hathaway Point Rd. off Rt. 36, St. Albans, Vermont
- **Distance:** 14 miles (22.5 kilometers)
- **Take out:** Van Everest F&W Area (Lake Rd., Milton, Vermont)
- **Alternative launch sites:** St. Albans Bay F&W Area (Hathaway Point Rd. off Rt. 36, St. Albans, Vermont), Georgia Municipal Recreation Park (Georgia Shore Rd., Georgia, Vermont)
- **Places to stop:** Above launch sites and St. Albans Bay Park, Mill River Falls Natural Area (PT, day-use only)
- **Highlights:** St. Albans Bay Park, Mill River Falls Natural Area, Lazy Lady Island (privately owned), Rock Island for potential tern sightings, scenic views of the Champlain Islands and the Adirondacks
- **Route:** This route follows the developed southeast shore of shallow St. Albans Bay. There are interesting wetlands around the entrance to Stevens Brook and the Mill River. South of Rock Island, a protected bird nesting site, the water gets significantly deeper. Beyond Mill River Natural Area the shoreline is lined with cottages and homes. Once in the Inland Sea, the land starts to rise sharply from the shore. There is no place to stop between Georgia Municipal Park and the Van Everest F&W Access (5 miles/8 kilometers), so doing this stretch in threatening weather is not advisable.
- **Comments**: Depending on the water level, solid land may be elusive in the Mill River Falls Natural Area; avoid stepping on fragile soil. Keep a safe distance from Rock Island to avoid disturbing nesting birds. St. Albans Bay is subject to algae blooms in warm weather. A strong south wind produces large waves in St. Albans Bay, particularly from Hathaway Point southwest. From St. Albans Bay Park south, the route is exposed to strong northwest winds and waves.

The Paddle:

In the early 1800s, when the town of St. Albans sat at the foot of the bay, St. Albans Bay was a bustling place and an important commercial port for the people in northwest Vermont. The 60-foot (18.3-meter) canal schooner *Gleanor,* built here in 1823, was the first boat to travel to New York City through the just-opened Champlain Canal. Today the city of St. Albans is three miles (4.8 kilometers) to the east, and the head of the bay is quiet. Even recreational uses are diminished, mainly because the water quality has suffered from increased levels of phosphorus seeping in from the many farms that surround the bay and date back to the middle of the nineteenth century.

▶ **St. Albans Bay to Milton**

A gentle southerly tailwind gives us a false sense of power as we slip almost effortlessly through the water. This trip in and out of the bay and down the east shore of the Inland Sea to Milton is going to be a piece of cake. Five miles (8 kilometers) and an hour and a half later, we finally turn the corner at the foot of the bay. It is longer than it looks. Stevens Brook feeds into the bay here, and despite its impaired status, appears to be a great place to explore. Once a popular state park, before excess algae and its resultant unpleasant odors made it an undesirable place to swim, St. Albans Town Park is almost deserted today.

An undeveloped shoreline marked by an extensive reed bed looms ahead. As Margy's kayak hits the reeds, they slant ever so slightly, disrupting the deer flies from their reedy perches. Ten yards behind her, I am the perfect target. There is a lesson to be learned here that I am not going to share with Margy.

The Mill River. Not until we are directly in front of the mouth of the Mill River do we actually see it. The river has a clear and distinct channel, about 25 yards (22.8 meters) wide, lined with reeds and water lilies that are just starting to bloom. There is no way to know that this is public space except by deduction—there is no development and there are no "posted" signs. We note how obscure some of Lake Champlain's greatest treasures are from the water. The 35-acre (14-hectare) Mill River Falls Natural Area was conserved in 2003 by Lake Champlain Land Trust and Georgia Conservation Commission, and is a day stop on the Paddlers Trail.

The water is an opaque brownish-green at the river's mouth with swirls of green algae following like ribbons through it. Not able to resist, we head up river, passing a huge beaver dam only surpassed in size by a still larger one about 100

Phosphorus and St. Albans Bay

Eurasian milfoil and other nuisance waterweeds were not a problem in 1823, but the bay's current battles with frequent blue-green algae blooms in the summer and the pervasive presence of Eurasian milfoil, both caused by excessive levels of phosphorus, are a long-standing problem. Efforts were first made in the 1980s to reduce the amount of phosphorus draining into the bay from the many farms that lie within the Stevens and Jewett brooks and Mill River drainage basins, as well as from city streets, lawns, and sewage treatment plants. Despite those efforts, the overall concentration of phosphorus in the bay has not been significantly reduced, according to recent studies. Part of the problem is that much of the phosphorus that has flowed into the bay over the past 150 years has been bound into the sediment at the bottom of the bay and is continuously being released back into the water. There is no quick solution to the problem.

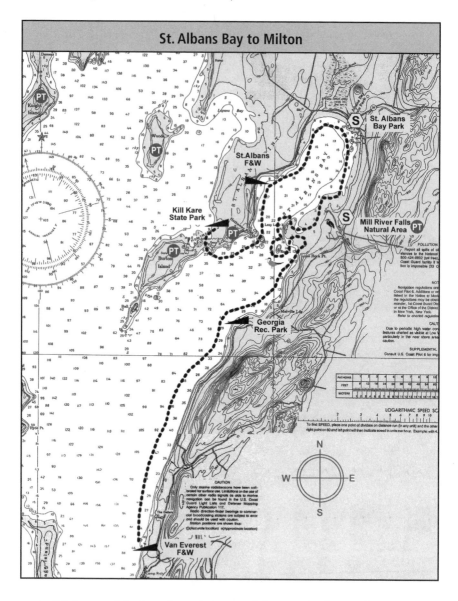

St. Albans Bay to Milton

yards (91.4 meters) farther along. Being careful to stay in the river's channel, we still run aground several times. About a half-mile upstream we are finally stopped by a tree across the water. Margy climbs over and then pushes her kayak under, only to declare it impassable. On our return we are met with an almost impressionistic image of the trees reflected in the brownish water with a slight ripple in the foreground. While this nutrient-rich murky water does not make a very good window, it is an excellent mirror. What a wild and peaceful place this is.

▶ St. Albans Bay to Milton

Over and under.

Lazy Lady Island. The improbably named Lazy Lady sounds more like the name of a boat than an island but, then again, in the eyes of their owners, little islands and big boats have a lot in common. From the northeast end, this privately owned three-acre (1.2-hectare) island looks like a giant snail with two tall cottonwood trees serving as its antennae. From the south side, it is clear that one of the antennae has a huge osprey nest in it. We see two birds in the nest, but no sign of others. The noisy protests from the bottoms of our kayaks attest to how shallow the water is around this island. Unlike the mouth of the river less than a mile away, here the water is so clear that we can reach out and pick up pebbles from the bottom.

Once past Lazy Lady Island, the water gets deeper. We pass Rock Island, conserved by the Lake Champlain Land Trust in 1999, being careful not to get too close. This small, aptly named island with little vegetation is one of the most important nesting sites for the common tern.

After a relaxing lunch stop at the Georgia Municipal Recreation Park, we continue on past the closely packed camp and house-lined shore as the south wind continues to challenge us all the way to Milton. With few landmarks and little traffic, our continuous paddling puts us in an almost trance-like state, which we interrupt from time to time by challenging each other to identify what exactly we see ahead without looking at our charts. The Van Everest F&W Access is a welcome sight at the end of the day, but we almost paddle past it before we recognize we are there.

14   ## Milton to the Sandbar
Naturalist's Delight

by Cathy Frank

- ■ **Launch site:** Van Everest F&W Area, Lake Rd., Milton, Vermont
- ■ **Distance:** 6 miles (9.6 kilometers)
- ■ **Take out:** Sandbar State Park ($, PT day-use only, Rt. 2, Milton, Vermont)
- ■ **Alternative launch sites:** Sandbar F&W Area (Rt. 2, Milton, Vermont)
- ■ **Places to stop:** None aside from launch sites
- ■ **Highlights:** Eagle Mountain, Sandbar Wildlife Refuge, views of the Champlain Islands, birding (particularly herons and osprey)
- ■ **Route:** This 6-mile gem goes past summer camps and the steeply rising west side of Eagle Mountain to the wetlands of the Sandbar Wildlife Refuge and Sandbar State Park. Water depth is about 10–20 feet from the Van Everest F&W Access until the shallow sandy shore of the Sandbar State Park, where it is no more than 1–3 feet deep. There is a great swimming area at the state park.
- ■ **Comments:** There is no protection on this route from strong south and north winds and waves. The Wildlife Management Area is off-limits to boats of any kind, including kayaks. Sandbar Beach is a favorite location for wind surfers and kite surfers in a strong north wind.

The Paddle:

The water feels cold despite the warm day and light wind, not surprising considering how slow Lake Champlain is to warm up in the early summer. We look west to Savage Island and beyond to Grand Isle; a turned-around view from what is so familiar to us is a good start at broadening our lake perspective.

Paddling south we pass clusters of camps and a scattering of farms, but mostly the shoreline feels wild and undeveloped. Ahead, Eagle Mountain rises almost 574 feet (175 meters) from the shore, its otherwise sharp, lakeside profile softened by a blanket of trees. Part of the Eagle Mountain Natural Area, a 225-acre (91-hectare) wildlife reserve, it offers hiking trails and panoramic views of the lake. The Lake Champlain Land Trust conserved it in 1998. Unfortunately, there is no lakeshore access to the trails, nor is there any place to stop along this section of shoreline.

Intertwining cedar roots exposed by the slow but steady natural erosion of this steep west-facing shore cling to the thin layer of soil. I am reminded of a puzzle where the object is to get two seemingly inseparable pieces completely apart. Part of me wants to try.

The number of great blue heron flying overhead increases the closer we get to the huge Sandbar Wildlife Refuge, where there is a relatively new and growing rookery beween the mouth of the Lamoille River and US Route 2. Belted kingfishers hover 10–20 feet (2–6 meters) above the water, beak and head pointed

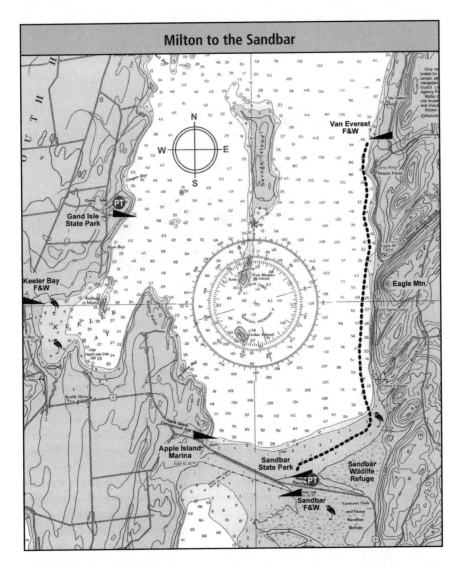

Milton to the Sandbar

down, before diving straight into the water to grab a fish. These birds make fishing look so easy.

The Sandbar Wildlife Refuge. Although not obvious from the water, this wildlife management area is huge—1,560 acres (331 hectares) in all. It is habitat for deer, red fox, coyote, beaver, mink, otter, and muskrat. Birds abound here, too. The great blue heron and osprey are the most obvious, because they are the biggest. But black, wood, ring-necked, and mallard ducks, as well as goldeneye and hooded mergansers, all breed here as well, according to Vermont's Department

Eagle Mountain.

of Fish and Wildlife, along with songbirds, reptiles, salamanders, and frogs. Even the rare, spiny, softshell turtle, most often associated with the Missisquoi Wildlife Refuge, is found along the banks of the river. Fish are plentiful, accounting for the many fish-eating birds and animals that frequent the area.

Seventy percent of the Wildlife Management Area—almost the entire wetland—is off-limits to the public. We are quickly reminded of this as we approach the opening to the 1.5-mile-long (2.4-kilometer) former branch of the Lamoille River that opens to the lake but no longer connects to the river. We sit for a moment wanting so badly to go beyond, but signs on the buoys warn us not to enter. Surely two thoughtful, slow-moving kayakers cannot do any harm to the inhabitants of this area. But, of course, we can ... sigh ... and so we don't. It is like standing at the locked door of a candy store, hands pressed against the window, straining to see all the sweet delights beyond the window display. Fortunately, the wildlife inhabitants are not constrained by its boundaries and there is much to see from where we are.

Not surprisingly, evidence exists of past human history in this rich wildlife area as long ago as 7,000–1,000 B.C. Later, seasonal and possibly permanent Abenaki settlements, and maybe Iroquois as well, grew along this shoreline of the lake and river.

From the western end of Sandbar Wildlife Management Area, it is only a short distance to Sandbar State Park's popular, north-facing, shallow, sandy beach. Were it not for the Lamoille River's washing of small sediment particles

▶ **Milton to the Sandbar**

downstream for over 10,000 years (since the last glaciers retreated), the park, the Sandbar Causeway, most of the 1,500 acres (607 hectares) of the wildlife refuge, and a good part of the land on the south side of the Lamoille River's mouth would not exist. I wonder what we would have seen had we paddled here 10,000 years ago.

It has definitely been a day of new views and insights. This was our first paddle away from the Champlain Islands, and although they were still within our sight, this paddle brought both excitement and a little apprehension as we cut the umbilical cord and set off to circumnavigate all of Lake Champlain. I'm glad we challenged ourselves to paddle beyond our island. This trip holds a special place in our hearts.

Cedar root tangle.

Islands of the Inland Sea
Seven Gems

What would the Inland Sea be without its islands? These gems give breadth and depth to the waterscape, adding greens and shadows to an otherwise blue sea. On islands in the foreground, the outlines of their trees and buildings make me wonder what they are like up close. Others, settling into the distance, look as if they are floating on the water. These islands add mystery. For us, they are a destination, always beckoning, teasing us to leave the shore and continue our investigation.

The Inland Sea is also where we heard our all-time favorite launch-site conversation between two fishermen, one coming in and one setting out:

"Any luck?"

"Yep."

"Find a good spot?"

"Yep"

The end. No further information was given.

Access to the islands of the Inland Sea can be found on every shore. St. Albans Bay, Milton, Sandbar, Keeler Bay, Knight Point, and City Bay in North Hero all provide easy access.

Cedar, Fish Bladder, and Savage Islands
Three in a Row

15

by Margy Holden

- ■ **Launch site/Take out:** Apple Island Marina ($), Rt. 2, South Hero, Vermont
- ■ **Distance:** 11 miles (17.7 kilometers)
- ■ **Alternative launch sites:** Keeler Bay F&W Area (Rt. 2, Keeler Bay, South Hero, Vermont), Grand Isle State Park ($, PT, State Park Rd. off Rt. 2, Grand Isle, Vermont), Van Everest F&W Area, Milton, Vermont (Lake Rd.), Sandbar F&W Area (Rt. 2, Milton, Vermont), Sandbar State Park ($, PT day-use only, Rt. 2, Milton, Vermont)
- ■ **Places to stop:** None aside from launch sites
- ■ **Highlights:** Views of islands, Green Mountains, waterfowl
- ■ **Route:** This is a deep-water circle route away from shore. Leaving the launch site and shore, the route passes by on one side of each island and returns on the other.
- ■ **Comments:** When heading into the middle of the lake, choose a calm day and watch the weather. This paddle is vulnerable to winds from all directions. The islands offer continually changing close and distant views.

The Paddle:

Cedar, Fish Bladder, and Savage islands make an inviting triumvirate strung out on a north/south axis down the middle of the southern end of the Inland Sea. On this beautiful autumn day, we change our usual practice of staying close to shore to paddle into the middle of the Inland Sea, reluctantly leaving the marina and the distractions of the shoreline behind, but anticipating the islands.

I focused on my kayak, because the scenery this far from shore changes slowly and the water is too deep to see the bottom. My kayak and I are a team, and we are merged with the water; a part of my body rests in the boat below the wet surface. I trail my hand through the water. The drips from my paddle keep me cool. As I lower one hip and then the other, my kayak snakes through the water and I feel like a fish. Pushing on one side and pulling on the other side of the paddle, the movement radiates through my arms, torso, hips, through my legs, and all the way to my toes that are pressing against the pedals. I savor the coordinated ballet that is kayaking. Each breath aligns with a stroke of the paddle, and body, boat, and water merge. Concentrating on my breathing I almost meditate, experiencing but not seeing the rippling of the water around me, unaware, even while all of my senses are engaged.

Cedar and Fish Bladder Islands. All too soon, privately owned Cedar Island's cliffs and wooded shores rise to greet us. As we paddle the eastern side, the island lives up to its name; the scent of cedars descends deliciously down to us pad-

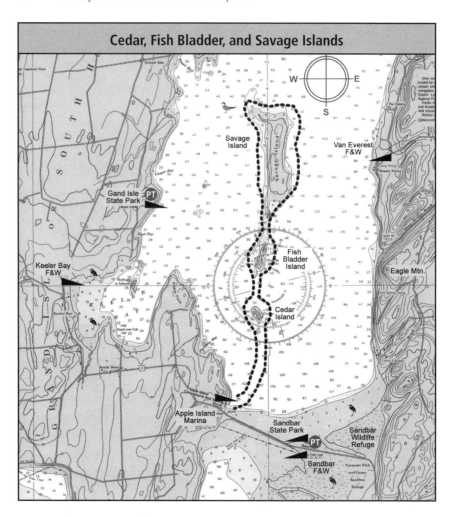

dling below the cliffs. In contrast to the rocky, low land of Burton Island, Cedar is more like a big, tree-covered rock jutting out of the water.

In less than a mile beyond Cedar, we reach Fish Bladder Island, also privately owned. We can see the top of a classic Adirondack lodge and hear the sound of a mower, confirmed by the scent of freshly cut grass reaching us on the water. "No trespassing" signs abound. How to take a break when island-hopping can be an issue. Sadly, the classic home on Fish Bladder caught fire in 2007 and, in spite of the best efforts of local fire departments, burned to the ground. Ironically, surrounded by water, the fire team could not get the necessary pumps to the island in time. Off the northeast end of Fish Bladder Island, a small rocky hummock called Upper Fish Bladder Island is conserved as bird habitat, but is off-limits to the public.

▶ **Cedar, Fish Bladder, and Savage Islands**

Savage Island. Savage Island, another mile north of Fish Bladder, is the largest of the three islands at 220 acres (89 hectares) and has been a year-round home for a long time. In 1810 it was owned by its namesake, James Savage of Plattsburgh, New York, who rented it to John and Elijah Minkler on condition that Minkler not cut standing trees. In 1822, James Savage's will bequeathed Savage Island to his daughter, Margaret Olive Freleigh, as long as it was not used to pay her husband's debts. (Did he believe in financial independence for his daughter, or simply distrust her husband?) A more recent owner, enamored of Lake Champlain and the idea of living on an island, bought Savage and made it home.

We see barns, a sawmill, and residences. There is an old airstrip, now not used. From the northwestern end of the island, a significant spit of land reaches out for Grand Isle. Common terns rise and swirl around us, the red beaks and legs of adults, still in their breeding plumage, add a dash of color to their distinctive black-and-white markings. Gulls and cormorants hold forth from the rocks. Smaller white birds with a distinctive spot on their cheeks catch our attention—a flock of Bonaparte's gulls. These gulls fly south all the way from their summer breeding habitat in the northern Canadian provinces. What a treat to see them this close.

From Savage Island, we turn back to the south, retracing our earlier paddle. The distant causeway connecting South Hero to Milton on the Vermont mainland at first appears to be just a few trees protruding above the water, but as we paddle closer it takes the shape of the familiar road that we drive so often.

These three private islands provide a good excuse to leave shore to circumnavigate a distant landscape.

Inland Sea Islands—Cedar, Fishbladder and Savage.

16	**Burton Island** *Island Haven*

by Margy Holden

■ **Launch site/Take out:** St. Albans Bay F&W Area, Hathaway Point Rd.
off VT Rt. 36, St. Albans, Vermont
■ **Distance:** 8 miles (13 kilometers)
■ **Alternative launch sites:** Kill Kare State Park ($, PT day-use only, Hathaway
Point Rd. off Rt. 36, St. Albans, Vermont)
■ **Places to stop:** Above launch sites and Burton State Park Island ($, PT)
■ **Highlights:** Burton Island State Park with walking trails, campsites, visitor center,
ferry; views of the Green Mountains and nearby islands
■ **Route:** The circle route follows the shallow, settled east side of St. Albans Bay
crossing the narrow opening to the Burton Island State Park, which can be circled
in either direction. Combine this with a paddle around privately owned Ball Island
(1 mile/1.6 kilometers) and publicly owned Woods Island (5 miles/8 kilometers),
conditions permitting.
■ **Comments:** When heading out to islands, choose a calm day and watch the
weather. The length of the fetch means that wind from south, west, and north
can build into big waves. Burton Island is a busy place when open. For lots
of company, go then; for a quiet paddle, go before the park is open or after
it closes. Perched just off the tip of the west shore of St. Albans Bay, Burton
Island became a Vermont state park in 1960. Original plans called for building a causeway to connect it to the mainland, but these were dropped in favor
of maintaining the island's natural appeal. There is now a state-run ferry service between Kill Kare and Burton Island to help the public get to the twenty-
six lean-tos and the seventeen tent sites on the island. The ferry also transports
day-visitors who want an island experience along with the opportunities to
hike trails or the 3 mile (4.8 kilometers) shoreline, visit the nature center and
museum, or rent a small boat. In addition, there are 15 boat moorings and
a 100-slip marina. It is the destination of choice for many weekend cruisers,
campers, and day-visitors.

The Paddle:
Finding the entrance to Kill Kare State Park padlocked, we turn back to the St.
Albans Bay Fish and Wildlife Access we have just driven past. We launch our kayaks
into peaceful water and admire the classic boats moored in front of old cottages.

On any given paddling day we check the weather forecast and hope to avoid
wind that is greater than 15 knots. Today, the wind gods double-cross us. Crossing to Burton Island, the water has a bit of chop, but does not feel like more than
we want to get into. When we reach a small point of land about halfway along
the southeast side of the island, we peer around it—into big waves. Even though

▶ **Burton Island**

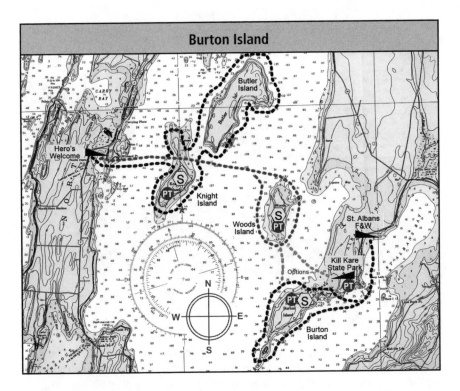

the waves appear to have increased in size significantly, we choose to go ahead.

Immediately hit by large waves, we keep an eye on the water and each other—and paddle as hard as we can. The waves make each stroke a big dig. We inch along. Ball Island is ahead and not that far, but in this wind it is too much of a pull and a risk. The size of the waves clearly exceeds our comfort level. If we had consulted the chart carefully, we would have seen the fatal fetch. These waves have had a long distance to grow. I remind myself that the worst thing that can happen is that I will go over, get wet, drift to shore, and have to pull my kayak into one of the wooded campsites to empty it. In front of us, Ball Island, which we want to circumnavigate, still looms as a tempting target, but these waves just seem to keep growing.

The wind is whistling in my ears when I hear a strange thud. Could that be the sound of Cathy's kayak hitting the bottom of a trough after crashing down from the top of a four-foot wave? These have to be the steepest waves we have encountered, because I have never heard that sound before. Instinctively, we point directly into the wind to keep our balance. Keep paddling—that's my mantra until it looks as if a turn will allow me to safely round the end of Burton. I wait for a series of smaller waves between the bigger ones, and quickly turn. Immediately, I am surfing, leaning back so I won't dig the bow in and do a face plant. It's a flying trip.

Rough water ahead.

In the lee. What a difference a protected shore makes. In this protected bay the *shush, shush, shush* of gentle waves pushing the pebbly stones against the shore replaces the whistling wind. We drop our paddles and take deep breaths. The last few minutes have been exhilarating and hard work, part of the adventure that Lake Champlain can dish up. In calm winds this trip would be a different experience. It is yet another lesson that this lake can change its mood and weather in mere moments.

In the wild waves we missed the south shore, but find the northwest shore of Burton Island lined with lean-tos and rustic campsites. Some look inviting, while others appear worn and overused. The occasional barbed wire and leaning fencepost are clues that the island was once farmed—first by the Burton family. Pigs, cows, and chickens lived here before the campers and boaters came along to claim the land for their recreational needs.

It is easy to see why the protected basin at Burton Island is a magnet for cruising boats. This beautiful harbor is open to the east with views of the lake, Kill Kare, and the distant Greens. It is deserted today except for a variety of herring, ring-billed gulls, a couple of great black-backed gulls, and double-crested cormorants; these birds command a sweeping bay of rock and sand. We drift peacefully through the basin, eating our lunch. Only some signs and a couple of small buildings remind us of its bustling seasonal use.

Without the wind, Burton makes a worthy short paddle—a chance to leave shore and visit an island without venturing too far. Add Ball Island, and it becomes an island-hopping day.

▶ **Burton Island**

Knight and Butler Islands
Roughing It

by Margy Holden

- **Launch site/Take out:** Hero's Welcome ($), Rt. 2 in North Hero village, Vermont
- **Distance:** 12 miles (19.3 kilometers)
- **Alternative launch sites:** Kill Kare State Park ($, PT day-use only, Hathaway Rd. off VT Rt. 36, St. Albans, Vermont)
- **Places to stop:** Above launch sites and Knight Island (PT)
- **Highlights**: Island and Green Mountain views, turtles, waterfowl
- **Route:** From the launch site, this circle trip crosses City Bay and open water to circumnavigate wild and publicly accessible Knight Island and privately owned and settled Butler Island. Between the two is little, privately owned Dameus Island. If launching from the St. Albans shore, include Woods Island in this trip.
- **Comments:** When heading into the middle of the lake, choose a calm day and watch the weather carefully. This route is vulnerable to winds from all directions.

The Paddle:

Knight and Butler Islands lie like twins close to each other in a north/south orientation, the most prominent islands visible from City Bay in North Hero. Hero's Welcome General Store and Café, in the center of North Hero, is definitely the closest and most picturesque place to launch, not to mention a supplier of all things imaginable. We start the day with something from their large selection of gooey goodies. Somehow the sugar seems to increase our appreciation of picturesque City Bay and the family of Canada geese that swim nearby.

Knight Island. About 1.5 miles (2.4 kilometers) later we reach the closest point on Knight Island, where we find a pristine, mostly uninterrupted wooded shoreline. Conserved by the Lake Champlain Land Trust in 1990, the State of Vermont owns and manages all but 10 privately owned acres (4 hectares) of this 185-acre (75-hectare) island. Only seven primitive campsites nestled along the shore, six of which are easy to spot because they have log lean-tos, a ranger's residence, and the dock, interrupt the treed shoreline. We could land our kayaks and choose to walk the perimeter trail, but the transparently clear water, through which we can see rocks and an occasional shell or minnow, and the sun glistening on its surface holds us in its thrall. We paddle on, appreciating the overhanging cedars and the musky smell of sun on soil in the bare campsites. Historically, Knight was farmed and later privately run as a primitive camping area with a managed lumbering operation.

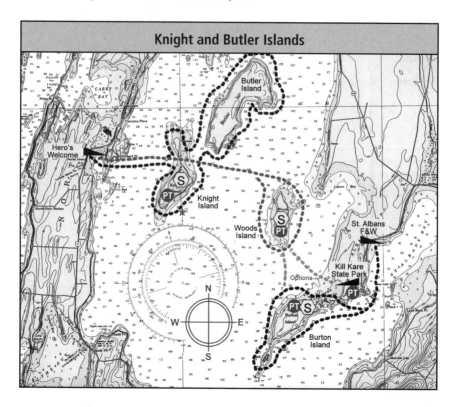

Knight and Butler Islands

Butler Island. We cross the half-mile gap between Knight and Butler islands, intrigued immediately by their differences. Butler is about twice the size of Knight and has its own outrigger island, Grammas Island, which sits a few yards offshore. We cannot land on either island. Permanent, privately owned camps line the shore of Butler Island. Like the campsites on Knight, they have no public electricity. We see generators, solar panels, some pumps pulling water from the lake, and even a barge loaded with building material. The pebble beaches and rocky shores look inviting, but this is a private island.

Conserved by the Lake Champlain Land Trust and owned by the Green Mountain Audubon Society, Grammas Island provides a sanctuary for the common tern and is off-limits to humans, so we keep our distance and enjoy the sight of an occasional bird in flight.

Dameas Island. On our way back from Butler, we circumnavigate small and private Dameas Island, which looks like an exclamation point just off the north end of Knight Island. We stop and stand in the shallow water off the deserted north end because, as law-abiding women, we don't want to land on private property. A couple of loons check us out. Between Knight and Dameas, we pass a rock that has been taken over by turtles. We name it, appropriately, turtle rock. Passing back along Knight, I think I see what may be a pair of migrating scaup ducks.

Compared to the rest of the lake, the islands of the Inland Sea provide a relatively protected area for waterfowl. Knight, Dameas, and Butler islands offer a lot of unspoiled territory to investigate and on Knight, one can do it on land as well as on water.

Clear water.

18	**Woods Island** *Emerald*

by Margy Holden

- **Launch site/Take out:** Hero's Welcome ($), Rt. 2 in North Hero village, Vermont
- **Distance:** 11 miles (17.7 kilometers)
- **Alternative launch sites:** Kill Kare State Park ($, PT day-use only, Hathaway Rd. off Rt. 36, St. Albans, Vermont), St. Albans Bay F&W Area (Hathaway Point Rd. off Rt. 36, St. Albans, Vermont)
- **Places to stop:** Above launch sites and Knight Island (PT), Burton Island (PT)
- **Highlights:** Island and Green Mountain views, turtles, waterfowl
- **Route:** From the launch site, this circle trip crosses City Bay, passes Knight Island and circumnavigates Woods. Include Knight and Butler Islands in this trip (14 miles/22.5 kilometers) or combine with Burton Island (9.5 miles/15 kilometers).
- **Comments:** When heading into the middle of the lake, choose a calm day and watch the weather.

The Paddle:

From City Bay in North Hero, Knight obscures our destination—Woods Island. We paddle directly toward the north end of Knight Island and pass our designated "turtle rock," which in this early morning is already populated with its namesakes. Once past Knight, Woods is in sight. We get into the rhythm of paddling in the calm water. The State of Vermont owns and manages Woods Island, which was originally conserved by the Lake Champlain Land Trust. Once there, it is a 2-mile (3.2-kilometer) paddle around the 125-acre (51-hectare) island.

Woods Island earns its name from a densely wooded, rocky shore with one sandy bay that truly invites a swim. Inland, bushy growth seems to be overtaking open areas of fields and wetland. The island was historically farmed, and remnants of a house foundation and drainage ditches can still be found. Now, the island is a unique habitat for plant life, including some species that are rare or threatened in Vermont. Trails provide a way to hike between campsites and across the island on berms that were built by a private developer. A few lucky campers occupy some of the five primitive campsites. As an avid skinny-dipper, I am careful to make warning sounds as we approach.

Having circled Woods Island, we head back to City Bay, but pause at the halfway point, Knight Island, to again watch the turtles—all seven of them.

Paddling around these gems of the Inland Sea proves to us that leaving the shore gives us time and space to better appreciate the experience of being out in a kayak, as well as satisfying our curiosity about what is out there and experiencing the peaceful setting that islands can provide.

▶ **Woods Island**

Woods Island

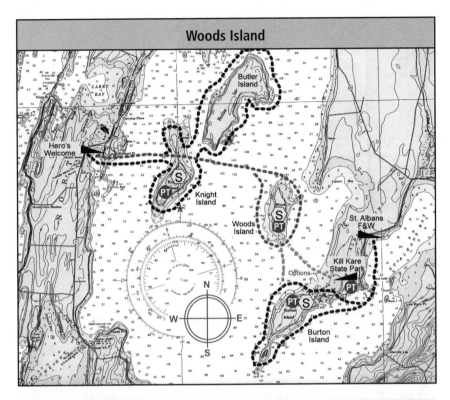

Woods Island campsite.

Rock, Popasquash, and Grammas Islands
Bringing Back the Common Tern

On three islands in the Inland Sea, Mark LaBarr, staff scientist at Audubon Vermont, supports the Vermont state-endangered common tern comeback on Lake Champlain.

Each island is unique. Quarter-acre Popasquash Island off the Maquam shore, where common terns have nested since the 1890s, is a chunk of shale with grass on the top. Quarter-acre Rock Island, with similar topography but more vegetation, and where the common tern has nested since the 1960s, sits in St. Albans Bay. Treed Grammas Island, the largest of the three, sits within a few yards of Butler Island. For the first time in thirty years, common terns nested and fledged on Grammas Island in 2007, lured by LaBarr, who placed decoys and a solar-powered sound system there to play their call 24/7. The Green Mountain Audubon Society owns the three islands; Audubon Vermont manages them under the Common Tern Recovery Project. They are definitely off-limits to humans.

Common terns breed in their third or, occasionally, their second year. The nests themselves are very simple—straw or dried grasses are placed in a shallow depression. The two to three spotted eggs, which hatch in about three weeks, vary in background color from almost teal to beige. If three chicks hatch, usually only two will fledge and live for an average of fifteen years. Once the chicks fledge, the family tends to move together to a new place.

Managing a tern island requires lots of work and can look funny, too. Double-crested cormorants pose a constant threat. To prevent their taking over an island, LaBarr constructs a wire grid two or three feet above the surface. This looks like a giant tennis racquet. Once the terns return in the spring, LaBarr and his interns monitor each island weekly. They number each nest, record its condition, and count the eggs (and hopefully the chicks). The scientists have to "tern walk" around each island, high-stepping over the wire grid lines, wobbling a bit to search for a clear place to put a foot so as not to step on a hiding chick, and crawling to search for the chicks, which blend perfectly with the brownish-gray ground. Found chicks get banded. On Grammas Island the researchers look a bit like astronauts on the moon, because they must "suit up" in heavy one-piece clothing to avoid being bitten by deer ticks. On Popasquash, they wear hard hats to protect themselves from dive-bombing common tern parents. This is not a comedy routine; it is science for the birds.

▶ **Woods Island**

Tern chick. Photograph courtesy of Chris Boget.

Unfortunately, black-crowned night herons and owls are able to penetrate the wire grid and take eggs and chicks. Great blue herons will also try, but usually can be "mobbed" away by the angry adult common terns. The grid also does not prevent four-legged predators like mink from getting onto Popasquash and killing chicks. Canada geese walk ashore on Rock Island, where they clumsily mash eggs with their big webbed feet. In order to discover what was eating the tern chicks on Popasquash, LaBarr and his intern set up a solar-powered night camera. They were successful in getting chilling footage of a glinting eye followed by a black-crowned night-heron moving stealthily from nest to nest gobbling down chicks. On a lighter note, on other nights they got close-up footage of spiders building webs on the eye of the camera, which completely obscured the action beyond.

Chicks that escape predators fledge by mid-July. Many, however, are lost to predation when they are only a couple of days old. Luckily, the common tern can re-nest up to three times. These tern islands sit just far enough apart to prevent a successful predator from destroying nests on all the islands at once, but close enough for re-nesting, which seems to be more successful at the end of the season.

The number of nesting common tern pairs increased from 50 in 1989 to 200 in the last twenty years. Almost 90 chicks fledged, in spite of a quarter of the nests being lost to predators. What a remarkable success the Common Tern Project is against great odds. Mark LaBarr and his colleagues have moved the Lake Champlain's common tern population much closer to stability. When thinking of vulnerable chicks that have just hatched, it is impossible not to appreciate the incredible challenges to survival that each one faces. This helps us to realize, yet again, how fragile our ecosystems are.

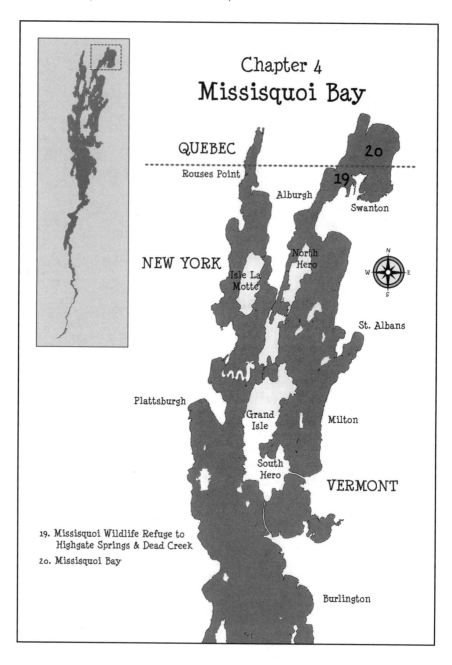

Chapter 4
Missisquoi Bay

QUEBEC

Rouses Point

Alburgh

Swanton

20

19

NEW YORK

Isle La Motte

North Hero

St. Albans

Plattsburgh

Grand Isle

Milton

South Hero

VERMONT

19. Missisquoi Wildlife Refuge to
    Highgate Springs & Dead Creek
20. Missisquoi Bay

Burlington

Chapter IV

Missisquoi Bay

With a 35-mile (56-kilometer) shoreline and a maximum depth of only 14 feet, Missisquoi Bay, known for its fishing, forms a large, shallow puddle separated from the rest of Lake Champlain by an opening that is less than a mile wide. The shoreline is often wet and wild. The combination of size, shape, and shallowness results in a diminished water quality. Three rivers, rich in beauty and agricultural phosphorus, also drain into Missisquoi waters. Two wildlife preserves dot its shores. Residents of about two-thirds of Missisquoi shores speak French as their native language.

Black tern.

Missisquoi Wildlife Refuge to Highgate Springs & Dead Creek — *Of Wet and Wild—a Watery World*

19

by Margy Holden

- ■ **Launch site:** West Swanton F&W Area, Rt. 78 adjacent to Missisquoi Bridge, Vermont
- ■ **Distance:** 17.5 miles (28.2 kilometers)
- ■ **Take out:** Louie's Landing, Missisquoi Wildlife Refuge (PT day-use only, on Rt. 78, West Swanton, Vermont)
- ■ **Alternative launch sites:** Charcoal Creek F&W Area (corner Rt. 78 and Campbell Bay Rd., West Swanton, Vermont), Highgate Springs Town Park (Shipyard Rd. off Old Dock Rd., Highgate Springs, Vermont)
- ■ **Places to stop:** Above launch sites and Mac's Bend Missisquoi NWR Access (1 mile on side road from Louie's Landing, off Rt. 78). Landing and walking on shore is off-limits in most of the reserve, but Mac's Landing is a year-round stopping place for boats.
- ■ **Highlights:** Most of this trip is along and/or through the Missisquoi National Wildlife Refuge, offering extensive wildlife including osprey and great blue heron nests, views into marshes, Dead Creek, and the Missisquoi River. Walking trails are accessible from the river or the refuge headquarters on Tabor Rd., which also has exhibits and handouts.
- ■ **Route:** This nature-filled, potential circle route follows the sometimes-settled shoreline northeast, reaching the border of the refuge just beyond the mouth of Charcoal Creek. From there it passes the three mouths of the Missisquoi River and turns south along mostly marshy shores through two large bays to Highgate Springs Town Park. The route then backtracks slightly to the mouth of Dead Creek, turns left and follows the shallow winding creek south to the river, where it turns right into the Missisquoi River and reaches the launch site.
- ■ **Comments:** There is not much chance for waves to build except in a north wind between the mouths of the Missisquoi River. Dead Creek is very protected. It can be a stiff paddle up the Missisquoi against wind and current. The entire route is through shallow water. The reserve is an important nesting site for ducks, heron and turtles, so it is important to heed signs, stay out from the shoreline, and not disturb or stress wildlife. While we used two cars, one can make this a circle trip using Louie's Landing, traveling out the Missisquoi River and returning by Dead Creek, or from Louie's Landing traveling out one branch of the Missisquoi River, around Shad and Metcalfe islands and back the other Missisquoi branch (12 miles/19.3 kilometers).

The Paddle:

Our impression of Missisquoi Bay, based on an earlier trip, is literally tainted—green. When we arrive at the Missisquoi Bay Bridge launch site, however, my first reaction is, "Wow, look at that." The water is clear. Well, not as clear as we have seen in other parts of the lake, but there is no sign of the dreaded algae.

Algae Blooms

In 1999 two dogs drank algae scum and died. In August 2004 and 2005 there were again health warnings about the algae bloom in Missisquoi Bay and in still waters beyond the bay. In 2008 the bay fared a bit better, with no toxic blooms reported.

The manure and fertilizer spread on agricultural fields near Missisquoi Bay washes into streams that flow into the bay and combines with the sun-warmed, shallow summer water. The runoff supplies phosphorus and nitrogen, which, combined with warm water, supports a potentially deadly stew of algae. Remedies to agricultural runoff exist, but sympathetic farmers who understand the problem and the remedies often lack the necessary capital to make these changes. The premier of Quebec and the governor of Vermont have pledged to work together, but signs of improvement are slow to materialize.

Missisquoi Bay provides a rich habitat for wildlife along the shores. We hope to see spiny softshell and map turtles, which nest nearby. We don't have to wait long. Just ahead, a man-made turtle platform rocks gently in the water. The platforms look as if the Oz tornado had dropped the Wicked Witch's house into Missisquoi Bay instead of Munchkin Land, leaving only the roof showing. We glide silently around it and are rewarded by a close encounter with three sunning, spiny softshell turtles. What a sight. Their distinctive narrow head ends in an upturned snout, a bit like a mole's head. Seemingly content in the sun, they ignore us as we float by holding our breath. (Later we learn that some of the platforms have turtle decoys on them to attract the real turtles. Did we, or didn't we, see the real thing?)

Leaving turtles and controversy, we pass the cottages around Sandy Point. When my husband's extended family spent happy summer vacations here, the main activity was fishing. Judging from the number of bass boats we encounter today, that hasn't changed, but the equipment has. Those old aluminum boats with 15-horsepower outboards have been replaced by faster, specialized boats and motors that send up plumes of spray as they speed by. Does it make a difference in how many fish are caught? In those old days, the reward was a perch

▶ **Missisquoi Wildlife Refuge to Highgate Springs & Dead Creek**

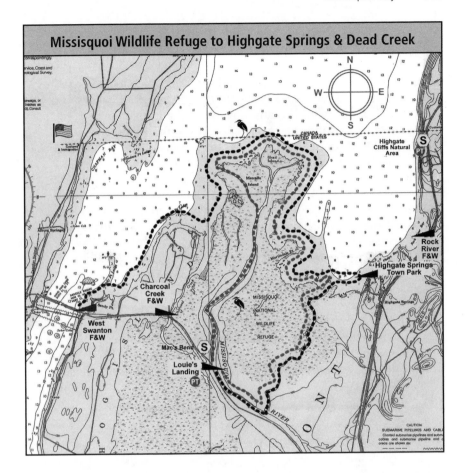

Missisquoi Wildlife Refuge to Highgate Springs & Dead Creek

dinner; today, cash is awarded to the winners of competitive tournaments that draw corporate-sponsored boats from afar.

My husband, Doug, remembers that "this was a watery, green kingdom, with trees bending over the water, trailing branches, darkness beyond. It was quiet, with striking individual sounds of wildlife, like the kingfisher, and the dense, damp smell of woods. We used to cross the delta at full speed to keep the draft of the motor to a minimum, wearing swimming goggles to keep the bugs out of our eyes."

Fifty years later the scenery is much the same, but we can't find any gog-gled boys, only rural shoreline in sharp contrast with the dense development on the south side of the mouth of Charcoal Creek. How different it appears from the wildness of the Missisquoi Wildlife Refuge ahead. A closer look at the chart reveals that the shoreline from the bridge to the refuge is actually the north end of Hog Island, separated from mainland Vermont and the Mis-sisquoi River by a swath of swamp, marsh, and creeks. Hog Island is about 8

The Spiny Softshell Turtle Controversy

Turtles bask in the sun for health and survival, which includes egg maturation. The spiny softshells used to sunbathe on the rocks of the old Missisquoi Bay Bridge causeway. When plans for a new bridge eliminated these surfaces, concern for these remarkable critters delayed the rebuilding of the bridge and provoked controversy over how much of the old bridge causeway to remove. Since these magnificent turtles are a threatened species in Vermont, with only about 300 left and most found near this bridge, turtle platforms provided a temporary sunning location. Since the completion of the bridge, the platforms have been removed, but much of the old causeway has been preserved.

Efforts have been made to protect the turtles' nesting habitat, too. Spiny softshells lay their eggs in the sandy gravel on the West Swanton and other beaches where the roots of weeds can interfere with digging to lay eggs. Steve Parren of the Vermont Department of Fish & Wildlife spends many a cold fall weekend weeding the nesting sites so that they will be in prime condition for the turtles to lay their eggs. Nothing like personal (and dedicated) service. Decisions must be continually made between the perceived needs of people versus other species.

Spiny softshell turtle — decoy or the real thing?

▶ **Missisquoi Wildlife Refuge to Highgate Springs & Dead Creek**

Watery world.

miles long (13 kilometers) and up to 3 miles wide (4.8 kilometers). For hundreds of years, Hog Island was a center of Abenaki life.

In the fall, the silver maples along the shore often take on a soft yellow hue. Not this year. These waterside maples on the far side of Charcoal Creek couldn't be more brilliant. We must sound as if we are watching fireworks with our *oohs* and *aahs*, as around every bend we are greeted by yet another colorful display.

Missisquoi Wildlife Refuge. Civilization disappears when we enter the Missisquoi Wildlife Refuge. The 88-mile (142-kilometer) Missisquoi River drains 1,200 square miles (310,799 hectares) of Vermont and Quebec. Shallow, sandy deltas mark the three mouths of the mighty Missisquoi, although reeds and other grasses obscure them. Huge old tree trunks, probably cottonwoods that have traveled downriver, rest at angles on the sand. Cormorants look as if they are playing "king-of-the-mountain" on one of them. Interestingly, the delta continues to build north approaching the Canadian border.

The Missisquoi Wildlife Refuge has grown to 6,642 acres (2,687-hectares) of wetlands, river, and uplands that provide a rich habitat for migratory birds and resident animals. It has been designated an Important Bird Area (IBA) on Lake Champlain by the National Audubon Society. The uplands are managed to improve American woodcock habitat, and grasslands are mowed judiciously to keep them open for seriously declining species like the meadowlark and bobolink.

The Abenaki: The Displaced

Native Americans roamed the shores of the Champlain Basin for ten thousand years beginning with the Paleo-Indian hunters. Around 7000 B.C., they were followed by the Archaic People, who were hunter-gatherers, and the Woodland People, from 900 B.C., who were involved in agriculture, improved tool and implement-making, and created ornamental objects. Artifacts dating from 3000 B.C. define the little we know about the earliest people, while oral tradition and the sparse records kept by Europeans tell us much of what we do know about the last four hundred years.

At the time of European discovery, Lake Champlain formed the border and highway between the Iroquois, who dominated the land to the west and south, and the Algonquin to the north. Western Abenaki inhabited the Vermont shore. It is believed that there were as many as 4,000 Abenaki before European contact in 1609, but their numbers were then decimated by diseases introduced by Europeans. The name Abenaki means "People of the Dawn," which is what other tribes called them, but they called themselves Alnobak, or "ordinary people," and their homeland, Lake Champlain, Bitawbagok or "lake in between."

The Western Abenaki of Lake Champlain lived primarily along the deltas of Vermont's major rivers, including the Missisquoi, Lamoille, Winooski, and Otter Creek, where rich bottom land provided fertile soil for growing crops. In midwinter, family bands would disperse to patrilineally defined hunting grounds hoping to catch and preserve enough game to sustain them until the following year. In their villages they lived in extended family groups in wood and birch longhouses. They made tools and implements, including ornamental, to support their way of life. The Abenaki worshiped and treated with respect the natural and animal world around them, but many, converted by French priests, later added Catholicism to their religion.

For centuries Hog Island at the mouth of the Missisquoi River played a central role in the life of the Western Abenaki. In 1973 construction equipment operators uncovered a skull in Swanton in what turned out to be a sacred burial ground of ninety graves. These remains were identified as those of the earlier Abenaki Woodland People, who lived between 1000 B.C. and 1600 A.D.

Hog Island provided a geographically secure location for the Abenaki, separated from the mainland by swamp and marsh, and out of sight and sound behind the Alburgh peninsula from the main

▶ **Missisquoi Wildlife Refuge to Highgate Springs & Dead Creek**

north-south historic trade and war routes on Lake Champlain. The Missisquoi River basin supplied fertile cropland, while its waters, along with those of the nearby Pike and Rock rivers, gave easy access to refuge in Canada. In 1736 an estimated 800 Abenaki lived on Hog Island. Relics indicate that their croplands at times stretched inland along the river for 15 miles (24 kilometers). In 1743 a French priest, enticed by potential conversions among the Abenaki on Hog Island, established a mission at the falls in Swanton.

As the Abenaki from southern New England were displaced by European settlement, they fled north. There, the Lake Champlain Abenaki would increasingly feel the pressure of this growing population, of continually encroaching European settlements, and of the British/French/American battles that swirled around them.

Beginning in the early 1700s, hoping to discourage European settlement, warriors from Missisquoi led by the legendary Graylock traveled south to terrorize the settlements in southern New England. When soldiers and settlers retaliated, the Abenaki developed a strategy of gathering and dispersal. They could fall back on their winter hunting pattern and melt away in small bands into the wilderness or across the border into more secure settlements in Quebec. When things calmed down, they could return to the shores of Lake Champlain. The British, who considered the Abenaki to be French allies, retaliated in 1759, sending Rogers Rangers to wipe out the Abenaki settlements. Rogers found Missisquoi deserted, but killed the Abenaki in St. Francis in Quebec, temporarily eliminating a haven of retreat.

The demise of the Abenaki as a coherent community on Hog Island began in 1773 when the Allen brothers bought the lands around Swanton. Ira Allen reported that the Abenaki had fled to Canada to avoid a smallpox epidemic. While possibly true, this ignored the historic Abenaki defense of retreat and return. From that time on, both the Abenaki presence and their rights were denied as settlers began to take over their territory despite their protests.

Today we know that the Abenaki did not leave, but instead became "invisible" by ending their community life and retreating to a subsistence existence in the woods and fields. It took 200 more years for the Abenaki to assert their communal tribal pride by establishing a tribal council in 1976 and building a museum and cultural center in Swanton. In 2006 the Vermont Legislature officially recognized the Abenaki as a tribe. A year later the United

States Department of the Interior cited lack of evidence that a continuous tribe existed before 1900 in denying the Abenaki petition to be recognized as a legitimate tribe. It is ironic that the very skill that helped the Abenaki to survive for centuries—the ability to melt away to invisibility—now stands as an impediment to sought-after recognition.

The marshes and rivers provide refuge for up to 20,000 ducks that rest here during migration each year. Almost all of the black terns in Vermont build their nests here, along with the osprey and great blue herons. Nesting ducks include wood ducks, common goldeneye, hooded mergansers, and black ducks.

The Northern Forest Canoe Trail follows this shore. It begins at Old Forge, New York, and runs along 740 miles (1,191 kilometers) to Port Kent, Maine. Detailed maps of the trail with marked campsites and portages are available. Those paddling the 74-mile (119-kilometer) Lake Champlain section of the trail enter Lake Champlain in Plattsburgh, wind through the Champlain Islands, and leave along the Missisquoi River. It is called a "canoe" trail in honor of the Native Americans' main mode of water transportation, but it is equally appropriate for kayakers.

Shad and Metcalf islands sit like corks stuck in the mouth of the Missisquoi River, forming the three mouths. For a number of years, the great blue heron rookery on Shad Island had more than 600 nests. Most disappeared, but the rookery is making a slow recovery. I never tire of seeing the large but graceful great blue herons landing on a branch or nest in the treetops. Their wings flap, and the bough of the tree dips, then slowly comes up, dips again, and finally all ends up in delicate balance. Miraculous. In 2006 this area was also a nesting site for thirty-eight pairs of osprey. The osprey population had at one point been decimated, but they are making a strong comeback. The incredible high-speed dive they make into the water when they spot their prey is breathtaking.

In the high water I delight in creating "reed music." The reeds brushing my high-tech paddle give off a surprising variety of sounds. Added to that are the percussion sounds made by the reeds pushing the small carrying handle mounted on the bow of my kayak. It bounces against the kayak in a remarkably rhythmic fashion. The reeds brushing on the side of the kayak make a whishing sound. Mix in the lapping of the water and, at one point, the rather continuous chatter of a white-belted kingfisher, and I am at least a small paddling band unto myself. I am continually drawn back into the reeds by the promise of more music.

We are enclosed in swampy, dreamy serenity of trees, reeds, and water. The entire shoreline of the wildlife refuge is truly a watery world with uncertain definition between lake and shore, especially in this high-water fall, and particularly

▶ **Missisquoi Wildlife Refuge to Highgate Springs & Dead Creek**

from the perspective of a kayak. Where does the water stop and the land begin? There is constant movement. Swaying tree branches overhang the reeds that are also in motion, rocked by the water and blown by the wind.

The Return Trip: Our plan is to paddle back via Dead Creek, an old channel of the Missisquoi River that meanders from Goose Bay to about 4 miles (6 kilometers) upstream from the mouth of the Missisquoi. Since it is early enough in the afternoon and the wind is manageable, we decide to paddle across the bay to Highgate Springs and then double back to Dead Creek. We find Highgate Springs completely quiet. About 9300 B.C., Paleo-Indians occupied this spot and left their stone points as evidence.

It is submerged now, but I have seen the delta of Dead Creek populated with shore birds. Once again I am reminded of the old Heraclitus adage, "You can never put your foot in the same river twice." The weather and seasons will have their way; we are only observers in the moment.

The sun slanting through the silver maples lining Dead Creek makes mysterious shadows and moving reflections on the water. Water bugs skitter away from the bows of our kayaks. I slip under overhanging branches trying not to get enmeshed in the spider webs and hanging leaves. Wooded banks give way to cultivated fields and the sound of truck traffic on Rt. 78 as we approach the Missisquoi.

We head northwest with the current, but not the wind. A few minutes of strenuous paddling bring us to our take-out site. We quickly load the car and head out—to the raspberry stand on Rt. 78 on the west side of the Missisquoi Bridge. Nancy Bohannon Christopher, a childhood friend of my husband, appears once we announce our presence using the walkie-talkie that is taped to the countertop. There is a tense moment when the customer who precedes us announces how many pints he wants, but we determine that there is enough for all. What a juicy way to end our day of paddling the watery world of Missisquoi Bay.

20 Missisquoi Bay
An International Adventure

by Margy Holden

- **Launch site:** Highgate Springs Town Park, Shipyard Rd. off Old Dock Rd., Highgate Springs, Vermont
- **Distance:** 23 miles (37 kilometers)
- **Take out:** West Swanton F&W Area (Rt. 78 adjacent to Missisquoi Bridge)
- **Alternative launch sites:** Rock River F&W Area (Rt. 7, Spring St., Highgate, Vermont), Philipsburg Public Wharf (Canadian Customs, Rt. 133 to Avenue Montgomery, Philipsburg, Quebec), Venise-en-Quebec Public Wharf (Rt. 202, Avenue de Venise, Venise-en-Quebec)
- **Places to stop:** Above launch sites and Highgate Cliffs Natural Area (PT), Philipsburg Pier, Missisquoi Beach, Venise-en-Quebec Town Beach and food purveyors
- **Highlights:** Highgate Cliffs Natural Area, Highgate State Park, Rivière aux-Brochets Natural Area at mouth of Pike River, Venise-en-Quebec, Philipsburg, Quebec, wildlife, marshes, agricultural views, navigable rivers to explore
- **Route:** This fascinating circle route follows the shallow east shore of Missisquoi Bay north, passing the mouth of the Rock River, the cliff, the town of Philipsburg, the mouth of the Pike River and its park, settled Jameson Point, to the waterfront of Venise-en-Quebec. There it turns south and follows a lightly settled and agricultural west shore of Missisquoi Bay back to the Rt. 78 bridge and the launch site.
- **Comments:** Take your passport! Paddlers entering Canada are expected to stop at the Philipsburg Pier and check in at the yellow phone at the end of the pier. To register on return to the U.S., the Alburgh Springs Customs Office is identifiable by the flags on the nearby Canadian Customs office visible across a private field. Alternatively, one can paddle to the West Swanton F&W Area and drive to the Alburgh Springs Customs Station on Alburgh Springs Rd. (first right on the other side of the bridge). This paddle is open to wind from all directions. Don't forget to stop at the raspberry stand at the west side of the Missisquoi Bridge.

The Paddle:

Its length and crossing into and out of Canada defines this trip. While I often forge ahead with the conviction that everything will work out, Cathy does research. This leads us to the Vermont Route 89 Highgate Customs Office, where we learn that we have to register with Canadian authorities from a yellow phone in Philipsburg to legally enter Canada, and with the U.S. Customs Office in Alburgh Springs if we are to be allowed to reenter the Untied States. How we will do this is unclear, but we set out believing "everything will work out."

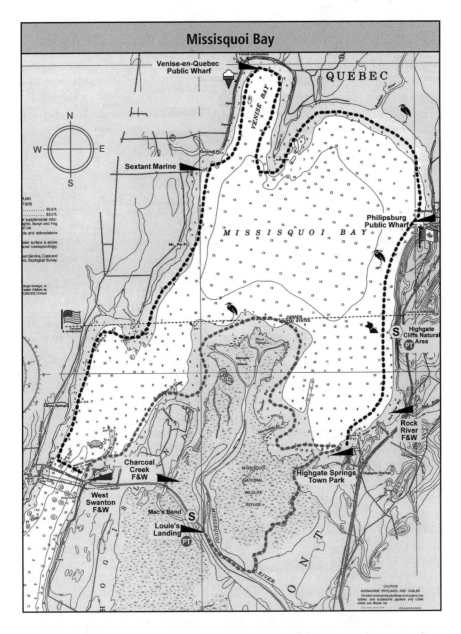

Algae Blooms at the Rock River. The greenish tinge of the water indicates an algae bloom, which becomes denser as we paddle out from shore. The nontoxic algae can become thick enough to make the water an unappealing pea-soup color.

A marshy area stretches from the waterfront of The Tyler Place, the lovely old family resort, most of the way to the mouth of the Rock River. This river flows through Quebec and Franklin County and, according to Candy Page in her *Burlington Free Press* series, in spite of its relatively small, 59-square-mile (1,528-hectare) drainage basin, transports more phosphorus per acre into Lake Champlain than any other river or stream. As a result, the Rock River is a focus of efforts to prevent phosphorus runoff. The obstacles are real. The uncertain farm economy, insufficient funding, uncoordinated efforts by federal and state agencies and nonprofits, and lack of a method to enforce compliance, all make cleaning up the Rock River a substantial challenge. Yet many farmers work within their financial ability to leave grassy corridors along streams to absorb runoff, and use machinery that inserts fertilizer below runoff depth. Federal, state, and provincial government subsidies make a difference, but the list of farmers who wish to comply far outstrips the number of experts available to design manure retention systems. While there are no reports that today's bloom is harmful, it is certainly not inviting to us and others who would like to swim. Some residents have been moved to action, forming the Friends of Missisquoi Bay. They bring attention to the issue and raise the funds to demonstrate beneficial practices.

Up to this point we have experienced Missisquoi Bay as a flat, marsh-like landscape. Suddenly that changes. Vertical dolomite cliffs over 200 feet high (61 meters), soar straight out of the water. What a surprise! The cliffs are designated the Highgate Cliffs Natural Area, part of the 37-acre (15-hectare) Highgate State Park. Turkey vultures soar along the cliffs on the winds' updrafts. They are just one of the bird species now found in Vermont as our climate warms. Birds are justly called an "indicator species," because they react in noticeable ways to changes in the environment. In 2006 one of thirty-four Vermont pairs of peregrine falcons actually nested here and successfully fledged two chicks. The stunning cliffs also provide the setting for a unique adventure. We find a yellow Labrador swimming in deep water, exhausted, trying to reach distant kayaks. We manage to find him safe footing beneath the cliffs and track down his owners.

O, Canada! From under the cliffs, we cannot see the wide swath of cleared land that marks the Canadian/U.S. border. There is no sign or symbol along the shore—not even a marker—that we are crossing into another country until we get to the Philipsburg Pier that looms above us by at least 15 feet (4.6 meters). As promised by the customs agent, there is a bright yellow phone on a post at the pier's end.

I pick up the phone, and a cheery male voice says *bonjour* and asks for our registration number. Hearing that our kayaks do not have registration numbers, he asks me to please wait. Could we really be kept out of Canada? If the fashion police were in charge, I would be. To cope with the 90°F (32°C) temperatures today, I wear a straw hat tied on with yarn and a man's shirt draped over my life preserver, giving me a bizarre, hunchback appearance.

The agent returns to the phone and tells us that we have been given an eleven-digit registration number, which we must have with us. Oh dear, how will we ever remember it? He spells the first part. K-A-Y-A-K. That is Quebec

▶ **Missisquoi Bay**

The yellow phone—permission granted.

ingenuity. The second part is numerical. I repeat slowly so that Cathy can help memorize: 208 (phew, the reverse of Vermont's only area code), 1960 (the year I graduated), 2006 (the current year). We've got it! We can actually paddle into Canada, and we have our very own registration number to prove it.

We walk back down the long pier and climb into our kayaks. The main street of Philipsburg looks serene. Beyond Philipsburg, the land is mostly marshy all the way to the mouth of the Pike River at the northeastern end of the bay. The reeds stretch out from shore, and I seize on the opportunity to make "reed music" once again with my kayak.

The Pike River. The wide mouth of the Pike River brackets the water that moves gently into the lake. I hum the song "Up a Lazy River," which fits this place. This river also flows through farmland, carrying runoff that it deposits in Missisquoi Bay. The Pike River is the only river emptying into Missisquoi Bay that has actually decreased in the last few years the phosphorus load that it carries.

Beyond the Pike River, Jameson Point stretches south for over a mile into Missisquoi Bay. When we finally round this long point, we see Venice-en-Quebec in the distance. Hungry, but reluctant to lose ground to the headwind, and with no public shore to land on, we are forced to paddle and eat at the same time.

We paddle steadily, hoping to find the ice cream stand I have promised Cathy is there. Just above a ramp in murky water, I see a sign for "Bar Laitier." We are like two women who have been lost in the desert as we stagger up to the service window to order the best milkshakes that either of us has ever had. The young owner has transformed a gravel parking lot into a floral wonderland of petunias.

Very reluctantly, we leave—without having seconds. At 23 miles (30 kilometers), this is our longest paddle, and the entire west shore of Missisquoi Bay is ahead. In the distance we can barely see our goal, the Rt. 78 bridge. Dwellings alternate with farmland most of the way. The water clarity varies from quite clear to islands of thick algae bloom. We search for the flags of Canada and the U.S. heralding the essential-to-us customs station. After paddling for some miles with no luck, we finally stop to ask for directions. A woman answers in unaccented English, which should be the first clue that we have overshot our objective. Considering our up-wind options, we decide to continue our illegal reentry into the United States.

Missisquoi cliffs.

▶ Missisquoi Bay

Safely covering the last 3 miles (4.8 kilometers) of this 23-mile (30-kilo-meter) trip, our tired arms shakily lift kayaks onto the car. We drive to Alburgh Springs and have to make a U-turn to get into the customs station right in front of two startled United States Customs officers. When we tell them our story, they teasingly respond that they won't arrest us this time, but they did see us paddling in Canada. What a complicated day for two normally law-abiding citizens. We head for Nancy Christopher's raspberry farm for our juicy reward. The proof of our exhaustion comes later that night when I find that, after going through customs, Cathy replaced her identification in my wallet and vice versa.

We did not look forward to paddling Missisquoi Bay, but found that the watery world of the National Wildlife Refuge is a wondrous place where water and land blend and wild things are protected. There is a mystery and beauty about it that we find nowhere else. The historic presence of the Abenaki is represented more strongly here than probably any other place on the lake (even though there is no visible evidence). The cliffs are such a contrast to all this. And it is fun to paddle into and out of another country.

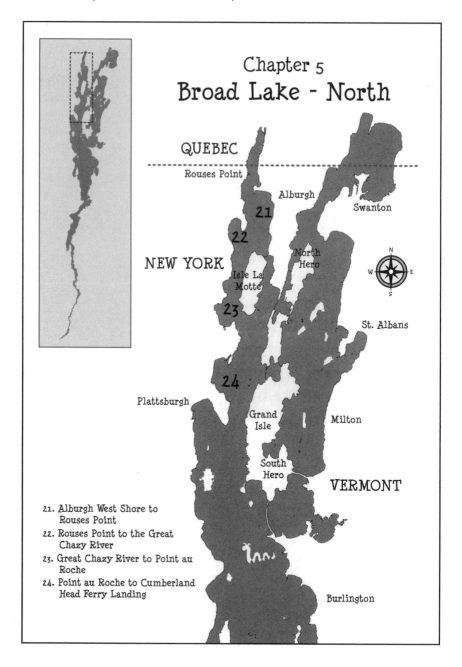

Chapter 5
Broad Lake - North

QUEBEC

Rouses Point

Alburgh

Swanton

21

22

NEW YORK

Isle La Motte

North Hero

23

St. Albans

24

Plattsburgh

Grand Isle

Milton

South Hero

VERMONT

21. Alburgh West Shore to Rouses Point
22. Rouses Point to the Great Chazy River
23. Great Chazy River to Point au Roche
24. Point au Roche to Cumberland Head Ferry Landing

Burlington

Chapter V

Broad Lake North

Main Gateway to Canada

The northern part of the broad lake is defined by the Champlain Islands to the east and the mainland of New York from Cumberland Head northward to the west. It is the gateway to Quebec, Canada. The farther north one travels on this part of the lake, the flatter the land becomes. The water is shallower and, as a result, much of its shoreline is marshy, although it has a lower concentration of invasive species than are found in other shallow areas of the lake. Although this northernmost section is still called "the broad lake" in deference to the fact that it is the main north/south channel, it is often not much more than a mile between some shores. Farms provide open space between cottages and homes along the shore.

Rouses Point Bridge.

Alburgh West Shore: Alburgh Dunes State Park to the Rouses Point Bridge — *Dunes and a Long Straight Shoreline*   21

by Margy Holden

- **Launch site:** Alburgh Dunes State Park ($), Coon Point Rd. off Rt. 129, Alburgh, Vermont
- **Distance:** 13.5 miles (21.1 kilometers)
- **Take out:** Kelly Bay F&W Area (Rt. 2, east end of Rouses Point Bridge, Alburgh, Vermont)
- **Alternative launch sites:** North Hero Marina ($, Pelots Point Rd., North Hero, Vermont), Horicon F&W area (West Shore Rd., Alburgh)
- **Places to stop:** None aside from launch sites
- **Highlights:** Alburgh Dunes State Park with dunes, beach pea and walking trails; views of Rouses Point, Isle la Motte, Island Line Railroad bed and Windmill Point Lighthouse
- **Route:** This route heads north through the channel between Alburgh and Isle la Motte, crosses under the bridge and then follows the shallow west shore of the Alburgh Peninsula along a road and agricultural land. It then turns briefly west along a marsh and the railroad bed before rounding Windmill Point and heading north again through the mile-wide passage to Kelly Bay and the launch site.
- **Comments:** The beginning of the route through the La Motte passage is relatively protected. Strong south or west wind can build waves over the shallow, mostly rocky shoreline north of that. There are no stopping places or facilities on this route, but lots of shallow rock or sand shallows on which to stand.

Alburgh Dunes State Park: What do you picture when you hear the name Alburgh Dunes State Park? If you're like us, the name conjures up an ocean beach scene of hills of sand, rather than a lake environment. But make no mistake—Lake Champlain too has sand dunes, although this looks more like a level, sandy beach. But note the plants growing on this slight mound of sand; they are beach grass and beach pea, which are commonly found on ocean dunes. This sand also behaves like dunes because it is ever so gradually moving into the wetland behind it, driven by the prevailing south wind and waves. So what are saltwater vegetation and sand dunes doing here on this freshwater lake? This special area is clear evidence that in Lake Champlain's fascinating geologic history, it was once the saltwater Champlain Sea.

A three-quarter-mile path from the dune area to the eastern boundary of the park provides a good way to see both the emergent dunes and the wetland behind the dune area. The wetland includes a black spruce bog, which is usually found in colder parts of Vermont. Scientists have taken core samples as deep as 26 feet (8 meters) into the bog and found evidence of vegetation dating back to the time of the glaciers. An upland white cedar forest provides habitat for the largest deer-wintering area in Grand Isle County. Wild turkeys also roam this area.

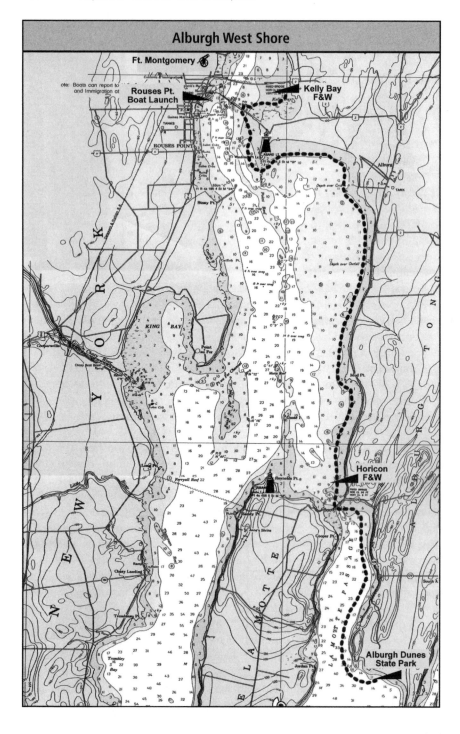

▶ Alburgh West Shore

The Paddle:

This 625-acre (253-hectare) property became a state park in 1996—barely in time to protect it from private development. We carry our kayaks across the almost-deserted beach to the edge of the water. The park attendant, who appears happy to have some business, tells us that most of the visitors are from Quebec.

The beach may be quiet, but the water is not. Large waves break on the shallow south-facing shore. We launch cautiously to avoid capsizing as we cross the breakers, which have had a good chance to build in the long fetch from the south. Our kayaks perform differently. Cathy's is about a foot longer and weighs a third more than even my new, improved kayak. We much prefer putting mine on the car, but hers is a far more stable boat in turbulent water. While I'm bobbing about, Cathy is cutting through the waves in a straight line, controlled most of the time by her rudder.

We wait for a string of smaller waves in order to make a quick turn north. From here we have a good view of our launch site and can better understand how the beach was created by sand washing up between two rock outcroppings.

With tail wind and waves astern, we make great progress through the half-mile-wide channel between the Alburgh and Isle la Motte shores. We pass the Alburgh Country Club, one of only four golf courses that can be seen from

Beachpea.

Lake Champlain Lighthouses

Lake Champlain's reputation for deep water belies the fact that numerous shoals and an irregular shoreline challenge mariners. As the hand-paddled small craft that plied the lake for centuries gave way to sail and steam, a hue and cry went up for lighthouses. The need was so great that captains themselves erected rough structures supporting improvised lights on such places as Isle la Motte and Windmill and Crown Points as early as the 1600s. In the mid to late 1800s, the United States Congress responded by appropriating funds to build a series of lighthouses on Lake Champlain. The first, on Juniper Island, was completed in 1826 and the last, Bluff Point Light on Valcour Island, in 1874. Twelve stand today, giving us a fascinating glimpse of history.

Most of Lake Champlain's lighthouses are privately owned. The exceptions—Bluff Point Lighthouse on Valcour Island and the Crown Point Lighthouse—welcome visitors. The private lighthouses can be seen from the water on Isle la Motte, Point au Roche, Juniper Island (hard to see through the trees), Cumberland Head, Split Rock, and Barber Point. Most have weathered limestone octagonal towers with attached homes for the keepers. Two reproductions of earlier lighthouses protect the north and south ends of the jetty in Burlington Harbor.

Some of the lighthouses were built twice, either because their location proved inadequate or they fell into disrepair. For example, the 1836 Cumberland Head Lighthouse turned out to be too far from the shore, and the 1838 Split Rock Lighthouse crumbled before being rebuilt in 1874. Quarries on Isle la Motte and Willsboro Point supplied much of the limestone for the lighthouses. The original Juniper Island Light was replaced by what is now the oldest surviving cast-iron lighthouse in the United States, built in 1846. The other cast-iron lighthouse, on Isle la Motte, sports a pinkish hue faded from its original red. Imagine the activity in1858, when Windmill, Point au Roche, Crown Point and sister Barber Point and Bluff Point lighthouses were built. Most of the lights shone through Fresnel lenses, which projected light for up to 15 miles (24 kilometers).

After the Civil War, injured veterans received preference as light house keepers. At least two of the veterans, at Cumberland Head and Bluff Point, died of their wounds and were replaced by their wives, who earned their official designation for having tended not only their ill husbands, but the lights for several years as well.

▶ Alburgh West Shore

Beginning in 1928 and continuing through the 1930s, steel towers with automated beacons replaced most of the functioning lighthouses. Many of the lighthouses passed into private hands and some into disrepair. The Colchester Light, a notable exception, was deconstructed, moved, and now stands proudly on the dry land of the Shelburne Museum not far from the steamship *Ticonderoga*. Not until the beginning of this century did a few of these beautiful structures achieve a renaissance through the efforts of their owners. Beginning

in 2002, automated beacons returned to the privately owned Windmill, Isle la Motte, Cumberland Head, and Split Rock lighthouses. Bluff and Crown Point lighthouses also reclaimed their beacons. What a thrill to come upon a view of one of these striking structures, rising above the water and still shining its beacon to provide safe passage for mariners.

Bluff Point Lighthouse.

the lake. I scoot under the Isle la Motte Bridge, making echoes, watching the barn swallows swoop, and enjoying the peace of the bridge's lee. Ah, the joys of kayaking.

From the Isle LaMotte Bridge northward, the shoreline and the vegetation change. Cottonwoods, looking a bit like sentries lined up along the pebbly water's edge, have great hollows in the base of their trunks formed by the battering from the water and ice. I imagine Quebec bootleggers of the 1920s stealthily stashing a barrel of liquor in one of those great hollows in the dark of night to be recovered at a later time.

The road between the Isle la Motte Bridge and Alburgh runs right along the almost straight shoreline, peppered with a string of houses and docks and interspersed with an occasional farm, until it joins Route 2 at the southern edge of Alburgh town. We pass a couple fishing from a ramp. When I see her catch and he take the wriggling fish off the hook and return it to the water, I know they have the kind of relationship I like. I bet he baits her hook, too. The Shoreline Chocolate and Lake End Cheese Store, unmarked from the water, when open provides the only public stopping place along the shore.

Alburgh, Vermont, is unique for reasons that we cannot see from the water. In 2006 the residents voted at town meeting to restore the "h" to the end of the town name, which then had to be approved by Vermont's Department of Libraries. Alburgh, spelled either way, is one of only three towns in the United States that you can access only by boat, by bridge—or by driving on roads through Canada.

Beyond Alburgh the shallow, sandy, reed-bordered shoreline swings west. The occupants of several motorboats who have rafted together greet us with cheerful *bonjour*. We meet many more people from Quebec on this northern part of the lake. Partially hidden behind the marsh, familiar, large chunks of granite remind us that we are following the Island Line rail bed.

Posted.

▶ **Alburgh West Shore**

Windmill Point, an upwind paddle today, juts south into the lake for almost a mile. At the point's tip we can see both the expansive view to the south and the historic stone lighthouse.

This view south gives us a sense of how strategic this location is. If one is traveling south, it is the first broad water. Beyond here to the north, the lake is more like a river. It must have been quite a sight for Samuel de Champlain and others who traveled south along the Richelieu River from Canada to finally reach something resembling the lake they had been hoping to find. Windmill Point was the location of one of the earliest French settlements on the lake. Its eastern shore offers protection from the north wind and a clear view of boat traffic to the south. Benedict Arnold chose the protection of this peninsula as an anchorage when on a scouting expedition before the Battle of Valcour. He discovered that the danger was on shore when a landing party from his craft *The Boston* was attacked by Native Americans allied with the British, resulting in casualties on both sides. The rest of the American party managed to get back to their boat and escape.

We paddle around Windmill Point through shallow water and choppy waves to head north again. We have a good view of the town of Rouses Point on our left and the cottages of Windmill Point on our right. A few minutes later we glide into calm water created by remnants of the old railroad bridge, which was used by both the Rutland and Central Vermont railroads between 1851 and 1964. Although the rails are gone, the uprights remain, each adorned today by a cormorant holding onto its territory in spite of our presence.

Tucked beneath the old railroad bed, wild morning glories bloom, watched over by common terns. As I pause to observe, Cathy takes off suddenly, paddling fast. I race to catch up, only to be attacked by the same deer flies she is trying to escape. We both paddle briskly and eventually outrun them. The Vermont Fish & Wildlife Access is just ahead at the base of the eastern end of the Rouses Point Bridge, almost hidden in the reeds. We take our kayaks out, load them on the cars yet again, and appreciate our tired muscles on our drive south.

22 **Rouses Point to the Great Chazy River**
Explorer's Route

by Margy Holden

- **Launch site:** Rouses Point Boat Launch, Montgomery St. off Rt. 2, Rouses Point, New York
- **Distance:** 10 miles (16 kilometers)
- **Take out:** Great Chazy River NY Boat Launch (off Rt. 9B, ¼ mile south of Coopersville, New York)
- **Alternative launch sites:** Kelly Bay F&W Area (Rt. 2, adjacent to Rouses Point Bridge, Alburgh, New York)
- **Places to stop:** Above launch sites and Stony Point Breakwater (Stony Point Wildlife Management Area, off Rt. 9B, Rouses Point)
- **Highlights:** Fort Montgomery, Rouses Point, Point au Fer, wildlife in King Bay marsh areas, historic sites
- **Route:** This historic route passes by the moored boats on the Rouses Point waterfront, around the long Stony Point Breakwater, along a marshy shore, around Point au Fer, and around King Bay into the Great Chazy River.
- **Comments:** A south wind can build waves, especially around Point au Fer. The entire route is shallow except around some of the marinas in Rouses Point.

The Paddle:

We look at the New York shoreline every day from our Vermont homes, but we have never before taken our kayaks across the lake. I want to know if what I imagine I see in the distance resembles what we will really see up close. It is roughly 34 miles (55 kilometers) from Rouses Point to Cumberland Head, and since we cannot find a public access at the midway point, we break the trip into three segments.

The New York shore is full of natural areas and history. It is the main channel through Lake Champlain. The Champlain Islands to the east narrow the lake, making for intriguing passages and superb views. According to a recent study, there are more boats moored and launched here than at other places on the lake with the possible exception of Malletts Bay. These northern shores are where many fishermen head, too.

We put our kayaks in the water at the immaculate New York State launch site at the north end of Rouses Point. As we push off, seven black ducks swim out of our way—barely. They may be more used to boat traffic than the ducks along less populated shorelines, where frightened ducks flee quickly. We are surrounded by moored and docked boats of all descriptions and sizes. Here they are more likely to fly the Quebec flag and sport French names, reflecting the proximity to Montreal. This can be a busy place, especially on weekends when boats moored on the Richelieu River travel south to enjoy Lake Champlain, or Americans go north to experience a bit of French culture.

▶ **Rouses Point to the Great Chazy River**

The modern Rouses Point Bridge soars 56 feet (17 meters) above us to the north, connecting Vermont and New York. It was built in 1987 to replace a fifty-year-old toll swing-bridge that had become completely impractical because of increasing recreational boat and auto traffic. Under the bridge we spy Fort Montgomery, or Fort Blunder as it is sometimes called, which is just to the north on Island Point.

Fort Montgomery

Fort Montgomery's impressive walls appear to rise directly out of the water. The Americans actually began building this fort two years after the end of the War of 1812 to counter the continuing British threat. Construction continued for several years, until a survey done to establish the actual location of the 45th parallel—the boundary at that time between the United States and Canada—found the blunder. The fort was three-quarters of a mile north of the border in Canada. The government ceased construction, but local residents seized an opportunity and removed much of the fort material to construct buildings in Rouses Point and nearby towns. When the boundary was resettled by the Webster-Asburton Treaty in 1842, Island Point officially became part of the United States. By that time, Fort Blunder was in such dire condition that construction had to be started anew. It was still ongoing at the end of the Civil War, but the British threat had passed and the fort was never completed. Since then, much of the Isle La Motte stone used to build the fort has again been carted away for local use. Fort Montgomery lives on, both as an historic structure and as a visible part of many other buildings.

Fort Montgomery.

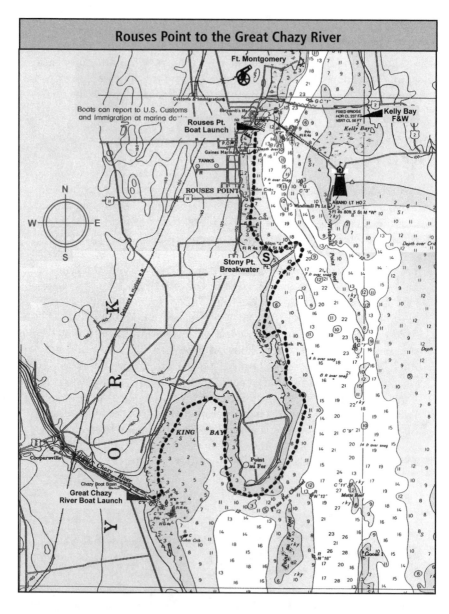

The history of Rouses Point demonstrates what changed when steam replaced sail, and again when rail replaced steam. First settled in 1783, Rouses Point became a bustling port for shipping and the railroad. An eighteenth-century traveler arriving by steamboat in Rouses Point reported that the level of activity and noise was comparable to what she had experienced on New York City's Broadway.

▶ **Rouses Point to the Great Chazy River**

Then, in 1875, when the Delaware and Hudson rail line was extended to Montreal, bypassing Rouses Point, and the northern terminus for steamboats was moved south to Plattsburgh, the city's fortunes declined precipitously. Today the loudest sounds we hear from our kayaks are water lapping on the shore, the ringing of the moored sailboats' rigging, and the occasional distant rumble of trucks shifting gears as they make the turn onto Route 11.

The chart of the shore of Rouses Point is lined with notations of "ruins" and "submerged cribs." In the calm of this quiet morning, we can see the remnants of rock cribs that once supported the piers. A bit farther along, we learn just how much the half-mile-long Stony Point Breakwater on the south end of Rouses Point is protecting the waterfront and us from wind and waves. Landing our kayaks on the small beach on the north side, we clamber along the huge quarried rocks discovering fossils and fishermen. When we paddle around its tip to the windward side, the south wind and waves hit us. We head south for the cover of Catfish Bay and push through the waves around Catfish Point before reaching Point au Fer. We peer into the marsh in Catfish Bay where Rogers' Rangers encircled and defeated French attackers in 1760. Rogers was on his way north to try to wrest Montreal from the French.

Point au Fer. Point au Fer (meaning "head of iron," or "weapon") points south into the lake, reaching toward Isle la Motte. Some believe that this area was

Counterbalance — Stony Point Breakwater.

actually named Point au Feu, after the signal fires built here, but was mistakenly renamed "Fer." Whatever the name, this point of land was well used by Native Americans, by the French and British, and later by the Americans and British as they traded and battled up and down the lake. The long view down Lake Champlain from Point au Fer makes it easy to spot approaching friend and foe.

The British constructed a stone fort here in 1774 that was nicknamed the White House. It changed hands during the American Revolution, but the British retook Point au Fer in 1776 and, incredibly, used it as a base of operations for controlling the lake in this area until 1796, almost twenty years after the American Revolution had ended. (Block House Point on North Hero was similarly held.) What an odd situation to have the British maintaining a fort on Point au Fer while Americans lived at the mouth of the Great Chazy River, less than a mile away across King Bay.

Point au Fer has beckoned to travelers for centuries. In 1775, Benedict Arnold stopped here on his way to capture St. Johns on the Richelieu River. In 1777, on its way to Montreal, a delegation from the Continental Congress that included Benjamin Franklin reputedly enjoyed a pint at a tavern owned by a Colonel Christie on Point au Fer.

On Point au Fer today, a gradual beach stretches in front of neat houses, camps, and an occasional large dwelling. We can see for miles down the lake to cliffs on both shores. And that is what made Point au Fer such a strategic place for forts, battles, and visitors.

The Great Chazy River. King Bay is formed by Point au Fer on the east and the delta of the Great Chazy River on the west. It is so large that we are amazed at the amount of time it takes to paddle around it. With a depth of 3 feet (1 meter) in many places, it is perfect for small boats. The shallow water defines the shoreline, which is an alternating mix of small cottages, houses, and marsh. Like Catfish Bay, it is too shallow and reed-filled for us to paddle very close to shore.

We enter the mouth of the Great Chazy River and take out at the New York State launch site on the south shore. The Chazy Yacht Club marina, docks, and boats line up beyond it. This lazy river invites exploration because it is rapid-free for the first six miles inland from the lake. As we take our kayaks out, I wonder if the owners of the trucks waiting in the parking lot know that this river is stocked regularly with brown trout. This is a relatively brief, but historic paddle.

▶ **Rouses Point to the Great Chazy River**

Great Chazy River to Point au Roche
Between Isle and Shore

by Margy Holden

- ▋ **Launch site:** Great Chazy River NY Boat Launch, off Rt. 9B, ¼ mile south of Coopersville, New York
- ▋ **Distance:** 11.5 Miles (18.5 kilometers)
- ▋ **Take out:** Point au Roche NY Boat Launch at Chellis Bay (Dickson Point Rd. off Point au Roche Rd. off Rt. 9, New York)
- ▋ **Alternative launch site:** Stoney Point F&W Area (West Shore Rd., Isle La Motte, New York). We could not find public accesses marked on charts in Trombley Bay and Chazy Landing. There are two commercial launch sites in Monty Bay, but we were refused access at one.
- ▋ **Places to stop:** Above launch sites and Mooney Bay Marina Store and Restaurant
- ▋ **Highlights:** Marshes with wildlife, agricultural shoreline with distant Adirondack views, historic houses of Chazy Landing, views of Isle la Motte and Green Mountains beyond, tire breakwaters in Mooney Bay
- ▋ **Route:** The route follows a consistently shallow and initially marshy to later rocky shoreline, ending at the cliffs at the north end of Point au Roche. The initial agricultural shoreline with long views to mountains becomes increasingly settled.
- ▋ **Comments:** A strong north or south wind will create waves, but the contour of the shore and the proximity of Isle la Motte offer some protection. We were unable to find accesses marked on the map in Chazy Landing and near Wool Point, and were refused access at one of the private marinas in Monty Bay. If this situation persists, there is no shore access on this paddle.

The Paddle:

The water along the shore between the mouths of the Great Chazy River and the Little Chazy River is shallow and filled with reeds wherever there is protection from the south wind. In most places on Lake Champlain, shoreline cliffs limit the view inland. That is not so here. Along this Chazy shore, the land sweeps back, field after field, to Rand Hill and Lyon Mountain and, to the north, the flat plain of the St. Lawrence River. We share this impressive view from our kayaks with cows grazing ever so close to the water. There appears to be no land barrier from seeping manure. If the Great Chazy River meanders, the Little Chazy River slithers into the lake. The smaller Little Chazy River curves this way and that, upstream from the mouth. Duckweed flourishes, and there is little discernible current.

It is a short paddle to Chazy Landing, which looks charming from the water. "Landing" indicates that it was once a stopping point for sailboats and steamboats. Matthew Saxe built the first steamboat wharf between Whitehall and St. Jean in 1805 here. We can still see his house, which is very near the water, and

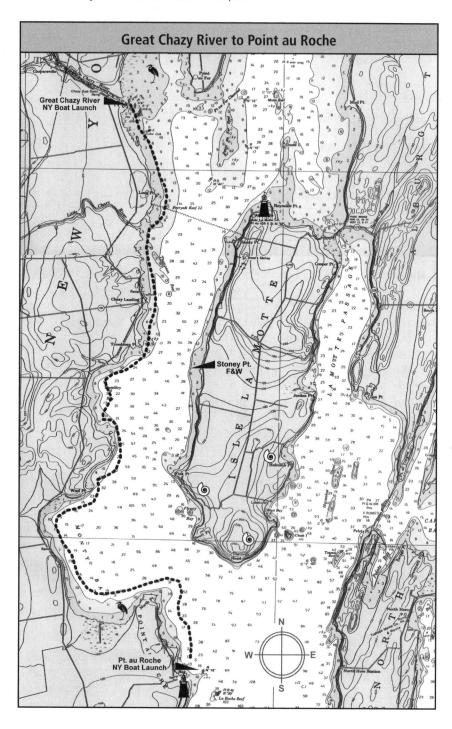

▶ **Great Chazy River to Point au Roche**

under my kayak are the rocks that must have supported the wharf. We try to find a launch ramp that is marked on the charts, and think we do—with a flowerbed planted in it.

Homes dot the shoreline all along Trembleau Point and into Trembley Bay, south of Chazy Landing. My mind wanders as I speculate about why the names are Trembleau and Trembley. Did two brothers live here, one on the point and one in the bay, with the brother in the bay anglicizing his name? The shore is lined with cottonwoods and the ground is pebbly. It is just a little over a mile from here across the water to where we can see the Vermont fishing access on Isle la Motte and Camel's Hump rising many miles behind it. The juxtaposition of New York and Vermont, with Canada not far off, makes this main channel on the northern part of Lake Champlain all the more interesting to paddle.

Monty Bay is memorable for a specific reason. It is the land of tires—lots and lots and lots of tires. They are tied together by resourceful marina owners to form breakwaters of many lengths and descriptions. Surely, not many pesky waves penetrate these man-made, floating sculptures. In places they almost look like extensions of the land. Are they attractive? That depends on your taste. Does it work? Yes, and it also uses tires that would normally end up in a landfill. On the south end of Monty Bay, reeds that wave in the breeze for almost as far as we can see are a natural contrast to the man-made tires.

Point au Roche looks like an anvil tipped on its side with the top facing North Hero. *Roche* means rock, and indeed the shores are rocky. Just ahead, the first promontory at North Point is an indication that we are leaving the flat shores of a river plain in a transition to the foothills of the Adirondacks. These small cliffs put into perspective how low the land along the northern New York shoreline has been. Between North Point and Chellis Bay we paddle through a number of small bays with good views to the east of North Hero. We end our day at the New York State access ramp.

Lakeside farm.

24 | Point au Roche to Cumberland Head Ferry Landing
Parkscape and Settled Shore

by Margy Holden

- **Launch site:** Point au Roche NY Boat Launch at Chellis Bay, Dickson Point Rd. off Point au Roche Rd. off Rt. 9, New York
- **Distance:** 13 Miles (21 kilometers)
- **Take out:** Cumberland Head Ferry Landing (Rt. 314, New York)
- **Alternative launch sites:** Point au Roche State Park, New York ($, PT, off Point au Roche Rd. off Rt. 9)
- **Places to stop:** The entire shoreline of Point au Roche State Park
- **Highlights:** Point au Roche State Park with walking trails, interpretive center, sand and rock beaches, Deep Bay (sometimes called Lake Champlain's fiord), Point au Roche Lighthouse, views of the Green and Adirondack mountains and The Gut, wildlife
- **Route:** Leaving the launch site, the route follows the scenic shore of Point au Roche Park, along the western rocky shore, around the point, through Deep Bay, and to the sand beach of the Park. It then follows the shallow, suburban shores of Treadwell Bay and Cumberland Head.
- **Comments:** Walking trails and small museum in the state park are accessible from the water. The entire shore of Point au Roche State Park is accessible, but there are no stopping places after the park. The western shores of Point au Roche State Park and Cumberland Head are exposed to north and south winds.

The Paddle:

We launch our kayaks in Chellis Bay and head south. Almost immediately we round a bend and find ourselves looking up at 50 feet (15 meters) of blue limestone rising directly above us. The octagonal Point au Roche Lighthouse is so close to the water that we can almost touch it. Unfortunately, it is structurally deteriorating. In 1989 the light was moved to a buoy that we can see bobbing offshore to mark the La Roche Reef. Ahead we can see the masts of the sailboats docked at the Mooney Bay Marina. In season, a restaurant and ships store offer amenities to the paddler.

Point au Roche Park. Mooney Bay marks the northern boundary of the 835-acre (338-hectare) Point au Roche State Park. We leave there and paddle around one more point to a beautiful little cove at the north end of Conner Bay. What a good spot for a lunch stop. A gradual, slab-rock shore makes it easy to land. I can't wait to get into the sparkling water. This is one of the prettiest spots we have stopped at on the lake. A trail along the shore offers an opportunity for those who want to explore. I watch a dragonfly investigate my knee before it darts away.

▶ **Point au Roche to Cumberland Head Ferry Landing**

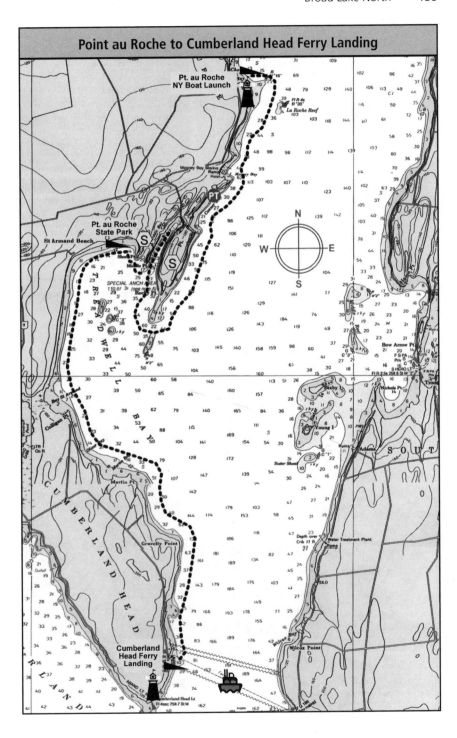

Point au Roche to Cumberland Head Ferry Landing

The south end of Connor Bay is the beginning of Long Point, aptly named because it is over a mile long. Along with adjacent Deep Bay, it is often called Lake Champlain's only fjord. Long Point has walking trails that are used in summer by walkers and in winter by cross-country skiers. Its cedars stand in contrast to the predominant cottonwoods and maples that line the shore to the north. From the tip of Long Point, North Hero and the entrance to The Gut are to the east, and Cumberland Head to the south.

Deep Bay wraps us in its cedar scent, warmth, and calm. Its 20-foot (6-meter) depth is surprising for such a long, thin body of water. It's really quite wondrous, a world apart. A chattering belted kingfisher leads the way. There is access to the Point au Roche trails at the inner end of Deep Bay. It's probably not always this quiet, however, because it is a destination for cruising boats.

Long Point has two, much smaller, mimics to the west—Middle Point and Short Point. It reminds me of the three bears. We paddle around each, thoroughly enjoying the ins and outs. The view from the tip of Short Point is the crescent of sand beach at Point au Roche State Park shimmering invitingly in the sun. There is a bathhouse, concession stand, and another boat launch ramp. In addition to this good swimming beach, the park offers campsites and a nature center. The nature center's collection is an intriguing array of items, including a taxidermy display of local animals, rock specimens, and an old, well-mounted but disintegrating butterfly collection. From 1952 to 1970, before becoming a state park, this area was Fantasy Kingdom Amusement Park, complete with

Deep Bay, Point au Roche.

▶ Point au Roche to Cumberland Head Ferry Landing

Point au Roche.

homes for the three little pigs and Captain Hook's cove. Today the homes are gone, but some of the same area is set aside for dune regeneration.

We leave Point au Roche Park and paddle along the developed shore of Treadwell Bay, yet another huge bay along this shoreline, just a few minutes drive from Plattsburgh. The Treadwell Bay Marina is unusual on Lake Champlain. In addition to moorings, it has a capacity for over 400 boats in an enclosed basin. It was a controversial development in the 1990s when the New York Department of Environmental Conservation issued a permit to incorporate part of a wetland in Cumberland Bay State Park into the project, making it possible to create the basin. Today, it is one of the larger marinas on the lake.

From Treadwell Bay, we can see the ferry crossing between Cumberland Head and Grand Isle at our distant destination. It takes a while, but we get there. The pebbly beach we land on next to the ferry dock is a welcome sight. There is just one issue. I think that everyone waiting in line for the ferry must be able to hear our creaking bodies as we unbend into standing position, but we both manage to maintain a small amount of dignity and balance.

We have chosen to take three days to paddle the shoreline from Rouses Point to Cumberland Head, the route of explorers, raiders, and recreational boaters. We have experienced first-hand what we usually look at from a distance.

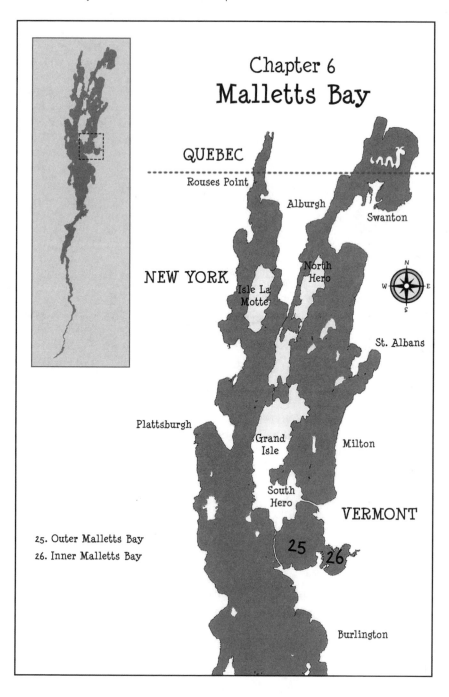

Chapter 6
Malletts Bay

QUEBEC

Rouses Point

Alburgh

Swanton

NEW YORK

North
Hero

Isle La
Motte

St. Albans

Plattsburgh

Grand
Isle

Milton

South
Hero

VERMONT

25. Outer Malletts Bay
26. Inner Malletts Bay

25

26

Burlington

Chapter VI

Malletts Bay

A Lake unto Itself

nner Malletts Bay is one of the best, naturally occurring, protected harbors on Lake Champlain. Outer Malletts Bay, on the other hand, is an enigma. It is a bay only by virtue of two man-made structures—the old Rutland Railway Causeway, which spans the 3.5-mile (5.6-kilometer) gap from Colchester Point to Allen Point in South Hero, and the Sandbar Causeway to the north, which connects South Hero to Milton. These two causeways have almost converted inner and outer Malletts Bay into an independent lake, fed by Malletts Creek and the Lamoille River with a drainage basin that extends all the way to the top of Mount Mansfield. The water is clear and for the most part void of nuisance invasive water weeds. Sand beaches, rock cliffs, an undulating shoreline, small islands, and spectacular views make this a boaters' paradise in the summer.

Marble Island.

Outer Malletts Bay
Created by Causeways

25

by Cathy Frank

■ **Launch site/Take out:** Sandbar F&W Area, Rt. 2, Milton, Vermont
■ **Distance:** 20 miles (32.2 kilometers)
■ **Alternative launch sites:** Sandbar State Park ($, PT day-use only, Rt. 2, Milton, Vermont), Apple Island Marina ($, Rt. 2, South Hero, Vermont), Allen Point F&W Area (off Martin Rd., South Hero, Vermont)
■ **Places to stop:** Above launch sites and Round Pond Natural Area, Malletts Bay Causeway, Rossetti Natural Area (Thayers Beach), Law Island (PT, just outside causeway)
■ **Highlights:** Birding at Sandbar Wildlife Management area, Sandbar Causeway and Round Pond State Park, Malletts Bay Railroad causeway and bike path with exceptional middle and distant views to the Adirondacks and Green mountains, swimming beach at Rossetti Natural Area, Mallets Head and Red Rock Point cliffs, Champlain Overthrust
■ **Route:** This long, circular route passes along the Sandbar Causeway, the marshy shore of Round Pond Natural Area, the camp- and house-lined South Hero eastern shore and the Malletts Bay Railroad Causeway before reaching the sandy north-facing shore of Colchester and Rossetti Natural Area's sandy beach. The entire route is shallow except for the crossing between the inner and outer bays and along the Red Rock cliffs. There is no place to stop between Rossetti beach and the Lamoille River delta (7 miles/11 kilometers).
■ **Comments:** This entire bay is exposed to strong northwest and south wind and waves. There is significant distance between stopping points. The 3.5-mile (6.6-kilometer) railroad causeway, itself a stopping point, offers scant protection from sudden storms. This is not a good route to take if afternoon thunderstorms are forecast. Boat traffic out of Malletts Bay marinas, heavy on weekends, creates large, choppy waves through the narrow opening between the inner and outer bays. Weekend traffic through the causeway cut is also heavy.

The Paddle:

A forecast of light and variable winds and no threat of afternoon storms make this a perfect day for this route. While delightful on a good day, the 3.5-mile (5.6-kilometer) causeway exposure means it's not a place we want to be if the weather changes abruptly.

Cars and trucks speed along the causeway in a rush to get somewhere, while we descend into the slower moving world of herons, ducks, and gulls and head west. (This is a great place to take pictures of great blue heron, because they are so accustomed to the steady traffic noise of Route 2 that they do not fly off when a paddler approaches.) Round Pond State Park and Natural Area, recognizable

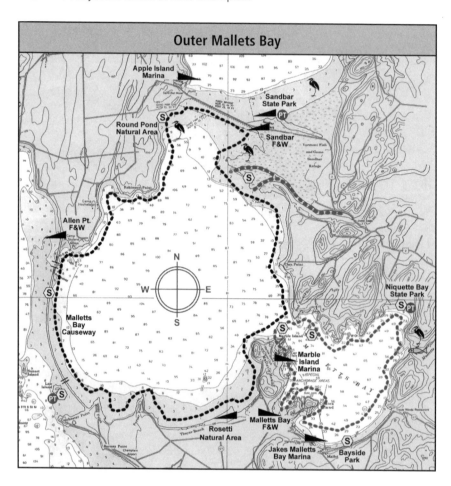

by its completely undeveloped shoreline, makes a good first stop on the South
Hero shore. (This is another example of a lack of signage for people approaching from the water.)

This relatively undeveloped state park consists of approximately 125
acres (50.6 hectares) of wetlands, fields, and woodlands, and 1,100 feet (335
meters) of Lake Champlain shoreline. A pebble beach at the south end of the
park is a good place to land, explore the walking trails, and swim. We take a
moment to play cat and mouse with the illusive, reed-lined, shallow shoreline to the north of the beach. The wetlands contain a native species of phrag-
mites, in stark contrast to the invasive species that is taking over many of the
lake's wetlands.

Conserved by a cooperative venture of four land trusts in 2002, beaver, nesting marshland birds, and migrating neo-tropical songbirds can be found here
during the appropriate seasons. A round pond about 20 yards (18 meters) in

▶ **Outer Malletts Bay**

from shore gives the park its name. According to island folklore, Round Pond is bottomless. Alas, in reality it is actually about 17 feet (5 meters) deep.

Despite the "light and variable" wind prediction, the south wind picks up to a steady 10–15 MPH (16–24 KPH) as we approach the railroad fill, so we stop and attach our spray skirts, a chore akin to trying to seal down a stubborn Tupperware lid. Two playful damselflies alight on the deck of my kayak, fly off, return in an instant, fly off, and return again. The damselfly's adult life is but a few days long, spent eating and mating. Are these delicate creatures attracted to my kayak-turned-procreation-platform by the splash of colors or because I am just a convenient refuge at sea?

The entire causeway is accessible to the public and is a great place to picnic, rest, or swim. In the wind and waves, however, it can be a little tricky pulling a kayak up onto the sloping marble and granite blocks. Today the south end of the causeway provides a welcome respite from the wind. We pop our spray skirts and grab a snack. This long, westerly pointing section of land, comprised of Colchester, Mills, and Porters points, is lapped by clear water that is usually only waist-deep as far out as 100 yards (91 meters) and has a sandy bottom all the way back to the cliffs of Malletts Head.

Rossetti Natural Area. From here, it is 3.5 miles (5.6 kilometers) to Rossetti Natural Area's sandy beach, the only public access on this side of the bay. Conserved by the Lake Champlain Land Trust in 1997, Rossetti's popularity as a municipal park for the Town of Colchester is clearly demonstrated by the number of boats anchored off the shore on this weekday.

Island Line Railroad bed, Mallets Bay Causeway. Photograph from John Gardner Collection, courtesy Local Motion.

After a lunch, we paddle east toward Malletts Head, looking forward to the added boost of the south wind at our backs when we swing north. When we get there, much to our dismay, the headwind from the morning has totally died. Unfair!

Malletts Head. The shoreline changes abruptly at Malletts Head, which looms almost 150 feet above the water at the northern end. Reportedly, Captain Jean Pierre Mallet, a Frenchman with rebel sympathies, lived on this point before and during the Revolution. He used a viewpoint near his home, now called "Captain's Lookout," to see who was approaching from both east and west.

We move our kayaks close together as we cross the opening between inner and outer bays to increase our visibility, keep our eyes peeled for oncoming traffic, and appreciate the panorama of the Green Mountains. On a weekend the boat traffic is so fast and heavy that crossing here in a kayak is akin to walking across an interstate highway. The cliffs at Red Rock Point on the other side are impressive.

Near Clay Point we spy another window into the Champlain Overthrust, an unusual rock formation of older, brownish-white, dolomite rock sitting atop younger, diagonal, gray-shale layers. (See "The Champlain Thrust Fault" sidebar in the "Burlington to South Hero" paddle.)

By mid-afternoon our pace is slowing. Oh for a swim, but the entire east shore from here to the Lamoille River is privately owned, and even though the water offshore looks less than 4 feet (1.2 meters) deep, the threat of sinking into muck, never to return, deters us. Hats full of water poured over our heads temporarily revive us. Picking up our pace we approach the large, reed-filled point of land that is part of the Lamoille River delta and Sandbar Wildlife Refuge, just to the north. A trip up the Lamoille River 3.5 miles (5.6 kilometers) to where Route 2 crosses the river offers good views into the refuge and provides a sheltered route on a windy day. Delta Island, the small triangular island at the mouth of the river, is open to the public as well.

Rather than paddling around the reeds, we try to find a channel through them, but we run aground repeatedly. It is incredibly peaceful as we sit for a moment, hidden in the reeds, invisible to the rest of the world, reluctant to move on.

A few minutes later we ease the bows of our kayaks onto the shore, pull our knees up to give our tired legs a rest, and sit motionless for a few minutes. This paddle requires a little transition time before we rejoin the world of rapidly moving traffic.

▶ **Outer Malletts Bay**

The Island Line and the Malletts Bay Causeway

The 3.5-mile Malletts Bay causeway is one of three causeways in the Champlain Islands built by the Rutland Railroad as part of their Island Line, creating train service between Burlington and Alburgh. Service began in 1901. Passenger service was discontinued in 1953, and freight service in 1961.

The original causeway contained a swing bridge across the 190-foot opening at the north end. This was one of four swing bridges on the islands. All have been removed.

The environmental impact of this causeway has been significant. With the exception of two relatively small openings to allow boats in and out of the bay, and one small opening under the Sandbar, this entire section of lake east of the causeway and south of Sandbar has been closed off from the broad lake. How and why did this come to be?

The advent of railroads in Vermont in the mid-1800s was a major step in ending Vermont's physical and economic isolation. Although many were built, two railroads, long known as the Central Vermont and the Rutland Railroad, came to dominate the scene. By 1849 each had lines across Vermont. For the rest of the century, they competed to extend their routes north to Canada and west to Ogdensburg, New York. The Central Vermont was the first to succeed, reaching Rouses Point via the Vermont mainland and St. Albans in 1851. In 1899–1900 the Rutland Railroad built the Island Line, choosing the Champlain Islands route because it was relatively flat.

The Island Line finally gave the Rutland Railroad the competitive connection north that it had sought for so long. It also had an enormously beneficial effect on the Champlain Islands by connecting them to Burlington year-round. Taking only thirty minutes to cover the distance from South Hero to Burlington, the train carried milk, ice, hay, and passengers on a regular basis. Today the Malletts Bay causeway is a recreational path with occasional ferry service across the northern opening. For more information on the Island Line, check out http://www.localmotionvt.org/islandline/history/index.htm.

26 | Inner Malletts Bay
Lake Champlain's Unpredictable Weather

by Cathy Frank

- ■ **Launch site/Take out:** Malletts Bay F&W Area, Lakeshore Dr., Colchester, Vermont
- ■ **Distance:** 12.5 miles (20 kilometers)
- ■ **Alternative launch sites:** Marble Island Resort and Marina ($, Marble Island Rd., Colchester, Vermont), Jake's Mallett's Bay Marina ($, Lakeshore Drive, Colchester, Vermont)
- ■ **Places to stop:** Above launch sites and Marble Island (north side), Beer Can Island, Niquette Bay State Park (PT), Bayside Park
- ■ **Highlights:** all of the above, plus scenic views to the east and west as well as wildlife around the entrance to Malletts Creek
- ■ **Route:** This is a deep bay with water depth averaging 20–40 feet along the shoreline. This circle route passes several marinas, the camp-lined east shore of Malletts Head, across the narrow opening to the north shore and then along the less developed north side of the bay. Niquette Bay State Park sits in the northeast corner, offering picnicking, swimming and hiking trails. From there one passes the wildlife-rich opening to Malletts Creek, the camp-lined west shore, past the town beach, yet another marina, and around Coates Island. There are adequate stopping points evenly spaced around the bay.
- ■ **Comments**: There is heavy boat traffic on weekends and the potential for large and choppy waves at the neck between the inner and outer bays. Walking trails are accessible from the shore at Niquette Bay State Park. Strong northwest winds funnel through the bay's narrow opening, and a strong south wind creates sizable waves on the north side of the bay.

The Paddle:

For two weeks the forecast has been "mostly cloudy with chance of showers in the morning and showers and thundershowers by afternoon, wind south, 10–20 MPH (16–32 KPH)." One day there are thunderstorms with hail and high winds, another day only passing showers. We have run out of patience and, perhaps, good judgment. The sheltered waters of inner Malletts Bay look tame on the map, and the many camps, tightly packed along most of the shoreline, should provide opportunities for emergency take out if a storm approaches.

Inner Malletts Bay is one of the busiest harbors on the lake with several marinas taking advantage of its exceptional shelter. It is near Burlington and the rest of Chittenden County, and little more that an hour's drive from Montreal. One needs to consider the heavy boat activity when paddling here. Fortunately, the first 20 yards (18.2 meters) from shore are usually free of traffic, as the water is too shallow for most boats.

▶ **Inner Mallets Bay**

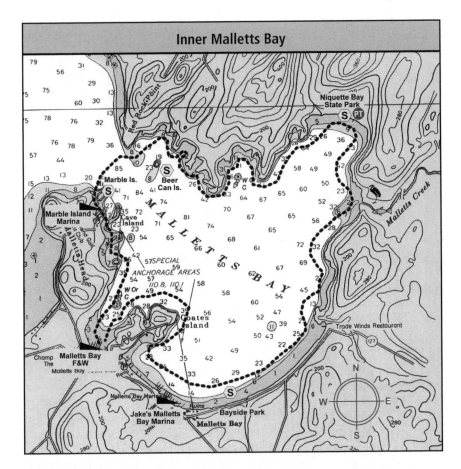

We see dark clouds building over New York even before we push off from the boat ramp between Coates Island and Malletts Head. Immediately to the west are the sharply rising cliffs of Malletts Head. Small cedars cling to cracks partway up the 30-foot (9.1-meter) wall of rock. The spring high-water mark, 2 feet (.6 meters) above the current water level, is visible on the rocks. The shore soon opens up to a series of little bays created as much by five small offshore islands as by the shoreline itself. Our imaginations run free, concocting a pirate history for aptly named Cave Island. Unfortunately, Cave, like all of the other islands except Marble Island, is privately owned.

Marble Island. Marble Island, the last and largest island along this shore, is a natural area managed by the Lake Champlain Land Trust. Kayakers and canoeists are welcome to stop on "Picnic Rock" on the north end of the island, but because of five rare plant species, steep cliffs, shallow soil, and dense woods, the rest of the island is off-limits. Sixty-foot (18.3-meter) high cliffs loom large behind us. Evidence of the quarrying of the island's dolomite rock in the late 1800s still exists on the south side of the island.

The North Shore. When we cross the half-mile opening to Red Rock Point and the northern side of the inner bay and turn east, sizable waves start to hit us broadside as we are no longer protected from the south wind. Instinctively we move into our "watch every wave" mode. Beer Can Island off to our right, also conserved by the Lake Champlain Land Trust, is worthy of a circumnavigation, if not a stop, but not today. Despite the fun of rolling with the waves, we are both taking on water. Ducking behind an anchored houseboat, we attach our spray skirts and move on, turning our heads frequently now to note the progress of the dark clouds that are slowly working their way east. This convoluted, tree-covered northern side of Malletts Bay has a relatively steep topography and, unlike the closely packed camps on the eastern side of the bay, homes and camps are well spaced and much of the shoreline is undeveloped.

Niquette Bay State Park. Once around the last point of land on the northwest shore, waves propel us toward the pristine sand beach of Niquette Bay State Park. Today we have this normally popular place to ourselves. Established as a small, little-used park in the 1970s, Niquette Bay State Park grew by an additional 290 acres in 2000 when the Lake Champlain Land Trust conserved the additional land and gave it to the state. There is an extensive network of hiking trails and, in the springtime, the wildflowers are exceptional. We take a well-deserved "back break" and dive into our lunch. Unfortunately, the dark cloud that has been following us all morning feels disconcertingly close now. So we inhale the rest of lunch and resume our trip, paddling south-southwest into the wind for about 3 miles (4.8 kilometers) to get back to the busy, developed, south side of the bay.

To the west a heavy rainstorm has enveloped South Hero and the outer bay, but we hear no thunder and see no lightning. We paddle on with a bit of an adrenalin rush past the entrance to Malletts Creek, the sole body of water feeding into inner Malletts Bay. This exceptional wetland, the first 70 acres (23.8 hectares) of which were conserved by the Lake Champlain Land Trust in 2003, has an extensive wild rice marsh, making it attractive to wading birds including the American bittern, least bittern, and black-crowned night heron. It is also a spawning ground for many fish species including northern pike, largemouth bass, and yellow perch. I-89 and a large power line carrying electricity from Quebec to Vermont cross this wild area about a half mile in from the bay. What a juxtaposition! We can see several osprey nests on the platforms built for them atop the huge power poles.

We hug the shore, paddling hard against the wind, continually looking back and forth between the approaching clouds and possible take-out places. We can no longer see Malletts Head, 2 miles (3.3 kilometers) to the west. Still we see no lightning and hear no thunder. Finally, we run out of both nerve and will,

▶ **Inner Mallets Bay**

pull into a tiny cove with a pebbly beach, turn our kayaks toward the oncoming clouds, and talk casually about something totally inconsequential to relieve the tension as we wait to see what happens. Watching the impenetrable gray curtain approach, we are suddenly engulfed in torrents of water falling from the sky— but no wind, no hail, no thunder, and no lightning. So, drenched to the core, the dramatic clouds still overhead, we set off once again.

South Hero to the west and the Adirondacks have reappeared. Meanwhile, to our east, Mount Mansfield fades in and out of visibility. As the storm finally passes us, we begin to feel more relaxed, enjoying that carefree and invincible feeling one gets after danger has passed. Just after we pass Colchester's Bayside Park and sandy beach, we notice that the cloud to our east is getting bigger and darker and moving in our direction, in exactly the opposite direction of the previous storm. So, once again, adrenalin flowing, we paddle faster, hoping to get back to the boat launch before the new rainstorm hits us. The cloud continues to grow to immense size and color and, just as we round Coates Island, the rain and wind begin. Fortunately, there is still no thunder or lightning, so we press on, knowing we are almost home.

The rain stops just as we get to shore (of course), and by the time we have the boats back on the car, the sun is out and we are almost dry. Our trip around inner Malletts Bay greatly exceeded our expectations. The clouds added a mystical quality, and the rainstorms a sense of high adventure, as we discovered that not all of Malletts Bay is congested and busy. In fact, most of it is spectacularly beautiful.

Niquette Bay State Park Beach.

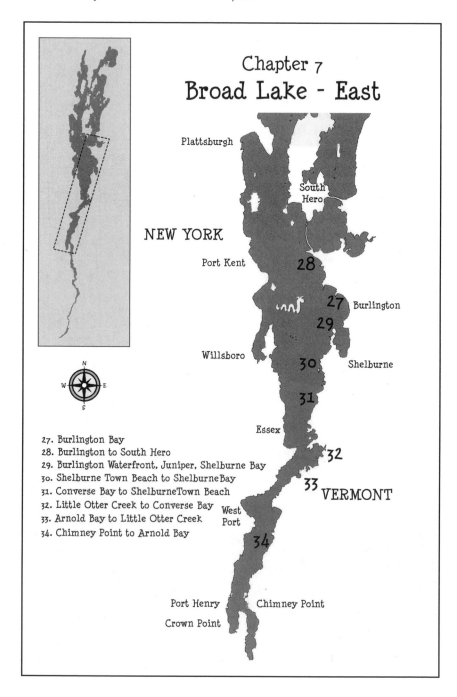

Chapter 7
Broad Lake - East

Plattsburgh

South Hero

NEW YORK

Port Kent

28

27 Burlington

29

Willsboro

30   Shelburne

31

Essex

32

33 VERMONT

West Port

34

Port Henry   Chimney Point

Crown Point

27. Burlington Bay
28. Burlington to South Hero
29. Burlington Waterfront, Juniper, Shelburne Bay
30. Shelburne Town Beach to ShelburneBay
31. Converse Bay to ShelburneTown Beach
32. Little Otter Creek to Converse Bay
33. Arnold Bay to Little Otter Creek
34. Chimney Point to Arnold Bay

Chapter VII

Broad Lake East

History and Development

The landscape of the east shore of the broad lake varies from the suburban shores of Colchester on the north to the agricultural fields of Addison County in the south. The spine of the Green Mountains rides majestically in the distance. The fertile valley between the lake and the mountains provides the answer to why the Vermont shore historically was and today is more densely settled. More people live on this east side of the broad lake in Vermont than anywhere else in the Champlain Valley, concentrated in Burlington, but spreading out in concentric circles from the center of the city. The population results in a lot of boating traffic on weekends. Most of the shoreline gleams with layered gray shale. Offshore, the bottom of the lake plunges to deeper levels than to the north or south. Many bays offer intriguing paddling.

A floating lunch.

Burlington Bay
Where the Action Is

27

by Cathy Frank

- ■ **Launch site/Take out:** Perkins Pier ($ for nonresidents), Maple St., Burlington, Vermont
- ■ **Distance:** 5.5 miles (8.8 kilometers)
- ■ **Alternative Launch Sites:** Burlington Waterfront Park Boat Launch (adjacent to Coast Guard Station), Blanchard Beach (PT day-use only, near Oakledge Park, Flynn Ave.), North Beach ($, PT, Institute Rd. off North Ave., Burlington, Vermont)
- ■ **Places to stop**: None aside from launch sites
- ■ **Highlights**: ECHO Center, Burlington Breakwater and lighthouses, red rock formations at Red Rocks Park, the Lois McClure Sailing Canal Boat when in port, views of Burlington's developed hillside and spectacular views of the Adirondacks
- ■ **Route:** This circular route passes along the industrial part of Burlington's waterfront, past lakeside homes, Oakledge Park, and South Burlington's Red Rocks Park and cliffs. For a longer trip, paddle north along the shore to Lone Rock Point, then loop back along the breakwater to Red Rocks Point and back along the shore to Perkins Pier (8.5 miles/13.7 kilometers).
- ■ **Comments:** Watch for heavy commercial and recreational boat traffic. Despite the breakwater, strong south wind and waves penetrate this bay.

The Paddle:

What a view—the Burlington Boat House and its adjacent marina, several excursion vessels, the ECHO Center (a state-of-the-art museum and aquarium devoted to Lake Champlain and its drainage basin), a recreation path that extends for miles in both directions, a functioning train track, sewage and water treatment plants, and to the north a public fishing pier and the Burlington Community Sailing Center. Additionally, the view across the lake to the Adirondack Mountains is unrivaled. Burlington's waterfront has a rich history. The second steamboat in the world was built and launched here in 1809. The Lake Champlain Transportation Company has been providing ferry service across the lake to Port Kent since 1825. From the early 1800s until well after the arrival of the railroad in 1849, sloops and then sailing canal boats filled the harbor. In the early 1800s developers added fill to create additional land to accommodate the rapidly growing shipping business. (Today that flat land west of Battery Street is filled with public parks, restaurants and other commercial enterprises.) A visitor in the 1850s would have found the harbor lined with stacks of lumber awaiting shipment.

We launch from Perkins Pier, the successor to the original structure (identified on an 1830 map as the only "Wharf"). Heading south, the old Burlington barge canal, infamous for the toxic coal tar residues left from the manufacture of gas between 1895 and 1966, grabs our attention. The Environmental

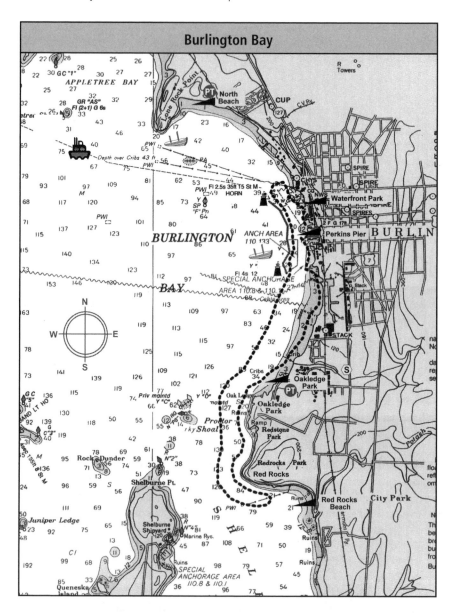

Protection Agency (EPA) declared this contaminated wetland a Superfund site in 1983. Figuring out how to clean it up took twenty years more and blocked the construction of a major highway into Burlington that has yet to be built. Temporarily draining the barge canal's turning basin and capping the coal tar in place solved the contamination problem. Today a small dam augmented by a beaver dam bars the entrance to the canal. What an impressive demonstration of the

▶ **Burlington Bay**

regenerative ability of the wetlands, as the canal once again becomes habitat for muskrat, beaver, and other small animals. Alas, in early 2009 a leak in the sand and silt cap was identified when coal tar was discovered in the canal's waters. Plans are underway to fix it.

Nearby, at least 200 Canada geese crowd onto a small beach and adjacent rocky spit of land, apparently oblivious to the former Superfund site. They honk as we approach. In the fall more geese than people are on the water. Canada geese can fly at a speed of 40–50 MPH (64–80 KPH) and cover 400 to 500 miles (644–805 kilometers) a day, certainly putting our efforts to shame. They do stop to eat and rest along the way, staying until cold temperatures urge them farther south.

We paddle past Burlington's popular Oakledge Park toward Redrock Point at the opening of Shelburne Bay. When we close in on the rocks, their color springs alive in layers of deep maroon-red, pink, cream, beige, and white, all reflected in the water below. This incredible work of art can only be truly appreciated from a very close perspective. The colorful Monkton quartzite was formed from sand in the shallow waters of the same 460-million-year-old southern sea responsible for so many of the fossils that we see along the lake.

We hear yelling and laughter on the cliffs beyond. Kids have been illegally jumping from them for generations, despite a significant number of tragic accidents. We hold our breath as a small figure walks to the edge, hesitates for a moment, and then leaps 50 feet (15 meters) into the water below. What a relief

Busy Burlington harbor.

when a head appears on the surface. The jumper swims to shore and starts the slow climb back up to the ledge to do it again. Meanwhile, another jumper launches.

We reverse course and head for the southern tip of the Burlington breakwater. Almost a half mile long (0.8 kilometers) and about 30 feet (9 meters) wide, this barrier defines the western side of Burlington Bay and in one form or another has protected it since the late 1830s.

When we are almost at the end of the far end of the breakwater, without warning the 18-foot (5-meter) Flying Juniors of the University of Vermont sailing team appear, looking like a swarm of large water beetles moving in unison. One turns, and they all immediately follow suit. How can we cut back to the Burlington shoreline without getting in their way, as it is not obvious what "their way" is as they tack back and forth? They pass, and we make a run for it. Fifty yards (46 meters) into our dash, the "water bugs" round their mark and run down the bay right at us, moving a lot faster than we are. We paddle harder. (Given the right incentive, we can always paddle harder) and just squeak by. Well downwind of us, several of them capsize. *Brrr.* The average water temperature is only 55° F (13° C).

Paddling back to the launch ramp, we can't help but notice a HUGE cigarette boat, about 60 feet (18 meters) long, tied up at the pier. Since we have never been this close to one of these big power boats, curiosity takes over.

"Wow, that's quite a boat. How fast can it go?"

"75 MPH," he responds, and without our asking (the price of gas having just reached $3.00 a gallon) he offers, "and it gets 4 MPG. And next year I will probably be riding in a boat like yours."

We all laugh at the advantages of our little kayaks, which get infinite mileage and never run out of gas. (Although the same cannot be said for the paddlers.)

▶ **Burlington Bay**

Burlington to South Hero
Paddling the Island Line

28

by Cathy Frank

- **Launch site:** Burlington Waterfront Park Boat Launch (adjacent to Coast Guard Station), Burlington, Vermont
- **Distance:** 17.5 miles (28 kilometers)
- **Take out:** Whites Beach (West Shore Rd., South Hero, Vermont)
- **Alternative launch sites:** Perkins Pier ($ for nonresidents, Maple St., Burlington, Vermont), Burlington Community Sailing Center (Lake St., Burlington, Vermont), North Beach ($, PT, Institute Rd. off North Ave., Burlington, Vermont), Leddy Beach ($, Leddy Beach Rd. off of North Ave., Burlington, Vermont), Auer Family Boat House ($, end of North Ave., Burlington, Vermont), Colchester Point F&W Area (Windmere Way, on Winooski River, Colchester, Vermont), Allen Point F&W Area (off Martin Rd., South Hero, Vermont)
- **Places to stop:** Above launch sites and Mayes Landing, Law Island (PT), Malletts Bay Causeway (Colchester/South Hero)
- **Highlights:** ECHO Center, Champlain Overthrust on Lone Rock Point, Auer Family Boat House, Delta Park (short walk from Colchester Point F&W Area via Windmere Way), Law Island, Malletts Bay Railway Causeway and bike path, views of Adirondacks and Green Mountains
- **Route:** This linear route passes inside the Burlington Breakwater along the public waterfront to North Beach, then around Lone Rock Point and a world-renowned rock formation, the Champlain Overthrust, and then to Leddy Beach. Once around Appletree Point, the Winooski River delta provides shallow water and abundant wildlife. Beyond, the water remains shallow and the bottom sandy as the route passes summer camps, until Colchester Point where the water becomes deeper. From Colchester Point, it crosses open but shallow water to Law Island. From there the route follows the Malletts Bay Railroad Causeway to South Hero. Break this trip in half at the Winooski River by using Colchester Point F&W Area or Auer Family Boat House (8 miles/12.8 kilometers).
- **Comments:** Significant waves can build in strong SW and NW winds. Additional waves can be particularly unpredictable around Colchester Point even in a moderate wind. There can be heavy boat traffic in Burlington Bay and the opening to Malletts Bay.

The Paddle:

Burlington Bay. We pull away from shore with strong strokes, giving the passing ferry a wide berth as we turn north. A young boy and man fish from the pier. "No luck so far," they respond to our obvious question. Already swimmers are enjoying the shallow water and large expanse of sand at North Beach, the oldest and largest of Burlington's three lakefront parks.

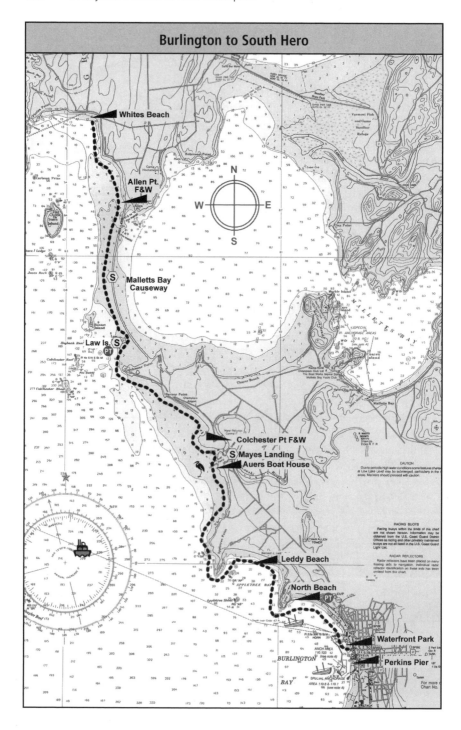

Burlington to South Hero

About a half mile off North Beach, yellow buoys mark the location of the sixty-four-foot Civil War-era *Burlington Bay Horse Ferry*. It is the only existing shipwreck of this once-common type of ferry—literally a "two-horse-powered" ferry, propelled by two horses walked forward on a huge circular platform. Setting the flywheel in motion caused a paddle wheel on each side of the boat to turn. This is a State of Vermont Underwater Historic Preserve open to the diving public. (Consult the State of Vermont The Horse Ferry, Underwater Historic Preserve Information and Diving Guidelines). A working half-sized model of this ferry exists at the Lake Champlain Maritime Museum.

There are believed to be over 300 shipwrecks on the bottom of Lake Champlain. Our respect for the forces of wind and water increases with each one we pass over. (For more information on shipwrecks, visit http://www.lcmm.org/.)

Shipwrecks

According to the Lake Champlain Maritime Museum's (LCMM) Web site, as many as 300 shipwrecks have occurred on Lake Champlain. Not all have been discovered and documented, but those that have give us insights into historic naval battles and tell interesting human stories.

Urged into action by the discovery of zebra mussels in Lake Champlain in 1993, LCMM was authorized three years later to conduct a lake-wide bottom survey to identify whatever undiscovered artifacts lay below before they became encrusted in zebra mussels. That work is ongoing and documented on the LCMM Web site.

Perhaps the most historic shipwreck, the gunboat *Philadelphia*, sunk during the Battle of Valcour in 1776, is displayed in the Smithsonian in Washington, D.C. A replica is anchored at the LCMM.

New York and Vermont together have created the Lake Champlain Historic Preserve System, spearheaded by the Lake Champlain Maritime Museum. Its goal is to allow divers to view these historic treasures, while at the same time protecting the artifacts from anchor damage and pilfering. Nine shipwrecks, marked with yellow buoys, are available for qualified divers to explore.

Rounding Lone Rock Point, at the northern tip of Burlington Bay, we get our first clear view of the world-famous geologic overthrust, the Champlain Thrust Fault. A thick layer of cream-and-grey dolomite, a limestone-like rock, sits atop a band of layered black calcite-streaked shale. The dolomite is much older than the shale beneath it, having been thrust up and over it by tectonic forces over 400 million years ago.

The steep, forested western shore of Lone Rock Point is undeveloped save for a walking trail that winds around the point. Thanks to the Episcopal Diocese of Vermont, which owns it, we are blessed with this long, undeveloped stretch of shoreline within the largest population center in Vermont.

The Champlain Thrust Fault

The Champlain Thrust Fault is an approximately 200-mile-long, north-south-oriented geologic formation running from Canada to the Catskill Plateau in New York State along a significant section of the eastern side of Lake Champlain. The fault is characterized by two types of rock. The top layer of gray Dunham dolomite, a limestone-like rock that formed 565 million years ago on the shallow shores of a tropical sea south of the equator, rests on top of 430-million-year-old calcite-streaked black shale. This reversal of the expected order—older rock sitting atop younger rock—was created when one tectonic plate (the Laurentia plate) was squeezed by a colliding plate. As a result of the pressure created on the Laurentia plate, the plate cracked in many places, causing the resulting pieces to be thrust up and over each other.

Lone Rock Point presents an exceptional view of the fault. You can see signs of the thrust elsewhere on the east side of the lake in Outer Malletts Bay, Shelburne Bay and Shelburne shore.

Champlain Overthrust, Rock Point.

▶ Burlington to South Hero

Beyond, Burlington's Leddy Park sits on the bluff above the public beach. Bikers and walkers move in both directions on the Island Line Trail, which runs along the shoreline from Burlington to the opening in the Malletts Bay Causeway. Approaching Appletree Point, familiar layers of shale extend vertically 30 feet (9 meters) in stark contrast to the horizontally oriented shale layers of the Champlain Overthrust. These delicate layers can be found at all angles along the Vermont shoreline. Passing a fisherman standing and casting from his boat, we note with some amusement that he has a significant "overthrust" of his own.

Appletree Point to Colchester Point. A noticeably shallow and marsh-like sandy bottom characterizes the long stretch between the rocky cliffs of Appletree and Colchester points to the north. Over thousands of years the outflow from the mouth of the Winooski River, which lies between the two points, has created a delta of sand and silt that extends more than a half mile into the broad lake. Great blue herons and egrets fish amongst the reeds. Accustomed to the small boat traffic in this area, these lovely creatures do not fly off as we approach.

After paddling for 8 miles (13 kilometers), the pedestrian/bike bridge spanning the Winooski River, with Auer Family Boat House nestled beneath, comes into view. We need a break.

Auer Family Boat House. The Boat House, a much-loved landmark that sits on the south side of the mouth of the Winooski, has been a fixture on the lake since the 1920s. With the exception of a few coats of fresh red paint applied over the years, it looks the same as it did then. Once owned by their father, now siblings Charlie and Christine run it in the summer months. When we step into the building, we step back in time. We are greeted by an eclectic menu of snack foods including a counter full of penny candy, along with hotdogs, Clif Bars, and Gatorade, plus live worms and other basic fishing supplies. Margy marvels at the cash register, which will only ring up to $5. What a relic. Colorful kayaks and a few canoes have replaced the original rental rowboats.

Back in our kayaks, we detour under the bridge to inspect Mayes Landing, conserved in 2000 by the Lake Champlain Land Trust and now a city park. The Winooski River itself is navigable for about 11 miles (18 kilometers) to the falls and the dam in the heart of the city of Winooski. A quarter-mile upriver, the Colchester Point Fish & Wildlife Access is a good place to break this trip.

The Winooski River. This junction of lake and river marks one of the most historically significant locations on the lake. Archeological evidence, dating back to 1400 A.D., reveals that the Abenaki Indians cleared land and planted corn along the river in the nearby Intervale. The Abenaki named the river *Winooski,* meaning "Onion River," because there were wild onions growing along its shores. Additionally, this has also been an historic haven for smugglers. (See "Smuggling on Lake Champlain" sidebar in "St. Albans to Missisquoi Bay Bridge" paddle.)

Auer Family Boathouse.

Delta Park. We head northwest on the lake along the sandy shore of the 55-acre (22-hectare) Delta Park, part of the Winooski Valley Park District. Migrating birds stop here, including the endangered common tern. Delta Park also provides an important turtle nesting ground for painted, snapping, and map turtles, and is home to a threatened tiger beetle species and to several rare plants, including the beach pea. (This shoreline is a protected wildlife management area. Stopping here is not permitted, but there are raised walkways through the park that are accessible from the Colchester Fish & Wildlife Access and the pedestrian/bike path (see http://www.wvpd.org/). Numerous trees, fallen in place or washed ashore, lie at angles to each other, looking like a neglected set of giant pick-up sticks.

A section of shore, lined with a bizarre mixture of old, unassuming camps and large new homes, epitomizes the struggle created by urban development pressures and the resultant rising lakeshore property values. We pass a small sand dune area to the north, dotted with older camps. Sand dunes are found on several places along the lake, although you have to look carefully to see them.

▶ **Burlington to South Hero**

Colchester Reef and Lighthouse

From 1871 to 1932, the Colchester Lighthouse marked Colchester Reef, one of Lake Champlain's most notorious hazards. This two-story, four-bedroom house sat approximately one mile from shore atop a rock-and-concrete-filled wooden crib, which itself sat on a rock seven feet below the water's surface. There are innumerable stories told about the challenges light keepers and their families faced living on this precariously placed lighthouse. One of the more extraordinary stories, reported on the lighthousefriends.com Web site, centered around Walter Button, light keeper in 1888, and his wife Harriet.

Mrs. Button went into labor in late January of that year. It was agreed that Walter would ring the fog bell to alert someone on shore to call the doctor. When the doctor and assistant reached the shore, they found the ice too thin to cross by foot, yet there was not enough open water to get a boat through. With no good option, they proceeded gingerly across the thin ice by foot. A large chunk of ice broke off the main section, leaving them stranded about halfway to the lighthouse. They drifted north as their patch of ice began to break into smaller and smaller pieces. Jumping from floe to floe, they eventually arrived on the South Hero shore four miles north.

Meanwhile Myrtle Edna Button was born that night without incident or medical assistance.

The lighthouse now graces the grounds of the Shelburne Museum.

Colchester Point: Both Colchester Reef and Shoal sit a mile offshore fully exposed to the long reach of the broad lake in both directions. In a strong wind, waves build up into unpredictable heights.(When we want to know what the real wind conditions are on Lake Champlain, we listen for the wind speed on Colchester Reef as reported by the National Weather Service.) Even a moderate wind can create challenging waves. (On a 1798 map of this area, Captain William Chambers, RN, named this location, most appropriately, Caution Point.) A 51-foot (15-meter) flashing light marks the reef.

Law Island and the Island Line Trail. Once past Caution Point, the Malletts Bay Causeway dominates the view to the east. The 3.5 miles (5.6 kilometers) of marble-lined railroad bed, busy with bikers, spans the once-wide opening of outer Malletts Bay. The old rail trail sits about 10 feet (3 meters) above lake level without any significant vegetation to block views in all directions. To the west the view extends 10 miles (16 kilometers) across the lake to the Adirondack Mountains. To the east we see Mount Mansfield and the long ridgeline of the Green Mountains across the 8 miles (13 kilometers) of outer and inner Malletts bays. The gently sloping fields of South Hero mark the north.

Law Island is a perfect lunch spot just 100 yards (91 meters) off the south end of the causeway. John Law bought and farmed the island in 1787. In the beginning of the twentieth century, there were a number of summer camps on it. This island was conserved by the Lake Champlain Land Trust in 1994 and is a site on the Lake Champlain Paddlers Trail.

With no south wind to contend with, we stop on the steeper, rockier, south side of the island to take advantage of the view southwest. (There is a sheltered pull-out with a shallow grass and pebble beach on the north-east side, but it is prone to deer flies in the summer.) The delicate layers of calcite-drizzled shale that are so common on this section of lake rise steeply 15–20 feet (5–6 meters) above the water on the western and south shores. Stepping out onto the submerged, sloping, slippery, rock shelf is challenging, but the day and water are both warm, and an unplanned swim is refreshing. (We go to great effort to avoid deer flies and make swims exciting.)

Forty-five minutes later, dried out and well-fed, we head north, staying about 100 yards (91 meters) off the causeway, passing privately owned Sunset and Stave islands. We arrive at Whites Beach, delighted with our 17.5-mile (29-kilometer) journey. What a day. What a paddle. For all the diversity it has to offer, this is one of the most interesting stretches of shoreline to be found anywhere on Lake Champlain.

Burlington Waterfront to Juniper Island & Shelburne Bay
A Magical Day

by Cathy Frank

■ **Launch site:** Perkins Pier ($ for nonresidents), Maple St., Burlington, Vermont
■ **Distance:** 11 miles (17.7 kilometers)
■ **Take out:** Shelburne Bay F&W Area (Bay Rd., Shelburne, Vermont)
■ **Alternative launch sites:** Waterfront Park Boat Launch (adjacent to Coast Guard Station), Blanchard Beach (PT day-use only , near Oakledge Park, Flynn Ave., Burlington, Vermont), Red Rocks Park Beach (Central Ave. off Queen City Park Rd., South Burlington, Vermont), North Beach ($, PT, Institute Rd. off North Ave., Burlington, Vermont)
■ **Places to stop:** None aside from launch sites
■ **Highlights:** Rock Dunder, Juniper Island, Red Rocks Park, incredible views of the Green Mountains and Adirondacks, interesting layered shale rock on Juniper Island
■ **Route:** This exposed, deepwater loop heads straight out from shore around Juniper Island and Rock Dunder and back to the mainland at Red Rocks Park. From there, it heads down the east shore of Shelburne Bay. The entire route except for Shelburne Bay, which is protected from the south wind, is exposed to wind from any direction. Be sure to paddle close to Red Rocks Point to see the full beauty of the rock formations. An alternative trip is to launch from Shelburne Bay F&W Area, at the inner end of the bay, paddle out one side of the bay and beyond to Juniper, and return via the other side of Shelburne Bay (10.5 miles/16.9 kilometers); alternatively, one can do a loop of Shelburne Bay only (8 miles/12.8 kilometers).
■ **Comments:** When heading into the middle of the lake, choose a calm day with no threat of storms and watch the weather carefully.

The Paddle:

This warm, sunny, late-September morning has a magical aura about it. The Port Kent to Burlington ferry arrives just as the tour boat, *Ethan Allen III*, pulls out from its dock. We pause to admire the 88-foot-long (27-meter) replica of an early Lake Champlain sailing canal boat, the *Lois McClure*, tied up at her dock. The Lake Champlain Maritime Museum involved the community in building this replica here on the Burlington waterfront. Since then it has toured Lake Champlain and beyond and been the setting for living history lessons for thousands of children and adults. We long to see her under sail on one of our trips.

Out of the busy harbor, we feel like we are the only boats on the entire lake. Heading straight toward Juniper, we pass within a few yards of the south end of the breakwater. The near perfect reflection of the navigational light in the shape

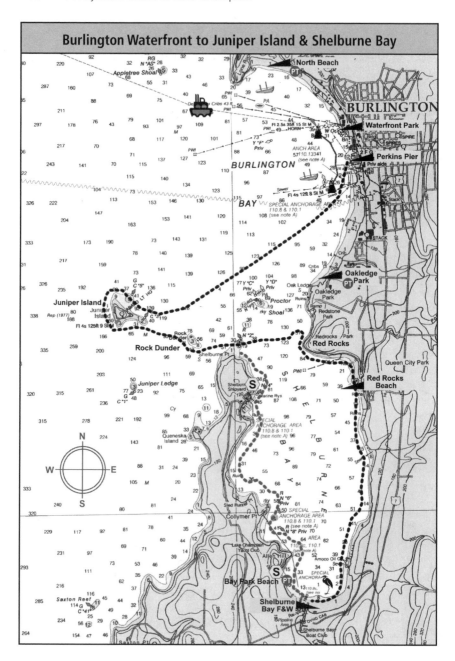

Burlington Waterfront to Juniper Island & Shelburne Bay

of a miniature lighthouse creates a peaceful image, as if announcing to those who pass, "This is a safe place." Just to the north, however, yellow buoys mark the State of Vermont Underwater Preserve of the shipwrecked *General Butler*.

▶ **Burlington Waterfront to Juniper Island & Shelburne Bay**

The Wreck of the *General Butler*

On a fateful winter night in December 1876, this 88-foot sailing canal boat with five people onboard sailed down from Isle La Motte with a load of marble for the Burlington Marble Works. A sudden winter gale caused the boat's steering mechanism to break just as the boat approached Burlington. A jury-rigged tiller failed, and the boat struck the south end of the breakwater. As the force of the wind and waves lifted the boat repeatedly onto the rocks, one person after another leapt to the top of the ice-coated breakwater. Miraculously, all made it to safety before the *General Butler* sank. It rests there today, on its keel in 40 feet (12 meters) of water. Thanks to the heroism of two people on shore who rowed out in the gale, all five of the cold, wet survivors on the icy breakwater made it safely to shore.

It does give us some pause to pass this sunken ship just as we leave our shoreline security blanket behind and head straight out into deep water and the open lake. Strong north and south winds and the threat of afternoon storms have prevented us from venturing out to Juniper all summer.

Juniper Island. Juniper Island sits about 3 miles (5 kilometers) off the Burlington shore, a little over a mile from Shelburne Point. A substantial shallow shelf on the northern side, and a long finger of shallow water extending to the east, form a navigational hazard for boaters coming from the south who want to turn into Burlington Harbor or Shelburne Bay. For that reason the United States government bought the island in 1826 for $200 and built the first lighthouse on Lake Champlain there the same year. In 1959 the government replaced the lighthouse with a 115-foot (35-meter) automatic light, and auctioned off the island in a controversial bidding process. The successful bidder, a former state senator, died in 1974 without a will or having filed a deed for the land. The island remains in limbo without clear ownership. In a further complication, the original deed places the island in Chittenden County, but not in any particular municipality, so this valuable piece of real estate produces no tax revenue.

The land rises gently behind a boathouse and dock that sit on the east side of Juniper. Steep shale cliffs dominate the rest of its shoreline, one of the most exquisite examples of this type of rock formation on the lake. On the west side the shale layers run vertically, but change their orientation, becoming even wavy in places as we paddle south and then east. How could the forces of plate tectonics have produced so many angles in so small a space? Some of the ever-present white calcite streaks look like mini lightening bolts in the dark gray shale, while others are soft and graceful. The lines and layers continue down beneath the water, where they begin to be obscured by significant accumulations of zebra mussels.

Rounding the south side of the island, the incredible view of Burlington takes our breath away. As we move a few hundred yards north or south, we create whatever mountain backdrop we like for this picture-perfect view. What should it be—Mt. Mansfield, Camel's Hump, Mt. Abraham? We skip lunch on Juniper's dock, because others have gotten there first.

Rock Dunder. "Let's have lunch on Rock Dunder." Oops, cancel that idea. Within 100 yards (91 meters) of Rock Dunder we are overwhelmed by its pungent ammonia stench. We are not about to challenge the malodorous domain of the gulls and cormorants today, so we settle for a "floating" lunch. "Settle" is not quite the right word here, however. Motionless in our kayaks, far from shore, with the jet contrails reflected in the near calm water, with limitless views of mountains and lake, and not another boat in sight, this scene is unrivaled by and unlike any other, bar none.

Rock Dunder was named *Odziozo* by the Abenaki Indians after the great creator of land, water, and life. According to Abenaki legend, the "Spirit of the Rock" created storms and destroyed the canoes of any who did not leave corn and tobacco offerings when they passed. We hope baby carrots will do. That's all we have left.

Paddling east, we swing by Red Rock Park to get yet another close-up view of these multicolored rocks, and then turn south, paddling along the east side of Shelburne Bay. It is 3.5 miles (5.6 kilometers) as the crow flies, but clearly longer

Rock Dunder.

▶ **Burlington Waterfront to Juniper Island & Shelburne Bay** when measured by an end-of-the-day kayaker's yardstick. This popular, heavily-used bay is fed by three streams (Potash, Monroe, and Bartlett brooks) and one river (the La Platte), all of which wend their way through a good part of heavily developed Chittenden County, particularly South Burlington and Shelburne. Shelburne Bay is ground zero for the urban storm-water runoff debate.

Both Potash and Monroe brooks have large flocks of Canada geese feeding at their mouths. Margy worries that convincing us Chittenden County urbanites that we are major contributors to the pollution problem is difficult when the 60–160-foot (18–49-meter) water depth dilutes the visual effect of so much phosphorus, but at least Vermont now bans the use of laundry detergents and dishwashing soaps that contain phosphorus.

We pull our boats out of the water at the Fish & Wildlife Access at the mouth of the La Platte River. It is a day neither of us will forget. Paddling out into the middle of the broad lake on a perfectly calm day, with no other boats or people close enough to infringe on the sounds and silence of the natural world, was an almost spiritual experience.

Urban Runoff: A Case in Point

Potash Brook exemplifies impaired waterways and contaminated storm water, as the development pressures of Chittenden County come up against prudent environmental practices.

Excessive amounts of nutrients (particularly phosphorus), pathogens (bacteria, viruses, and other disease-causing organisms), toxic substances (lead, mercury, zinc, and PCBs [polychlorinated biphenyls]), and sediments (soil particles from fields and stream banks) compromise the water quality of Lake Champlain. When it rains, these contaminants are washed off impervious urban surfaces such as paved parking lots, sidewalks, roadways, rooftops, and eroding stream and river banks and then flow, untreated, into streams and rivers that feed into Lake Champlain or directly into Lake Champlain itself. For every square foot of land we pave and build on, we remove a square foot of ground and vegetation that can filter contaminants out of water runoff. And while farm fields and casual agricultural practices have been blamed for the excess phosphorus that causes algae blooms and excess plant growth in the shallower and more rural northern and southern parts of the lake, a significant percentage of this so-called non-point-source phosphorus pollution comes from urban runoff. Yet studies show that we urban inhabitants are generally unaware that many of our innocent-seeming behaviors exacerbate the problem. Unfortunately, the solutions are neither simple nor cheap.

30

Shelburne Town Beach to Shelburne Bay
Around the Point

by Margy Holden

- ■ **Launch site:** Shelburne Town Beach (open only to residents in season), off Beach Rd., Shelburne, Vermont
- ■ **Distance:** 13.5 miles (21.7 kilometers)
- ■ **Take out:** Shelburne Bay F&W Area (Bay Rd., Shelburne, Vermont)
- ■ **Alternative launch sites:** None
- ■ **Places to stop:** Above launch sites and Shelburne Shipyard Store, Shelburne Bay Park Beach (PT day-use only, Shelburne Bay)
- ■ **Highlights:** Shelburne Farms, exposure of Champlain Overthrust, Shelburne Shipyard, wreck of the steamboat *Adirondack*, magma dike, cliffs, rock formations, views of the Adirondacks, Green Mountains, and Burlington Bay, walking trails accessible from water at Shelburne Bay Park
- ■ **Route:** Leaving the launch area, this varied, beautiful route turns north and follows a shallow, scenic shore of alternating cliffs, pastoral views, and estates. Rounding Shelburne Point, the route turns south, passing the shipyard, homes, and the yacht club, until reaching Shelburne Bay Park with its cliffs and boat ramp. Launch from Shelburne Bay F&W Area at the inner end of the bay and paddle to Burlington, returning along the other side (10.5 miles/16.9 kilometers) or do a loop of Shelburne Bay only (8 miles/12.8 kilometers).
- ■ **Comments:** The route is exposed to south, west, and north winds until Shelburne Bay. The Shelburne Bay Park offers places to stop, but the west side of Shelburne Point is privately owned. The trails on Shelburne Farms are open to the public and accessible from the Welcome Center at the intersection of Harbor and Bay Roads, Shelburne.

The Paddle:

The west shore of Shelburne Point has a surprising amount of open land, even though it is only a few miles from Vermont's largest city. Some of the land is agricultural, some is wooded, and some surrounds large homes. The east side of Shelburne Point, south of the Lake Champlain Yacht Club, has been conserved as Shelburne Bay Park. This open space is the result of thoughtful planning, aggressive preservation, and the generosity of many people. Shelburne Point could be called incomparable. The views of the Vermont shoreline provide just one facet of this paddling gem; the views of the Adirondacks, rising across the lake behind the New York shore, are breathtaking. Whiteface Mountain reveals its pointy peak in the distance.

The Shelburne Beach lies at the inner end of Meach Cove, an often tranquil, cup-shaped bay marked at the south end by Meach Island and at the north by shale cliffs. A fishing loon ignores us. Throughout the day, white-throated king-

▶ **Shelburne Town Beach to Shelburne Bay**

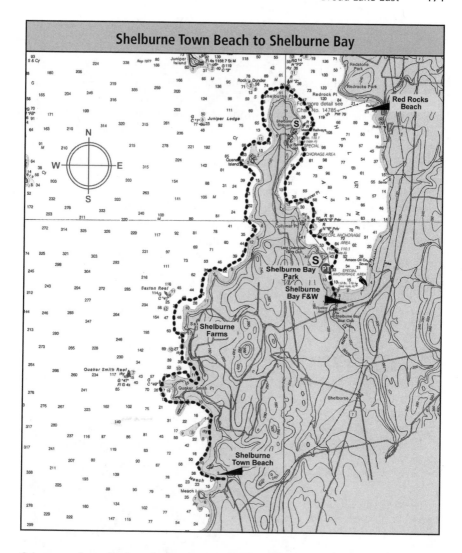

Shelburne Town Beach to Shelburne Bay

fishers arc from limb to limb, chattering. Cliff, tree, and barn swallows swoop by, catching flying insects. Kingbirds flutter in the overhanging cedars. We later see three more loons and two egrets.

What a rock tale we can tell about today's paddle. The layers of twisted shale along the shoreline cliffs give us a graphic demonstration of ancient forces that shaped the Champlain Valley millions of years ago. Within a short distance the layers of gray-black stone are contorted into innumerable opposing angles. We also pass big boulders resting at water level, some a light salmon color sparkling with shiny flecks. This rock, so different from the gray shale, reminds us that the glaciers transported stone from one place to another. We see some beaches covered with

Lake Champlain's beautiful white and gray stones ground smooth by water, wind, and rock. I imagine these stones with their little white lines as presents, fashionably wrapped in gray and tied with a white ribbon. They are gifts to us.

Scanning the cliffs, we are concerned by the signs of erosion that appear everywhere. Brown dirt cascades down some faces. The rock gives way completely in places, leaving heaps of stone at the foot of the once-majestic cliff. Some cedars hang tenaciously by a root, but others have lost their grip and are dead at the water's edge. How long have these changes been happening on these cliffs that have been here for millions of years? Have we humans put the process into fast-forward, or is this simply a natural process, the result of time passing and the forces of wind and water?

For the first five miles of our trip north from the Shelburne Town Beach, we pass surprisingly undeveloped shoreline. We have William Seward and Lila Vanderbilt Webb, who were early estate builders, and their descendants to thank for much of the open space. They created Shelburne Farms in the 1890s, which originally encompassed all the land between the tip of Shelburne Point and Shelburne Village.

Shelburne shore shale.

▶ Shelburne Town Beach to Shelburne Bay

Beyond Quaker Smith Point, fields rise to Lone Tree Hill. From a sheltered bay, we admire two landmarks of Shelburne Farms—the historic inn with its porches, turrets, and formal gardens, and the coach barn with its majestic clock tower. Beyond Shelburne Farms, palatial homes and grounds replace the rolling fields. A bit farther on we discover another example of the Champlain Thrust Fault, where an older rock has been thrust up over newer rock. How obvious it is—we just did not expect to find it here. Ahead, Queneska Island perches just offshore. Its name is derived from the Abenaki *Quineaska-took,* meaning "the long joint," referring to Shelburne Point. Preserved in the center of the island is an oak and hickory forest that represents a natural community once more common on Lake Champlain.

Erosion—Nature at Work

Lake Champlain has a continuously moving shoreline. Waves and ice at the waterline wear away and eventually undermine the rock and dirt layers until the land above it gives way. Even the layers above the water's reach deteriorate during the winter as the slanting daytime sun melts ice and the cold of night refreezes it. Gradually, layers of shale and dirt begin to crumble and fall. It is a rhythm of nature. Erosion has been happening since the Champlain Valley was formed. It impacts the clarity of the water; it takes fragile flora in its path.

While it is a natural process, some erosion surely has been hastened by our actions. We latecomers have built dwellings close to the shore and cut the forests along the water's edge to take advantage of the view. Banks denuded of trees no longer have roots to hold the soil together. Forests that trapped rain and snowmelt, allowing water to slowly sink into the ground, have been cut. Now the water runs directly into the lake, taking the soil with it. We see buildings hanging over the lake, not because they were built there, but because they may have been built too close to the edge, abetting nature's work. Erosion occurs naturally, but we have speeded the process.

At the tip of Shelburne Point, Juniper Island rises across the water to the northwest; closer to us is storied Rock Dunder. Crystal clear water sparkles around us. As we pass the point, the incredible panorama of Burlington Bay and the city opens up in front of us.

The overhanging cedars of Shelburne Point give way to the Shelburne Shipyard. What a busy place. Operating for nearly two centuries, the shipyard now serves recreational boaters with docks, moorings, a repair shop, and store. In 1814, Thomas Macdonough over-wintered his fleet here before the Battle of

Shelburne Farms

By the turn of the century, the Webbs' estate had become one of the finest in the country. They hired Robert Henderson Robertson to design the buildings and Frederick Law Olmsted, the designer of Central Park, to create a landscape plan. Some of the statistics from those early years stagger the imagination. By 1892 the Webbs had planted 25,000 trees and had created a nursery of 100,000 young trees. In the same year, 3,000 barrels of apples were harvested and sent to New York City for sale.

In succeeding generations the land was divided among heirs. When the property taxes in the 1970s became so high that the then-current owner of what is now Shelburne Farms could no longer afford them, he commissioned a plan to sell the land for development. The owner's children and other community members who believed deeply in the values of local agriculture, education, and the environment, worked to find an alternative vision. A solution was found in which some of the land was sold for development, some was conserved, and some was put into the nonprofit entity known as Shelburne Farms. Today Shelburne Farms stands as a model for local agriculture, a place where children and educators learn about sustainability through hands-on activities, and people can walk along fields and through managed woods, attend concerts, take a workshop, and participate in many other activities.

Plattsburgh. Between 1825 and 1906 the Shelburne Shipyard built thirteen steamboats, including the *Ticonderoga*, which we can still see at the Shelburne Museum. The shipyard also built ships for World War II and the Korean War.

Houses of many descriptions line the shores of Shelburne Bay. Just to the east of Sledrunner and Collymer points, we spot the low rock outcropping named Collymer Island. The wreck of the 222-foot-long steamboat *Adirondack*, which can be seen beneath the water on a calm day, lies between the island and the shore. The masts of sailboats moored at the Lake Champlain Yacht Club fill the bay in front of us. Begun in 1887, the yacht club today hosts an array of water-related activities for members. The 104-acre Shelburne Bay Park with its winding trails stretches along the shore from the yacht club to the Fish & Wildlife Access. A haven for walkers, the park also harbors significant geological anomalies.

On the second point beyond the yacht club, we see a familiar, small, cave-like opening sitting a few feet above the shore. This magma dike was formed when molten rock forcibly thrust up from deep beneath the surface of the earth. A sharp eye will find other examples located in Shelburne Bay. Just around the

▶ **Shelburne Town Beach to Shelburne Bay**

point, we have to look closely higher up to see yet another example of the Champlain Thrust Fault, our second sighting of the day. Farther into Shelburne Bay, we look up to Allen Hill with its crown of cedars.

Just before reaching the Shelburne Bay Fish & Wildlife Access at the mouth of the LaPlatte River, we pause to admire a great egret stalking prey among the reeds. Behind it, an outcropping of Monkton quartzite, a 500-million-year-old rock that originated near the equator, marks the edge of the access area. Originally "The Plot," the name LaPlatte commemorates a defensive plot hatched to take vengeance on an invading war party that had landed their canoes here to attack early settlers. When the repulsed war party tried to escape across Shelburne Bay, their canoes quickly sank from the holes that the defenders had made in them.

It is possible to paddle upstream to see wildlife and a variety of plant life through the 211-acre wetland, which is preserved by The Nature Conservancy. It is also possible to launch a canoe or kayak into the river from a ramp beside Route 7 and travel downstream to Lake Champlain.

What a wealth of surprises we have enjoyed around Shelburne Point.

Champlain Overthrust on Shelburne shore

31 Converse Bay in Charlotte to Shelburne Town Beach
Summer Lakeside Communities

by Margy Holden

- **Launch site:** Converse Bay F&W Area, off Converse Bay Rd., Charlotte, Vermont
- **Distance:** 7.5 miles (12 kilometers)
- **Take out:** Shelburne Town Beach (open only to residents in season, off Beach Rd., Shelburne, Vermont)
- **Alternative launch sites**: none
- **Places to stop**: Above launch sites and Charlotte Town Beach
- **Highlights:** Historic sites, Adirondack views, Meach and smaller islands, covered bridge, ferry
- **Route:** This route follows the north shore of scenic Converse Bay, around the Cedar Beach community, through historic McNeil Cove, and along a suburban shore. After passing the town beach, the suburban shore continues until Meach Island marks the entrance to the cove and the Shelburne Town Beach take-out.
- **Comments:** Waves can be large in strong winds outside Converse Bay. There can be significant boat and ferry traffic in McNeil Bay. The water depth drops off close to shore in some places.

The Paddle:

The Fish & Wildlife Access off Cedar Beach Road has to be one of the prettiest places to launch a boat on the Vermont shore. Tucked into Converse Bay and facing southeast, wetlands frame one side of the launch site and woods the other.

Converse Bay gradually reveals its placid water as we paddle away from the launch site. Garden and Cedar islands to the south, reflected in the water in the morning light, float in front of Thompsons Point. Unfortunately, we don't see any of the bald eagles that are known to roost in the tall cedars of Garden Island. We paddle under the steep cliffs of the north shore of Converse Bay. A beautiful Victorian-era house crowns the high point above the steep cliffs on the north shore. We admire Picket Island (called Dead Man's Island by locals) on our left, a favorite spot for picnickers and even a few overnight campers courageous enough to brave the mosquitoes and poison ivy. Mostly though, this lovely little island surrounded by shallow water provides a haven for paddlers. It is also a favorite spot for the youngest boaters with their brightly colored life jackets—an exciting first solo outing on a calm day.

Lake Champlain, always our teacher, provides us with another lesson. The calm water changes personality when we pass out of the lee. A long, straight fetch from the south builds waves that crash against and rebound from this point. We could have anticipated this. How happy we are to again enter the lee off the Cedar Beach.

▶ **Converse Bay in Charlotte to Shelburne Town Beach**

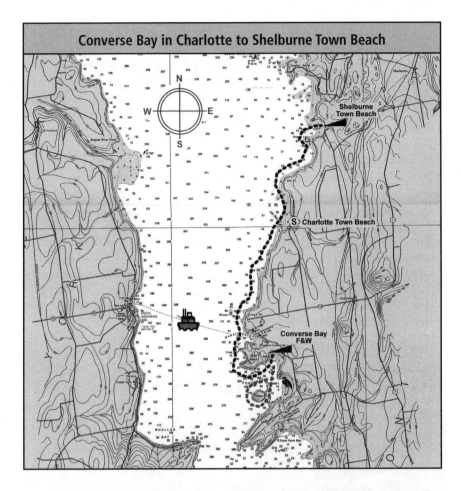

Converse Bay in Charlotte to Shelburne Town Beach

There is already activity on the dock this morning, the flag having been hoisted at dawn. The Cedar Beach Association, a lakeside summer colony originally called The Jolly Club, was started in the late 1800s by a group of families from Burlington. They commuted to and fro aboard the *Ticonderoga*, even bringing their cows aboard at the beginning and end of the summer. At first the summer colony consisted of a single shared kitchen with separate tents used by the camping families. What is most interesting about this and other summer colonies along the lakeshore—such as the Thompson's Point Association, also in Converse Bay—are the strict covenants among the campers that forbid converting homes for year-round use. Even 150 years later, the Cedar Beach Association regards this as an important tenet in their quest to retain a simpler life, where families gather to share meals and to respectfully use the lake, and kids entertain themselves with diving contests and a brisk game of kick the can. The roads remain unpaved, and a tree committee decides which trees can be cut down.

We round Pease Point and reach the protected lee of McNeil Cove, otherwise known as "the ferry bay." The cove is filled with moored boats, part of the Charlotte Sailing Center. Today it is almost serene, but on a warm, summer weekend, when the boat owners are ready for a sail, this place is hopping with activity. Add to that activity the Lake Champlain Transportation Company ferries to Essex, New York, which leave and arrive every thirty minutes.

There has been a ferry operating from here to the New York shore since John McNeil established the first ferry in 1790. Between 1821 and 1827, horses powered the ferry. Three horses on each side of the deck walked side by side on a treadmill that turned the paddlewheels. What a sight that must have been. From our kayaks we see a very different kind of boat filled with people and cars. Many walk-on passengers take this ferry just for the pleasures of admiring the magnificent views of the Adirondacks and the Green Mountains, enjoying a stroll around Essex, New York, having lunch or ice cream, and then riding the ferry back.

The Georgian Revival-style McNeil Homestead—on Wings Point, which borders McNeil Cove on the north—was built around 1800 and is on the National Register of Historic Places. A low, shale slab of land just off the Wings Point shore, named Sloop Island, looks just like its namesake.

Meach Island.

▶ **Converse Bay in Charlotte to Shelburne Town Beach**

When a 1960s proposal to build a nuclear power plant between Wings Point and the Charlotte Town Beach became known, the public reaction was strong and swift. As a result, the owners of the land decided not to make it available for that purpose. It was a good example of people working together to advocate for this beloved lake.

The picturesque Holmes Creek Covered Bridge is at the south end of the Charlotte beach. It, too, is on the National Register of Historic Places. The empty beach today may be thanks to the cool temperatures. A favorite place for birders during migration, we see neither birds nor birders today. Hills Point, beyond the beach, with its moderate-density housing, exposes us to more wind from the south.

Meach Island sits off the southern end of Meach Cove. The wife and children of Judge Meach, who owned the island in the 1820s, are buried here. A scenic private island to paddle around, it protects Meach Cove from south winds, which could be one of the reasons that Moses Pierson chose this site for his homestead in 1768. This gently sloping land on the east side of Lake Champlain also attracted many more potential farmers than the steep slopes of the western shore. But the times were not peaceful, with tensions growing in the Champlain Valley between the British and those who would soon be rebels.

In 1776 the Pierson family retreated to safer lands. During the winter of 1777, they returned with two teenage sons and a baby to thresh their crop, accompanied by Colonel Sawyer, his lieutenant, and fourteen soldiers. It wasn't long before they were discovered and a fierce battle ensued against the British and their Native American allies, lasting all night. At one point the blockhouse was set on fire, but the fire was doused by the defenders using Mrs. Pierson's freshly brewed beer. All of the Piersons survived, even though spent bullets were found in the baby's bed. They later learned that their attackers had all been British soldiers, with some disguised as Native Americans. What a contrast to today, as we paddle by an empty swimming raft and a beautifully maintained beach to the shaded launch ramp, talking about yet another gorgeous day on the water.

32 Little Otter Creek to Converse Bay
Rivers and Bays

by Margy Holden

- **Launch site:** South Slang (Little Otter Creek) F&W Area, Hawkins Road, Ferrisburg, Vermont
- **Distance**: 10 miles (16 kilometers)
- **Take out:** Converse Bay F&W Area (off Converse Bay Rd., Charlotte, Vermont)
- **Alternative launch sites:** Lewis Creek F&W Area (off Lewis Creek Rd., Ferrisburg, Vermont), Kingsland Bay Town Beach (Town Beach Rd. off Sand Rd., Ferrisburg, Vermont)
- **Places to stop:** Above launch sites and Point Bay Marina store, Kingsland Bay State Park (PT)
- **Highlights:** Abundance of marsh areas with wildlife potential, side channels for exploring in Little Otter Creek, Lewis Creek, Adirondack and Split Rock Point views, small bays, islands
- **Route:** The varied and scenic route passes through marsh to the mouth of Little Otter Creek, past Gardener Island and the mouth of Lewis Creek, around Long Point, through small bays, Town Farm Bay, along the south side and around the tip of Thompsons Point and through Converse Bay, passing its islands.
- **Comments:** The convoluted shoreline offers many intriguing bays, but makes this trip appear shorter than it is. The segment of this paddle in Little Otter Creek is protected from wind. McNeil Cove is open to the west wind, and the south shore of Thompsons Point can be dangerous in a strong south wind because of the long fetch and the wind channeled between cliffs in this narrow section of the lake. The north shore is open to the north wind. The water is shallow close to shore, with the notable exception of the tip and north shore of Thompson's Point where, in a heavy wind, a paddler would have to stay in deep water to avoid the turbulence of waves rebounding from the cliffs.

The Paddle:

The many enticing channels of Little Otter Creek trail off through the marshes, inviting us to explore. Delicate white water lilies line the twisty, narrow route from the launch site into the broader bay. They almost gleam in the dappled sun. Tiny insects crawl among the stamens. In spite of their dainty appearance, these tough lilies ride the ripples tethered by their flexible, firmly anchored stems. To the right, the bridge on Hawkins Road marks the entrance into the South Slang, a pond-like area that is rich in wildlife, a good place to explore, and accessible under the bridge when the water is low enough.

The Little Otter Creek Wildlife Management Area surrounds us. The marshy shores, protected water, and upland forest are home to coots, grebes, and bitterns. We see osprey fishing. This is a prime resting place for birds migrating

▶ **Little Otter Creek to Converse Bay**

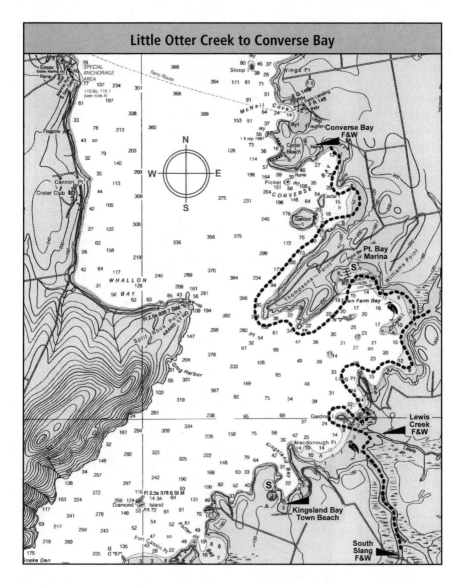

Little Otter Creek to Converse Bay

along the Atlantic flyway. Mallards, mergansers, teal, wood ducks, and black ducks nest here and also migrate through here. Otters do still live in Little Otter Creek, along with mink and muskrat. Fishermen like this water, too. Frogs hidden in the reeds croak their presence as we pass. To our right, East Slang, another side channel, offers yet another chance to explore.

Just ahead we see the broad channel where Little Otter Creek flows almost due north. In this broader, deeper water, aquatic plants gently undulate for many yards toward land before the land becomes dry enough to support distant trees.

The largest cattails that I have ever seen dwarf us in our kayaks. Pickerel weed not only shows off its spade-shaped leaf, but also its dainty pink flowers, which add a bit of color. Clusters of vegetation create little islands to slalom between. What a joy to paddle in this wild protected area. One could easily spend many hours investigating the small channels.

Little Otter Creek offered a protected location to hunt and forage and to access transportation routes through a network of rivers for Archaic Native Americans at least 10,000 years ago, as well as the later Abenaki. We keep a sharp lookout for some of the wildlife but, unlike the Native Americans, our survival does not depend on it, so our skills are not sharpened by need.

Hawkins Bay and Gardiner Island. It's almost a mile from where we launch our kayaks in Little Otter Creek to Hawkins Bay in Lake Champlain. We move right along, and gradually the channel widens, exposing Gardiner Island in the distance. As we emerge into the lake, a huge flotilla of double-crested cormorants basks in the lee of Macdonough Point. When we try to sneak by, those closest to us start, flap, and run across the water to become airborne, flying to the far side of the flock.

We paddle around privately owned Gardiner Island, searching for fossil remains on the limestone ledges. On the inland side we almost miss the mouth of Lewis Creek, because the marsh on both sides looks like a continuation of Little Otter Creek. The Abenaki originally called Lewis Creek the Fish Weir River. It rises in Starksboro, Vermont, in the foothills of the Green Mountains, and flows through farmland and hemlock-shrouded chasms before reaching Lake Champlain, draining eighty square miles.

Long Point. Beyond Gardiner Island and the marshes of Lewis Creek, Long Point juts out like a finger, due north into the lake. The cottages clustered close to the shore remain seasonal because the communal water supply is turned off in the winter. The crenulated shore from here north to Town Farm Bay guarantees that we paddle in and out of rock- and marsh-lined bays. A new sight greets us around each bend, while each bay has its own personality. On an unusual straight stretch of heavily wooded ledge, we admire the silhouette of a classic sailboat moored offshore and wonder what has kept further development at bay.

The wind has been surreptitiously building behind us, unnoticed until now. By the time we reach open water in Town Farm Bay, the wind has exceeded the forecast—and our comfort level. We head in among the moored boats at the Point Bay Marina, hoping their hulls will break the waves.

Thompsons Point. As we start out along Thompsons Point, we learn just how exposed this shore is. It is yet another great lesson in the power of the fetch. There is a very long uninterrupted stretch of water to the south of Thompsons Point that gives the waves a chance to build. I had been looking forward to see-

▶ **Little Otter Creek to Converse Bay**

Little Otter Creek.

ing historic cottages on this point, but instead we focus on each wave as it hits us broadside. Later, looking at our charts, we question whether the wind might also increase here because it is forced into a narrow gap between the heights of Split Rock Mountain in New York and Thompsons Point in Vermont. It is also possible that we are paddling against the current of the internal seiche, which must move faster here between these opposing cliffs.

We make steady, if slow, progress into the southwest wind, giving arms, shoulders, and torso a workout. On the tip of Thompsons Point, the high rock headland provides a springboard for the waves, sending them back out against those incoming. We head out from shore to avoid the chop and then turn quickly north—our kayaks take off, planing in the waves. What an exhilarating mix of thrill and fear. The outer end of Thompsons Point looks like a sea serpent with its mouth open, waiting to eat two women in kayaks. We paddle hard to keep our balance and our bows on top of the waves until we reach the lee, where we let out a whoop of relief. I don't know when I have more enjoyed quiet water in the dappled shade.

Originally named *Kozowaapska*, the "long stony point," Thompsons Point was an obvious stopping place for Abenaki and earlier Native Americans. A 2,000-year-old pot was found in water nearby. Thompsons Point, like Cedar Beach, is an historic summer community, but Thompsons Point land is owned by the town of Charlotte, unlike Cedar Beach, which is owned privately. Ralph

Nading Hill quotes longtime resident Jessie Gibbs, who told of the fate of the carriages of the young Charlotte men who liked to go on the steamboat outings to Port Kent and Ausable Chasm. In order to board with the attractive women of Thompsons Point, the Charlotte men would park their carriages near the clubhouse, but while the Charlotte swains were gone, the Thompsons Point boys would have a mischievous outing of their own riding the horses and switching the wheels on the different-sized carriages so they would wobble.

While not visible from the water, one aspect of Charlotte history is very clearly related to Lake Champlain. In 1849 railroad construction workers found a strange skeleton in a layer of blue clay surrounded by the shells of what were later identified as cold saltwater animals. Burlington naturalist Zadock Thompson identified the mysterious bones as those of a Beluga whale. That skeleton can still be seen at the University of Vermont, where Thompson carefully reconstructed it. The discovery of the Charlotte whale, as it is known, was a step in understanding that the Champlain Valley had once been at the bottom of the Champlain Sea.

Garden Island. From the north shore of Thompsons Point, we see 35-acre (14-hectare) privately owned Garden Island dead ahead. One of the five houses on this island dates from 1850. We admire the combination of dramatic cliffs and very accessible beach. Bald eagles reportedly nest here. Close-by Cedar Island resembles a smaller sibling.

We find the Converse Bay Fish and Wildlife Access quiet after our exciting trip around Thompsons Point. This morning we chose to head north through a relatively protected area, putting the south wind behind us. Did we consider the possible winds around Thompsons Point with its long fetch and funneling cliffs? No.

▶ **Little Otter Creek to Converse Bay**

Arnold Bay to Little Otter Creek
The Convoluted Shore

33

by Margy Holden

- **Launch site:** Arnold Bay Boat Launch, Adams Ferry Rd., Panton, Vermont
- **Distance:** 15 miles (24 kilometers)
- **Take out:** South Slang F&W Area (Little Otter Creek, Hawkins Road, Ferrisburg, Vermont)
- **Alternative launch sites:** Button Bay State Park ($, PT, Button Bay Rd., Vergennes, Vermont), Fort Cassin F&W Area (Fort Cassin Rd., Ferrisburg, Vermont), Kingsland Bay Town Beach (Town Beach Rd. off Sand Rd., Ferrisburg, Vermont)
- **Places to stop:** Above launch sites and Lake Champlain Maritime Museum, Kingsland Bay State Park (PT)
- **Highlights:** Historic sites, wildlife, fall geese migration, Maritime Museum with its extensive displays, Button Bay and Kingsland Bay state parks, walking trails, beaches, scenic narrows between Vermont and Split Rock Mountain, mouth of Otter Creek
- **Route:** Leaving historic Arnold Bay, the scenic, shallow-water route follows a visually sparsely settled shore, by Button Bay State Park, Basin Harbor, Fields Bay, the mouth of Otter Creek, and several other bays along the shores of Kingsland Bay and into Little Otter Creek.
- **Comments:** This route is exposed to both the south and north wind. It is one of the deepest parts of the lake, but it is possible to paddle in shallow water close to shore. It may be tempting to cross to New York, but heavy wind would make it dangerous.

The Paddle:

Tiny Arnold Bay is steeped in history. It was here, in the afternoon of October 13, 1776, that Benedict Arnold scuttled and burned most of his fleet when fleeing the British two days after the Battle of Valcour. (Three of his ships actually made it to Fort Ticonderoga.) Arnold reportedly waited until the last minute to strike the American colors, and then fled overland with his remaining men to Fort Ticonderoga, New York, and safety. Even before this event, in 1776, an elderly Benjamin Franklin stopped and spent the night at the house of Peter Ferris, then located here. In 1859 the body of John Brown was brought here to be taken across the lake on the Adams Ferry that ran from here to Westport, New York.

We turn our kayaks north and head for Button Bay. The shore is steep and wooded much of the way. We pause to watch the life-and-death struggle of a tiny mole that has fallen down a cliff, holding our breath each time it struggles up the steep slope only to fall back again. Above us, an incredible fall panorama unfolds. Wave upon wave of geese fly overhead, until the air above us is filled with their sound. As they land near us, we can't help but be amused by their feet-out-in-front landing.

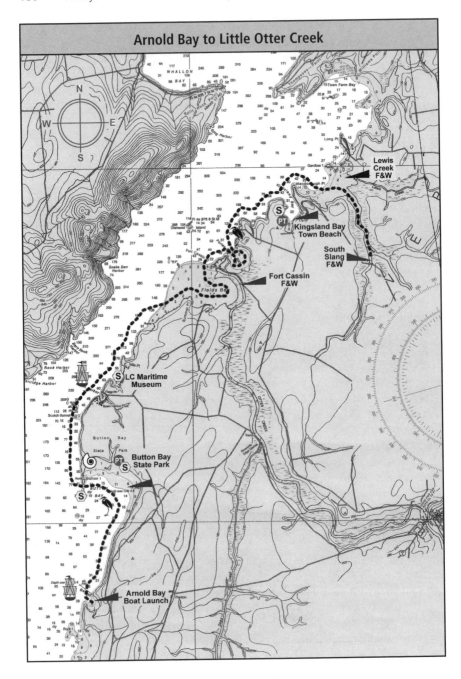

Arnold Bay to Little Otter Creek

Button Bay State Park. At 235 acres (95.1 hectares), Button Bay State Park has three distinct sections—the day-use area, the campground, and a natural area. The original name, Button Mould Bay, comes from the clay concretions that used to be found here in the shape of old button molds. This protected, south-facing bay has been an historic haven for travelers. We float offshore in our kayaks imagining all kinds of questions we would like to ask Samuel de Champlain, Benedict Arnold, General Burgoyne, Benjamin Franklin, and Ethan Allen, if only we had been around when they sought shelter here.

Mature oaks, hickories, pines, maples, and a nature center mark the Button Point Natural Area on the 14-acre (5.7-hectare) point on the west end of the state park. We land on the point and are torn between looking up at the flocks of geese that continue to pass over us, or down at the smooth rock where we find a trilobite fossil. We paddle around two-acre Little Button Island, just offshore, which is another remnant of 480-million-year-old coral reefs.

Heading north, the cottages of the Basin Harbor Club announce that we are approaching the resort. Owned by the Beach family since 1882, the Basin Harbor Club is steeped in tradition and informal elegance. Nearby, the replica of the gunboat *Philadelphia* is moored at the lakeside entrance to the Lake Champlain Maritime Museum, which is on the grounds of the resort. The gunboat was built in 1991 under the auspices of the museum. A volunteer aboard the boat talking to visitors as we approach spies us and hollers, "Friend or foe?" With the cannons of the *Philadelphia* pointed directly at us not more than ten yards away, how could we answer anything but "friend?"

The original gunboat *Philadelphia* was built in Skenesboro (now Whitehall, New York) in 1776 as part of Benedict Arnold's fleet. It was a 54-foot-long (16.5-meter) flat-bottomed rowboat, outfitted with a single mast and square sails designed to sail before the wind. Its 44-member crew fought in the Battle of Valcour, where the *Philadelphia* was sunk. It was found in the 1930s, raised from its watery grave, and moved to the Smithsonian Museum.

The museum's outstanding interactive history of Lake Champlain and its collection of significant watercraft just up the path from the shore merit a visit. Its marine archeological research, preservation, and publishing functions add much to the knowledge about Lake Champlain's maritime history.

Otter Creek. Dwellings line the shore between the Maritime Museum and Fields Bay. Behind the homes stretch the marshes and farms of Addison County. Ahead of us the Otter Creek delta juts into the lake, creating two bays. We paddle through the reeds of shallow Fields Bay to the south.

The most convoluted shoreline along Lake Champlain stretches between here and Converse Bay. When we use a string to measure our route close to shore, it comes to more than thirteen miles (about 20 kilometers), but if we straighten out the string, it measures only four miles (6.4 kilometers). Where better to investigate Lake Champlain's small bays?

Button Bay.

Otter Creek is 90 miles long, but flows serenely for the last seven miles (11.3 kilometers) between the dramatic falls in Vergennes and Lake Champlain. The falls were the site of frenzied shipbuilding as Thomas Macdonough prepared to face the British in Plattsburgh Bay in 1814. When wintering just below the falls, he was ordered to build several ships without being provided with supplies, equipment, or shipbuilders. Shipbuilders as well as patriotic local farmers turned out to help. Miraculously the 734-ton (665.9-tonne) *Saratoga* was built and launched in only forty days, along with many other craft.

Most of the land at the mouth of Otter Creek is part of the Lower Otter Creek Wildlife Management Area, a 695-acre (281.3-hectare) wetland and floodplain owned by the State of Vermont. Samuel de Champlain named Otter Creek *La Riviere aux Loutres,* or the "River with Otters." Otters still live in Otter Creek, as do beavers. We see a sleek brown mink skittering along the shore. Mergansers, mallards, and blue-winged teal breed here.

Artifacts found at the mouth of the creek indicate that Native Americans gathered here, as well as at Little Otter Creek, for centuries. Otter Creek provided a watery highway for Native Americans to reach other parts of New England.

The cliffs of Fort Cassin Point separate the mouth of Otter Creek from Porter Bay to the north. On May 14, 1814, Captain Pring, leading a British fleet, attacked the simple earthwork fort, but was driven off by Lieutenant Cassin and

▶ Arnold Bay to Little Otter Creek

his men. From the 1990s until recently, Porter Bay had a colony of nesting great blue herons that was protected by an emergent marsh. Fortunately, the marsh is preserved by The Nature Conservancy. We see bulrush, cattail and, again in the distance, silver maples.

Lake Bluff Cedar Pine Forests. From here to Kingsland Bay we paddle into and out of at least four more small bays. In its 264-acres (106.9 hectares), Kingsland Bay State Park includes all of Macdonough Point to the west and the east shore of Hawkins Bay. Walking trails follow the shore of Macdonough Point. The undeveloped east shore is part of the Kingsland Bay Natural Area. It is one of the best, unspoiled examples of a lake bluff cedar pine forest on Lake Champlain. The trees and plants grow on limestone and dolomite outcroppings, which also support rare plants. The soils are shallow, and the bedrock is either visible or just below the surface.

A choice location for homes, this type of lakeshore plant community barely survives throughout the Champlain Valley. Once the land is disturbed, invasive species can take over. Lake bluff cedar pine forest sites in Vermont total no more than 360 acres (145.7 hectares) and are mostly found along Lake Champlain. The marked campsite along the inner shore is a site on the Paddlers Trail.

The success of École Champlain, a camp for young women, kept this land in one piece until it was purchased by the State of Vermont in 1970. The historic Hawley House, built in 1790, still graces this day-use park. Shallow soils prevent building the kind of infrastructure required by camping.

We take out at the Ferrisburg Town Beach, at the innermost end of Kingsland Bay, and walk our kayaks over the mowed grass to the car. This was the day of bay after bay after bay.

| 34 | **Chimney Point to Arnold Bay**
Historic Point to Historic Bay |

by Cathy Frank

- ■ **Launch site:** Chimney Point F&W Area, Rt. 17, Addison, Vermont
- ■ **Distance:** 10 miles (16 kilometers)
- ■ **Take out**: Arnold Bay Boat Launch (Adams Ferry Rd., Panton, VT)
- ■ **Alternative launch sites:** Crown Point Campground Boat Launch ($, Bridge Rd., Crown Point, New York)
- ■ **Places to stop:** Above launch sties and D.A.R. State Park (PT), Mud and Woods Islands
- ■ **Highlights:** Hospital Creek, Fort St. Frederic and Visitors' Center, Chimney Point Museum, Rock and Mud islands, views of Green and Adirondack mountains, wildlife
- ■ **Route:** This linear route offers a narrow, shallow shelf of water as one paddles along the Panton Shore scattered with farms, new homes, and old camps. Mud and Rock islands offer interesting stopping places. Arnold Bay is historic, picturesque and filled with turtles.
- ■ **Comments:** This route is exposed to strong north and south wind and waves.

The Paddle:

From our vantage point at the Fish & Wildlife Access under the Champlain Bridge, rust abounds, not a reassuring sight as we hear the cars pass overhead. The Champlain Bridge, built in 1929, arches high over the lake, a striking sight from all directions.

Pausing to admire the view of Port Henry, New York, to the west, we let the gentle south wind give us an effortless start northward. We paddle by Hospital Creek, a mile-and-a-half inlet that was used in 1759 to house sick English soldiers during the French and Indian War so that they would not infect the remainder of General Amherst's army at Crown Point. This rich wildlife habitat makes a great paddle in its own right.

We are not the only ones taking advantage of this sunny, warm day. We pass fishermen, cormorants, gulls, bikini-clad teenage girls, adults reclining in chairs and reading, an osprey, a bald eagle, half a dozen kingfishers, a muskrat, an oriole, and a small train of merganser chicks seemingly pulled along by a mama engine. Wild yellow iris and white daisies dot the shoreline. The white fluffy seeds of cottonwood trees spread across the water, while patches of duckweed float close by. We startle a great blue heron, which flies from his fishing spot. Interestingly, it was not startled by the barking of a nearby dog, which must be a normal part of the bird's environment. The distant whistle of a freight train gets louder as it passes us headed north on the Delaware and Hudson tracks across the lake. On the Vermont side, the distant Green Mountains live up to their

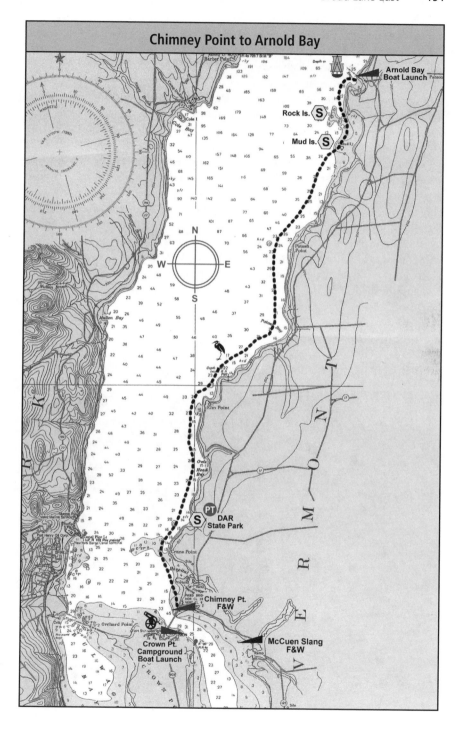

Chimney Point to Arnold Bay

name. The long flat ridgeline of Mt. Abraham confirms we are paddling along the Panton shore. Dotted with large new homes and clusters of older summer camps, it is not unlike the shoreline tension between old and new found in more populated Chittenden County.

Two hours of paddling require a chocolate fix. Pulling together for the first distribution of the day—and the new season, I hand one square of rich, dark, 70-percent chocolate to Margy, who does not grab it quite as quickly as I let go of it. Oh no! Chocolate does not float. What a devastating discovery!

Two small islands sit about a half mile offshore, just before Arnold Bay. We eagerly paddle out to the first, Mud Island. Despite its solid tree cover, it doesn't look more than 1 or 2 feet (.3–.6 meters) above the water level. We land on the north end and discover a large mound of dirt in the middle of the island, perhaps five feet above water level and about the size and shape of a large beaver lodge. The rest of the island, bordered by a shale beach, looks vulnerable to the unusually high water level (98 feet / 30 meters). We have discovered a playhouse just our size. The crystal-clear water reveals an endless supply of thin shale skipping rocks. (We have an undeclared contest to see who can skip a rock the greatest number of times. The winner will remain anonymous.)

Back in our kayaks, we linger over the view of Rock Island, a half mile to the northwest. With its elevated shoreline and tree-covered top, it looks much more substantial than Mud Island. There is a small landing area on the northeast end.

Turtle rock, Arnold Bay.

▶ Chimney Point to Arnold Bay

The Lake Champlain Land Trust has conserved both islands, which are nesting sites for waterfowl and are accessible to the public.

We arrive at Arnold Bay tired and ready to quit, but this historical bay, named after Benedict Arnold, has one more treat in store. Even before we can reflect on its history, we see what looks like a slew of turtles sunning themselves on a rather large rock sticking up in the water about 20 yards (18 meters) off-shore. As quietly as possible, we paddle closer, fully expecting that what we want to be turtles will turn out to be small rocks. Yes! Much to our amazement and delight, we see three big turtles with shells about 8–10 inches (20–25 centimeters) in diameter and about 4 or 5 smaller turtles piled on top of the larger ones. They look as happy to be soaking up the sun today as we are. They seem in no hurry to leave, despite our approach, but finally move off the rock one at a time as we get closer. One little guy tips over in his attempt to get off quickly, landing upside down at the edge of the rock. Legs flailing frantically, he struggles to roll himself over. I want to reach out with my paddle to help him, but resist the temptation. He finally flips over and slips into the water.

From the turtles, it is a short paddle to our take-out at the north end of this small bay. Before getting out of our kayaks, we take a moment to reflect on this bay's history and to inwardly acknowledge the debt we owe our brave band of "Rabble in Arms," many of whom never made it to this bay after the Battle of Valcour in 1776.

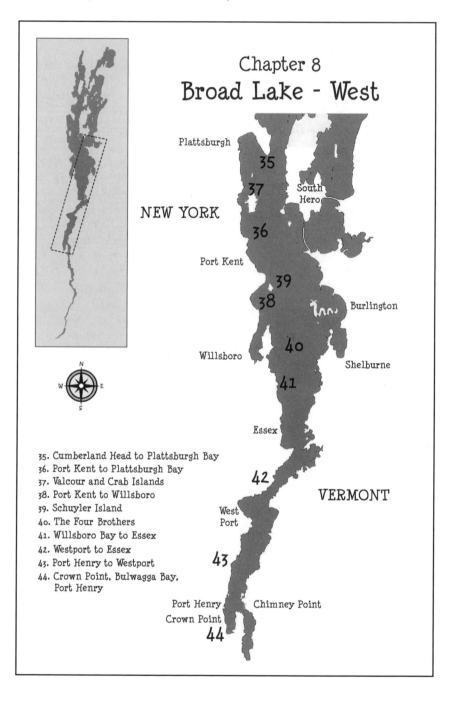

Chapter 8
Broad Lake - West

Plattsburgh

35

37

South
Hero

NEW YORK

36

Port Kent

39

38

Burlington

Willsboro

40

Shelburne

41

Essex

42

VERMONT

West
Port

43

Port Henry
Crown Point
44

Chimney Point

35. Cumberland Head to Plattsburgh Bay
36. Port Kent to Plattsburgh Bay
37. Valcour and Crab Islands
38. Port Kent to Willsboro
39. Schuyler Island
40. The Four Brothers
41. Willsboro Bay to Essex
42. Westport to Essex
43. Port Henry to Westport
44. Crown Point, Bulwagga Bay,
    Port Henry

Chapter VIII

Broad Lake West

The Battleground

Much of the deepest water on Lake Champlain can be found along the New York shore. Some of the cliffs rise to over a thousand feet and, in other places, lower foothills of the Adirondack Mountains and the Adirondack Park extend all the way to the lake. A number of picturesque villages are tucked between the mountains and the shore. One small city, Plattsburgh, New York, occupies the transition area between the mountainous shores of the broad lake and the flat fields of the northern part of the lake. Much of the remaining shore is undeveloped because of the Delaware and Hudson Railroad right-of-way that closely follows the shoreline. Whether because of the events during the American Revolution or the dramatic cliffs found along this route, or a combination of both, this is a fascinating section of Lake Champlain shoreline.

New York Palisades from Button Bay.

Cumberland Head to Plattsburgh Bay and Return
Winds and War

35

by Margy Holden

■ **Launch site/Take out:** Cumberland Head Ferry Landing, Rt. 314, Plattsburgh, New York
■ **Distance:** 9 miles (14.5 kilometers)
■ **Alternative Launch Sites:** Cumberland Bay State Park / Plattsburgh City Beach ($, PT, Rt. 314, Plattsburgh, New York), Lung Healthy Trail and Wilcox Dock (Cumberland Ave., Plattsburgh, New York), Dock St. Landing & Waterfront Park (off Bridge St., Plattsburgh, New York)
■ **Places to stop:** None aside from launch sites
■ **Highlights:** Site of historic battle, Cumberland Head Lighthouse, Cumberland Bay beaches, dramatic Adirondack, Crab Island, Valcour Island and Green Mountain views
■ **Route:** This shallow, circle route circumnavigates the tip of Cumberland head and follows the settled and shallow southeast shore into the bay and the Cumberland Bay State Park.
■ **Comments:** Some of the largest waves on the lake build in a south wind.

The Paddle:

Cumberland Head reaches out from the New York shore north of Plattsburgh and then drops south, narrowing Lake Champlain from 6 to 2 miles to the east and forming 3-mile (4.8-kilometer) wide Cumberland Bay to the west. New York and Vermont each have their own name for the ferry that connects them. It is called the Grand Isle Ferry by Vermonters and the Cumberland Head Ferry by those on the New York side. Thus, we cross on the Grand Isle Ferry, but launch from the Cumberland Head Ferry landing.

The beach is a deep pile of stones that have been smoothed and rounded by Lake Champlain, the artist. We launch and paddle south from the ferry landing for less than a mile, around the tip of Cumberland Head, and then head north and west toward the Cumberland Bay State Park.

The noise of the busy ferry landing quickly fades into the sound of water lapping on the rocky shore. The view down the broad lake almost 30 miles (48 kilometers) to the narrows between Split Rock Mountain and Thompsons Point is priceless. The rock formations are dark, layered shale. As we near the tip of Cumberland Head, Crab Island, where the casualties of the Battle of Plattsburgh Bay were treated or buried, and Valcour Island, where Benedict Arnold delayed the British advance in 1776, are directly in front of us.

Cumberland Head Lighthouse. The Cumberland Head Lighthouse, which is still in use, dominates this point of land. The 1867 lighthouse had an attached, Vic-

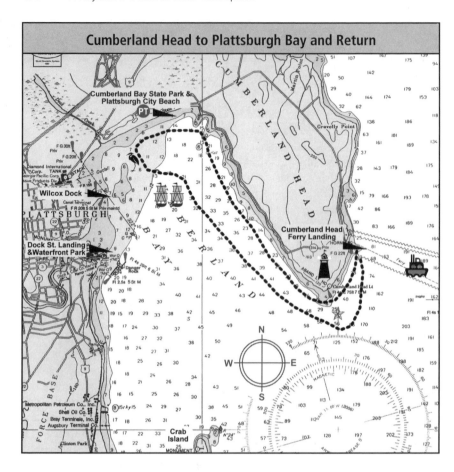

Cumberland Head to Plattsburgh Bay and Return

torian, four-bedroom house filled to capacity by the keeper, William Tabberah, a disabled Civil War veteran, his wife, and eight children. His disability, a musket ball lodged in his hip, did not keep him from climbing the tower to do his job. When he died in 1904 of surgery to remove the musket ball, his wife, Emma, was appointed keeper, serving with the help of some of her children until 1919. That Victorian house had been her home for almost fifty years.

We pass the tip of Cumberland Head and turn north. This is a prime housing area with its rocky shores and southern exposure, located within minutes of downtown Plattsburgh. The dwellings we pass include summer camps and a monolithic, white, cement, multistoried structure clinging to the rocks. We see all kinds of architectural preferences and tastes.

The former main road to Plattsburgh hugs the shore and is studded with wave-beaten cottonwoods most of the way to Cumberland State Park. The echoes of the epic Battle of Plattsburgh Bay are vivid as we paddle through this historic stretch of the Lake. Is that the sound of cannons?

▶ Cumberland Head to Plattsburgh Bay and Return

The Battle of Plattsburgh Bay, 1814

In the War of 1812, Lake Champlain again became a battleground in the struggle between the defending Americans and the British invaders. If the British could capture Lake Champlain, it would be a step in a campaign to sever New England from the rest of the states.

Even though the Americans had won the Revolutionary War, the British continued to harass American shipping in northern Lake Champlain. After an initial set of skirmishes on the Richelieu River, Cumberland Head, and other sites, the British sent a force of over 10,000 troops south to occupy Plattsburgh, causing roughly 2,000 troops under the American Brigadier General Alexander Macomb and 2,500 volunteers from Vermont to retreat south.

Thomas Macdonough, a twenty-eight-year-old veteran who had been charged with creating an American fleet to defend Lake Champlain, chose Plattsburgh Bay as the site for a naval battle that proved pivotal. It had been a mere thirty-six years since the Battle of Valcour, during the American Revolution, less than 6 miles (9.7 kilometers) to the south.

Macdonough employed a strategy similar to that of Benedict Arnold in the Battle of Valcour (see "Battle of Valcour" sidebar in "Port Kent to Plattsburgh Bay" paddle). Believing that the British would wait for a north wind, Macdonough positioned his ragtag navy in Plattsburgh Bay. That would force the British to come about after passing the tip of Cumberland Head and tack north into the wind to get within firing range of the American ships. Each time they tacked, they would present the American ships with a broadside target. Unlike in the Battle of Valcour, however, the element of surprise was missing because the fleet was visible to the British troops occupying Plattsburgh. On September 11, 1814, the superior British fleet sailed south, confident when they spotted the American masts across Cumberland Head. They rounded the point, just as we have done on a beautiful fall day, and faced the fledgling American fleet.

Captain Downie of the British fleet led his ships, tacking upwind just as Macdonough had planned. Macdonough's *Eagle* fired the first shot, which hit the British ship *Confiance*. Other initial shots missed their mark, including a British one that destroyed the cage of a gamecock on an American ship. According to contemporary accounts, the gamecock fled to a perch at the top of a cannon, where it crowed in defiance. The men cheered. Unfortunately, Macdonough's ingenious system of anchors and pulleys designed to turn the American boats

so that fresh guns could be brought into play, was almost immediately destroyed.

The battle quickly became fierce and bloody. Macdonough was
knocked out twice, apparently once when hit with the severed head
of a fellow sailor. Macdonough survived, but the British Captain
Downie, whose ship *Confiance* was hit with 105 rounds of fire, was
killed. Macdonough's ship, *Saratoga*, was hit by 55 rounds of shot.
The battle raged for two hours and twenty minutes until not a mast
on either fleet was usable. After punishing fire from both sides left
the fleets so damaged that they could neither withdraw nor pursue,
the British surrendered. When the British presented their swords,
Macdonough, noted for his gallantry, told the enemy officers to keep
them. They had fought valiantly.

Fifty-four British and fifty-two Americans had been killed, and
almost 200 wounded on both sides. The British strategy had been
thwarted. In Plattsburgh, when General Prevost learned of his navy's
defeat, he led his 10,000 troops back to Canada, leaving behind a
great supply of food, drink, and weapons. I can find no account of
what kind of party might have ensued.

The sky is bright blue and the wind is beginning to pick up. The shore
becomes densely settled. Cumberland Bay State Park, which has been a distant
white strip of beach glistening in the sunlight, is directly in front of us. We are
treated to a fall spectacle of huge flocks of Canada and snow geese floating on
the water. Even though they appear to be one big flock, they rise and fly away
with their own species in a cacophony of flapping wings and raucous calls. We
watch, transfixed by their silhouettes against the blue, until they become mere
specks in the sky.

I wade ashore to feel the warmth of the long sand beach and take a swim.
The south wind has been increasing steadily and Cathy waits, wisely riding
with the gulls beyond where the waves are breaking, while I struggle to again
launch my kayak through them. We attach spray skirts before heading in a
straight line between the beach and the tip of Cumberland Head. It is quite
a pull into this south wind, and my arms can feel it. What happened to that
forecast of light and variable winds, which is one of the reasons we chose this
trip today?

If I had looked at the chart, I would understand why we are encounter-
ing such large waves. Along with the incomparable view to the south comes a
fabulous fetch. Those waves, stimulated by the wind, have nothing to do for 30
miles (48 kilometers) but build to this point. It is a wild ride around the tip of
Cumberland Head and onto the beach by the ferry dock, but both kayaks stay

▶ **Cumberland Head to Plattsburgh Bay and Return**

upright. We pull ashore, happy to be there while Cathy sputters, using such words as "capsizing," "terror," and "never have I seen."

We load our kayaks and get in line for the ferry, happy to be on dry land and anxious to learn what the Frank wind anemometer has recorded. Once home, Cathy calls to say that the top wind recorded was 28 MPH (45 KPH). Not light and variable by a long shot.

Rough water. Photograph courtesy of Doug Hyde.

36 Port Kent to Plattsburgh Bay
The Battleground

by Cathy Frank

- **Launch site:** Port Kent Ferry Dock, Rt. 373, Port Kent, New York
- **Distance:** 16 miles (25.7 kilometers)
- **Take out:** Cumberland Bay State Park / Plattsburgh City Beach ($, PT, Rt. 314, Plattsburgh, New York)
- **Alternative launch sites:** Peru, New York, Boat Launch (Rt. 9, Peru, New York), Lung Healthy Trail and Wilcox Dock (Cumberland Ave., Plattsburgh, New York), Dock St. Landing & Waterfront Park (off Bridge St., Plattsburgh, New York), Ausable Point Public Campground and Day Use Area (PT, mouth of the Ausable River, Ausable, New York)
- **Places to stop:** Above launch sites and Valcour (PT) and Crab islands
- **Highlights:** Wildlife around Ausable River Delta, heron rookery and Bluff Point Lighthouse on Valcour Island, Crab Island Monument to the dead from the Battle of Plattsburgh in 1814, Plattsburgh waterfront, wildlife in Cumberland Bay's wetlands
- **Route:** From Port Kent to Valcour Island, this scenic linear route passes over the shallow water created by the delta of the Ausable River and its many defunct branches. It continues up the deeper channel between Valcour Island and the mainland, past Crab Island and on to Plattsburgh's waterfront, and then into shallow and wildlife-rich Cumberland Bay to the town and state beaches. Once past the Ausable River, there is a narrow shelf of shallow water along the shore beyond which water depth drops to 15–50 feet. There is the option of paddling across the channel to Valcour Island. A loop of Valcour itself adds 8 miles (12.8 kilometers) to the trip.
- **Comments:** This route is exposed to strong north and south winds and waves. Watch for poison ivy on Valcour and Crab islands.

The Paddle:

A forecast of 40-percent chance of showers with thunderstorms arriving by afternoon has motivated an early start on this warm June day for one of the most historic sections on Lake Champlain.

Port Kent is a sort of geologic dividing line between the rocks found on the New York side of the lake. To the south, one-billion-year-old rocks, part of the Adirondack formation, rise steeply from the water in most places. Yet, to the north, the land is low, and a fairly wide shelf of shallow water extends both north and south from the mouth of the Ausable River, the result of the river's outflow for the last 10,000 years. The river's multiple branches and dead ends are visible evidence that it has chosen a number of ways to arrive at Lake Champlain over the course of geologic time. Wildlife abounds in these sheltered inlets.

▶ **Paddle name**

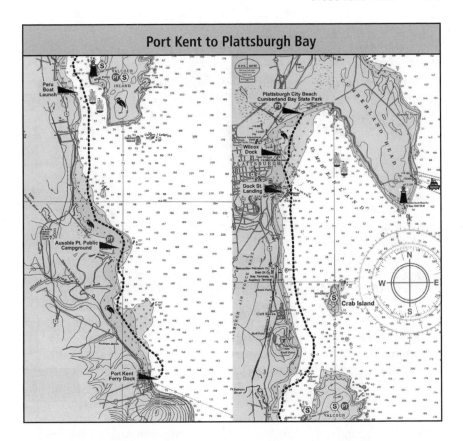

Passing a colony of small camps, seemingly untouched by twenty-first-century development pressures, we run aground trying to cut inside an offshore sandbar that is dotted with seagulls. A huge flock of cormorants is fishing just beyond the river. Curious as to what they are eating, Margy draws closer but, as she approaches, they fly off for safer waters. The noise of their wings slapping the water reaches a crescendo as more than a hundred birds fly over her head.

We approach this history-laden channel between Valcour and the mainland with reverence. The history that took place here in October 1776 is hard to see. It doesn't flutter in our faces like the fleeting flock of cormorants, commanding our attention. In fact, most of the evidence has either sunk to the bottom or sailed away.

We pause on the battle line for a moment and try to picture the string of ragtag American gunboats, strung out across the three-quarter-mile channel, attempting to stop the superior British Fleet from sailing south and controlling the lake in 1776. We have just paddled the same shallow sandy shore that the American fleet rowed by in their escape that foggy night after the battle. Our kayaks went aground without fog or dark of night for an excuse. I

Battle of Valcour, Revolutionary War Action on Lake Champlain

During the American Revolution both sides wanted to control Lake Champlain because of its strategic location as a natural transportation route connecting Canada and the mid-Atlantic colonies.

In the summer of 1776, a year after the war began, the Americans' minimal control of Lake Champlain was in serious jeopardy. They had withdrawn from Crown Point to Ticonderoga and were just managing, with the aid of four vessels taken from the British in 1775, to keep the British from advancing south on Lake Champlain. The British were preparing a fleet of warships on the Richelieu River (Lake Champlain's northern terminus) to sail south and take control of the lake and thus isolate New England from the other colonies.

Benedict Arnold, charged with building a fleet of ships to counter the anticipated British naval assault, had assembled 15 ships and 500 men, mainly farmers and carpenters. On October 11, 1776, those ships were anchored on the southeast side of the channel between Valcour Island and the mainland of New York, awaiting the British assault from the north. Arnold correctly surmised that the vastly superior British fleet, which outnumbered the American fleet by three to four times, would sail down the middle of the broad lake on a strong northwest wind and pass the southern end of Valcour Island before seeing the Americans spread out in a line across the channel well behind them. The British would then have to turn and sail upwind to engage the Americans in battle. (Macdonough used a similar strategy thirty-eight years later in the Battle of Plattsburgh Bay.)

To avoid early detection, the American fleet hid in the cove south of Bluff Point until the British fleet was spotted on the broad lake side of Valcour. The Americans fought fiercely for six long hours, but in the end the superior ships and guns of the British prevailed. The American gunboat *Philadelphia* (an exact replica of which is anchored at the Lake Champlain Maritime Museum) had been sunk, and the schooner *Royal Savage* burned. Most of the other American boats were badly damaged. With British soldiers securing the mainland, the Iroquois, loyal to the British, on Valcour, and the British fleet to the south, British General Sir Guy Carleton was content to wait until morning for an American surrender.

Meanwhile, with the help of a fortuitous fog, the American fleet took advantage of the cover of night and one by one silently rowed around the west side of the inattentive British line, hugging the New York shore. By mid-morning of October 12, the American fleet had

▶ **Port Kent to Plattsburgh Bay**

reached the north end of Schuyler Island, 8 miles (13 kilometers) south. There they made emergency repairs, scuttled two boats, and set off in desperate flight in hopes of reaching the safety of Fort Ticonderoga before the British caught up to them. Meanwhile, a surprised and angry General Carleton set off to the east the next morning hoping to find the Americans, but to no avail. Early on the morning of October 13, the British, now with fair wind, sailed south in pursuit, overtaking Arnold at Split Rock where fighting resumed. Realizing his fleet would be destroyed before reaching Ticonderoga (three ships actually made it to Fort Ticonderoga), Arnold set a course for Ferris Bay (now Arnold Bay) on the Vermont side. There, he drove his fleet ashore, burned his ships, and led the survivors overland to Fort Ticonderoga and safety. With the Iroquois in hot pursuit, the Americans endured a forced overnight march of nearly 25 miles (40 kilometers). Thanks to American fortifications on Mount Independence and Fort Ticonderoga, the British chose to return to Quebec to wait out the winter.

The Americans did not win the Battle of Valcour, but the resultant delay of one year in the British southerly advance gave the Americans the winter of 1776–77 to refresh their forces. The following spring, British General Burgoyne and his army were beaten at the Battle of Saratoga, one of the major turning points of the Revolutionary War.

Gunboat *Philadelphia* replica.

Valcour channel.

am thankful that Arnold's fleet did not do the same. Would we have different passports if they had?

We stop for lunch at the Peru Boat Launch, the west end of the battle line. Threatening clouds appear in the west and play games with us the rest of the afternoon. We paddle north past both Valcour and Crab islands, passing a lone kayaker heading south. High above on the western shore sits Clinton County Community College, formerly the Adirondack Hotel, a destination resort during the heyday of the railroad hotels. It is a distinctive landmark that can be seen from almost everywhere on the Vermont shore from Burlington north.

Plattsburgh's long, southeast-facing breakwater gives us some welcome respite from the now sizeable south waves as we duck inside for a few minutes to rest.

Approaching Cumberland Bay, we recall its recent pollution problems. Like history, pollution can be hard to see, especially if it is hiding on the bottom of the lake. In 1994 the concentration of PCBs (polychlorinated biphenyls), long-lasting industrial chemicals suspected of causing cancer, was found to be so high in Cumberland Bay that special fish consumption advisories were issued. The contamination stemmed from wood-product industries in the Plattsburgh area that dumped their industrial waste directly into the bay until 1973. A $35-million cleanup, completed in 2001, removed over 150,000 tons of contaminated sludge from the bay.

A few large breaking waves catch us as we approach Plattsburgh City Beach, but we accept our water-saturated state with pride, amazed at having covered 17.5 miles (28 kilometers) in four and a half hours, thanks to the south wind. No doubt the fatigue will hit as soon as we get home.

▶ Port Kent to Plattsburgh Bay

Valcour and Crab Islands
A Paddlers' Paradise

37

by Cathy Frank

■ **Launch site/Take out:** Peru NY Boat Launch, Rt. 9, Peru, New York
■ **Distance:** 13.5 miles (21.7 kilometers)
■ **Alternative launch sites:** Ausable Point Public Campground and Day Use Area (PT, Rt. 9 to Ausable Point Rd., Ausable, New York)
■ **Places to stop:** Above launch sites and Valcour (PT) and Crab islands
■ **Highlights:** Walking trails on both islands, Bluff Point Lighthouse and heron rookery on Valcour Island, War of 1812 military cemetery on Crab Island, lots of places to stop and swim
■ **Route:** This treasure-packed loop route first heads across open water to Valcour, where Bluff Cliff eventually gives way to a pebble beach with access to a trail to the lighthouse as one heads north. Crossing the 1.5 miles (2.4 kilometers) of open water to Crab can be challenging on a windy day. Crab's shoreline offers many opportunities to stop. Back on Valcour, campsites, on a first-come-first-serve basis, are scattered throughout the island, many along the shore. Rocky ledges and flat rock areas filled with 460-million-year-old fossils alternate with beaches along the east shore. Views of the Green and Adirondack mountains, nearby shores and the Champlain Islands abound. This trip can be done without including Crab, if the wind is moderate/strong.
■ **Comments:** Watch for poison ivy on both islands. Anchorages and campsites fill quickly. This route is exposed to strong north, west and south winds and waves. Crossing from Valcour to Crab can be challenging in a moderate-to-strong wind.

The Paddle:
We have just enough time at the Grand Isle Ferry for Margy to get a huge, hot, delicious, just-out-of-the-oven raisin bran muffin for us to split. (Kayakers should, at all times, be well-fed.) The day is warm, sunny, with 5–15 MPH (8–24 KPH) northwest wind.

From the Peru Boat Launch, we head east to Bluff Point, where Benedict Arnold hid his tiny armada to await the southbound British fleet. The remains of the entire hull of the American gunboat *Philadelphia* were found and removed from here. Arnold's flagship, the schooner *Royal Savage*, which ran aground and was burned by the British at the beginning of the battle, was discovered on the southwest tip of the island and has also been removed. Divers from the Lake Champlain Maritime Museum continue to search the bottom for other artifacts of this historic battle.

With the west wind behind us, it is an easy paddle to the newly renovated Bluff Point Lighthouse that sits directly ahead of us. The Clinton County Historical Society has restored the interior and developed several interpretive displays

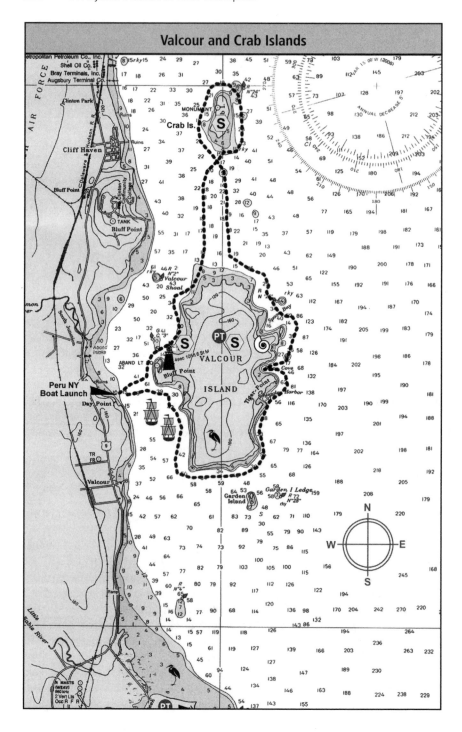

Valcour and Crab Islands

▶ **Valcour and Crab Islands**

about the lighthouse and its keepers. A small beach in the next cove north has a foot trail leading to the lighthouse. We head north along the west shore and then across almost 2 miles (3 kilometers) of open water to Crab Island. The wind and waves increase to a steady 20, gusting to 25 knots mostly from the west as we start across. We go into "watch every wave" mode to anticipate unexpected large waves from hitting us broadside.

Crab Island has its own rich history. It was here that the sick and injured were cared for during the Battle of Plattsburgh in the War of 1812. One hundred forty-nine American and British soldiers who died in that battle are buried together here in this federally recognized military cemetery. There is a granite obelisk to the fallen, and a huge flagpole on the west side of the island. We stop to read the memorials, being careful to avoid the prodigious poison ivy.

With some trepidation we leave the protection of Crab and head south, back to Valcour. With the wind a little more behind us than abeam, crossing back to Valcour is faster and easier than was the trip over. Still, we are greatly relieved once we get to Valcour and around to its leeward side. We have earned our lunch, and we stop at the first point of land on the east, just north of Spoon Bay. Climbing out of our kayaks onto some slippery underwater rocks, we find a long, flat, rocky ledge where we stretch out and relax our tired muscles while enjoying a

Crab Island Monument.

clear view of Grand Isle, South Hero, Providence Island, and the Green Mountains to the east. This place is seductive. Out of the wind, it is a perfect day.

Camera in hand, I get up to take some pictures and step onto a flat, wet, but not submerged rock. Suddenly, as if stepping onto black ice, my feet fly out from under me and I find myself flat on my back, head and camera in the water. Fortunately, no harm is done except to my ego and camera. (The memory stick full of pictures was fine, but the camera had taken its last picture.)

Meanwhile, Margy looks down at her left hand and lets out a yelp. We are sitting on fossils that are millions of years old. Valcour is made of the same 460-million-year-old limestone that is found at Fisk Quarry and Goodsell Ridge in Isle La Motte. Fossils abound. So, like two kids on a treasure hunt, we spend another hour or so scrambling along the shore, *oohing* and *aahing* at each new fossil find.

Valcour Island, owned by the State of New York and part of the Adirondack Park, has primitive campsites, many of which are located in protected harbors. It literally has a safe harbor for every wind direction. On the east side, pebble beaches buttressed by rocky cliffs and clear water provide a boaters' and campers' paradise. Lots of boats anchor in its many harbors, and the campsites, available on a first-come, first-served basis, are almost always full. Unfortunately, like all good Champlain Islands, it also has its share of lush poison ivy and mosquitoes. Arrive prepared.

We take our time on the east shore, going in and out of each cove and cranny, paddling around every rock that can be remotely called an island, seeing who can find the most unique and interesting spot. Eventually we find ourselves once again back in the northwest wind headed up to Bluff Point Cove. A great blue heron flies by and lands inland on a tall, dead tree, part of a once large heron rookery. Like other rookeries on the lake, this one appears to wax and wane. The heron blends so well with the tree that it looks like another branch. Realizing this, we look more closely at the entire grove of dead trees and discover many more herons perched on the higher branches. Nature's camouflage has done its work.

Before we know it, we are back on the New York shore. It is hard not to be overwhelmed when under the spell of Valcour Island.

▶ **Valcour and Crab Islands**

Port Kent to Willsboro
Almost Touch the Sky

38

by Margy Holden

- **Launch site:** Port Kent Ferry Landing, Rt. 373, Port Kent, New York
- **Distance:** 12 miles (19 kilometers)
- **Take out:** Willsboro Bay, NY Boat Launch (Boat Launch Rd. off Rt. 27, east side of bay, Willsboro, New York)
- **Alternative launch sites:** Port Douglas NY Boat Launch (Rt. 16, Port Douglas, New York)
- **Places to stop:** Above launch sites and Schuyler Island (PT), Port Douglas Town Beach
- **Highlights:** Spectacular cliffs on the west side of Willsboro Bay, rustic cedar shoreline, Port Douglas sand beach, cobble beach on north side of Corlaer Bay, black sand beach south of Port Kent
- **Route:** This route with a lot of unspoiled scenery passes a long black beach, rounds Trembleau Point with its few dwellings, follows the cedared, sparsely settled shore of Corlaer Bay, the Port Douglas Beach, and the dramatic cliffs of the west shore of Willsboro Bay, before ending near the marshy head of the bay.
- **Comments:** Include a paddle around Schuyler Island in this trip, if the weather is good (3.5 miles/5.6 kilometers). The relative natural state of the shoreline is a result of the proximity of the Delaware and Hudson railroad bed. This route is exposed to north and, until Willsboro Bay, south winds.

The Paddle:

There is something special about slipping into a kayak and taking the first strokes. The morning air holds warmth, moisture, and the promise of the rest of the day. Now we feel vindicated for scrubbing our trip yesterday when pea-sized hail banged against our windows. Now we're game, but wary.

Port Kent fills up hourly with cars as the Burlington to Port Kent ferry arrives and disgorges its cargo. Today we connect the dots by paddling between this popular destination and Willsboro Bay, another favorite haven of boaters.

The contrast between the New York and Vermont shores is most striking here. There are many cliffs, but few houses. The water is deep. We have the railroad track right–of–way to thank for much of the undeveloped land along the shoreline. The beach just south of Port Kent is long and shallow, with streaks of black sand as if a giant bottle of ink had been spilled. It is unique in our experience on the lake.

Just as we become accustomed to the wildness, we pass the tip of Trembleau Point and pause, enchanted by the riot of colors in well-kept gardens. We had planned to circle Schuyler Island, but out of respect for the line of angry black clouds blowing from the northwest over our right shoulders, we decide to stay close to shore. The height and proximity of the foothills block any distant

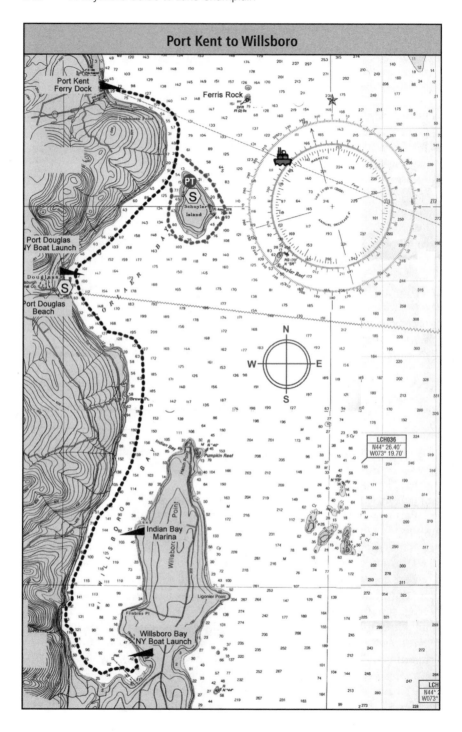

Port Kent to Willsboro

view to the west, making it difficult to tell what weather is approaching until it is upon us.

On the long, straight, southeast shore of Trembleau Point, with Schuyler Island behind us, the railroad again treats us to a wooded shoreline. The beach is covered with a deep bed of round cobblestones sculpted by wave action. On a 1776 map this stretch was aptly named Stoney Bay. Port Douglas is straight ahead, recognizable not for its many houses, but rather for its somewhat elaborate launch site and its sand beach.

Willsboro cleft.

The Delaware and Hudson Railroad and Lake Champlain Commerce

The amount of undeveloped land along the New York shore far surpasses that on the Vermont side. Puzzled at first, we soon discover that one of the reasons for this lack of development is the railroad bed of the Delaware and Hudson Railway. From just south of Plattsburgh through Willsboro Bay, and again from Westport to Whitehall, the railroad bed hugs the shore of Lake Champlain, making it a spectacular trip for rail passengers. The fortunes of the railroad deeply impacted the towns along the New York shore.

Through the time of sail and steam, towns like Rouses Point, Chazy Landing, Westport, Port Henry, and Essex (also a shipbuilding center) were popular ports where goods changed hands and passengers embarked and disembarked. When the Champlain Canal was completed, in 1823, opening a water route through Lake Champlain between New York City and Montreal, Whitehall instantly became a center of commerce as shipping increased throughout the lake. Ten years later there were more than 230 cargo-carrying boats on Lake Champlain, and the numbers continued to increase. When the iron industry took off in the mid-1800s, ore traveling from the mines through Port Henry onto canal boats and barges added to the volume.

Delaware and Hudson train—a constant companion.

▶ **Port Kent to Willsboro**

By 1853, railroads connected Burlington to Boston and New York City, but not on the New York side of Lake Champlain, where crossing the Adirondack foothills that hug the shore presented a greater challenge. Railroad magnates competed fiercely to complete railroad routes connecting New York to Montreal. The Delaware and Hudson was finally completed in 1875. Its construction was no small feat. Dynamite charges had to be lowered more than 100 feet from the top of the cliff to blast a shelf that was still 90 feet above the water. Workers were lowered to the shelf to clear the rubble and construct the track. We have found no account of whether there were lives lost. Today, peering up from the water, we marvel at the track and how slowly a train edges across it.

The completion of the Delaware and Hudson along the New York shore changed the fortunes of the lakeside towns. The efficiency of the railroad supplanted that of boats powered by sail and steam. Lake towns that had once been bustling ports fell into decline. While the railroad stopped in these towns, they were no longer essential transfer points except for Port Henry, which remained active until the iron mines closed. The greater legacy of the Delaware and Hudson to the boater may be the ribbon of green that remains along the tracks.

We paddle around the floating swim lines to the shore. It is a lovely spot, but where do the people live who take advantage of it? The view includes Schuyler and Providence islands, the South Hero shore and, across the widest part of the lake, the Burlington skyline. What a contrast in the population density between here and there. Just as I contemplate a swim in the clear water, it begins to rain. We run for the shelter, along with the two lifeguards. I ask how busy the beach gets, and they assure us that it doesn't and that is just fine with them.

When the rain lets up, we leave Port Douglas and continue south through Corlaer Bay, which is named in honor of Arendt van Corlaer, who was known in the 1660s for his great kindness to the Iroquois. He was drowned here on his way north to visit Quebec. Along Brown Point, which forms the south end of Corlaer Bay, we paddle through several tiny, picturesque bays where old Adirondack-style cottages are squeezed along the shore.

Willsboro Bay. When we enter Willsboro Bay, the cliffs change dramatically. The gentle hills that we have been passing fall behind, and we approach rock walls that stretch up almost as far as we can see. These cliffs are majestic. They rise so steeply that I leave only enough space to dip my paddle between my kayak and the sheer walls. Stopping, I let go of my paddle and reach out to touch the cliffs at shoulder level. These palisades don't stop beneath the water's surface, but plunge down for another 150 feet (46 meters). The water is clear, but the depth makes it look black.

I can actually *feel* that we are in deep water. The surface sways gently; the sound is a *slurp, slurp* as the water moves against the sheer rock and into the cracks. Every crevice seems to hide its own little waterfall. I can see about two feet below the cliff wall where the solid mat of zebra mussels begins. To see the tops of the cliffs, I have to do a kayaker's backbend, leaning the back of my head as close to the deck as possible. A great cleft in one cliff slices the rock from the top to deep under the water. I cannot resist back-paddling into this breach until my kayak's stern bumps the inner end of the cleft and I am out of sight. I am alone, floating on black water and surrounded by solid rock.

The railroad bed crosses these cliffs, at some points blasted out of rock that has fallen far down to the water. It is hard to see what supports the track, an impression heightened when we see two trains creep along bridges. When this section of the Delaware and Hudson track was built in 1874, drillers were lowered 90 feet from the tops of cliffs in order to set their charges.

Feeling a surge of energy from the thrill of these views, we paddle across the marshy inner end of Willsboro Bay into a stiff wind to the Willsboro Bay New York Access. From there we look back at the distant cliffs, surprised to see how ordinary they look from this distance. Yet, when viewed from the perspective of our kayaks, the west side of Willsboro Bay is one of the most impressive landscapes on Lake Champlain.

▶ **Port Kent to Willsboro**

Schuyler Island
Wild and Wonderful

39

by Cathy Frank

■ **Launch site/Take out:** Port Kent Ferry Dock, Rt. 373, Port Kent, New York
■ **Distance:** 7 miles (11 kilometers)
■ **Alternative launch sites:** Port Douglas NY Boat Launch (Rt. 16, Port Douglas, New York)
■ **Places to stop:** Above launch sites and Schuyler Island (PT)
■ **Highlights:** A completely undeveloped island with only primitive campsites, cobble beaches and views to the north, east and south; wildlife is prevalent
■ **Route:** Launching from either Port Kent or Port Douglas and paddling along the fairly steep New York shoreline, Schuyler sits only half a mile offshore at its closest point, surrounded by water as deep as 125 feet. The entire shoreline is low and accessible. Combine this paddle with a trip between Port Kent and Willsboro Bay, if the weather is good (15.5 miles/25 kilometers).
■ **Comments:** Trembleau Point and the foothills of the Adirondacks block the view to the west, so storms can appear suddenly. This route is exposed to strong north and south wind and waves. Watch for poison ivy.

The Paddle:
It is a perfect island-hopping day—sunny, hot, and mostly calm. Schuyler sits about a half mile offshore. Its shoreline is low and sloping, with a shelf of shallow water around the island buffering it from the deeper water, up to 170 feet, just beyond. This 123-acre island (50 hectares), about a tenth the size of its northern neighbor Valcour, is also part of the Adirondack Park and has a number of primitive campsites. Heading clockwise around the island, we stop for a swim at a pebble beach about halfway down the east side.

Standing waist-deep in the warm water and taking in the view east to Colchester, Burlington, and South Hero, we debate whether we are looking at Sunset or Law Island, enjoying the challenge of looking at a familiar place from a different perspective. *Vroom!* The roar of fast-moving bass fishing boats racing up the middle of the lake interrupts us. We count thirty boats by the time they have all passed. We note the irony of racing noisily around the lake at breakneck speed and expecting the fish to be quietly waiting.

Rounding the south shore, we pause to look below the water. It is so clear that we can almost count the blades of grass growing between the submerged rocks. Several large cottonwood trees stand in the water, one growing at an angle contrary to one's sense of stability. The ice and waves take their toll on trees that dare to grow so close to the water, eroding the soil from around their roots, which often have rocks and sticks wedged between them. Fortunately, the eastern cottonwood that grows as tall as 100 feet (30 meters) is very tolerant of

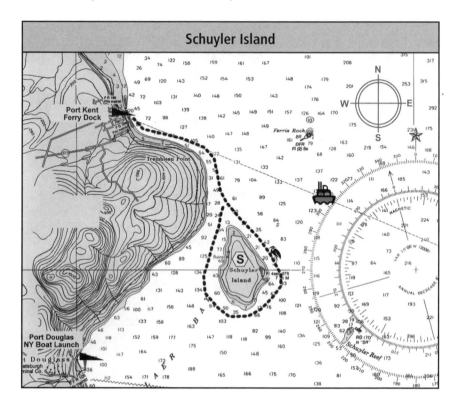

flooding, erosion, and flood debris. In late June and early July, their ubiquitous, white, fluffy seedpods look like snowflakes floating down from the sky. Interestingly, for trees this big, their root structure is disconcertingly shallow.

A long spit of pebble beach on the west side of Schuyler makes another great picnic spot and place to swim. Three cormorants perch on a high limb of a dead shoreline cottonwood just to the north. Are they thinking about colonizing the island? Please, no. There are so many large, healthy, deciduous trees on this lovely wild island, it would be a tragedy for them to be destroyed. Unfortunately, cormorants don't seem to do anything in moderation. (On the other hand, we humans do not have a very good track record either.)

After returning to the ferry dock, we wander over to the sandy public beach and look across the lake. We are reminded of the ferry that ran aground in the summer of 1977. Ferris Rock sits about 2.5 miles (4 kilometers) southeast of Port Kent and reaches nearly to the surface with surrounding depths of up to 150 feet (46 meters). It has ensnared many a boat over the years, the most famous of which is probably the Burlington–Port Kent ferryboat *The Valcour*. Crossing from Burlington at dusk, the ferry hit the rock. Once the distress calls were received, boats from Port Kent immediately went to help take passengers to shore. Their cars were removed from the stranded ferry by a crane on one of *The Valcour's*

▶ **Schuyler Island**

sister ships, and the ferry sat jammed up against the rock during a week of temporary repairs. It was eventually towed to Shelburne Shipyard. This lake of ours does not discriminate. Ferries as well as kayakers are vulnerable to its ways.

Schuyler Island cormorants.

<table>
<tr><td>40</td><td>The Four Brothers
Into the Middle</td></tr>
</table>

by Margy Holden

- **Launch site/Take out:** Indian Bay Marina ($), East Bay Rd., Willsboro, New York
- **Distance:** 10 miles (16 kilometers)
- **Alternative launch site:** Willsboro Bay NY Boat Launch (Boat Launch Rd. off Rt. 27, east side of bay, Willsboro, New York), Noblewood (PT day-use only, south of Willsboro, New York, off Rt. 22)
- **Places to stop:** None aside from launch sites
- **Highlights:** Views of the Adirondacks and the Green Mountains, Burlington Harbor, nesting area of several species of birds on islands decimated by the overpopulation of the double-crested cormorant
- **Route:** After passing along the settled and shallow east shore of Willsboro Bay, this route, filled with birds and waterfowl, heads around Willsboro Point and through deep water to, and around, the islands, which are close to the middle of the lake. There are no places to stop on this route.
- **Comments:** *Stay far enough from the islands so that the birds are not disturbed.* The route to these islands in the middle of the lake is exposed to the wind from all directions; this paddle should only be done in calm, clear weather by strong, experienced paddlers, as the islands are nearly in the middle of the broadest part of the lake.

The Paddle:

After launching in Willsboro Bay in light to moderate north wind, we find the water at the end of Willsboro Point rougher than expected. We pause, discuss, but never affirm continuing. We just do it. Is this good judgment, or are we prejudiced by all the effort it took to get here? We hope our decisions are informed by some version of good judgment.

Large, trailing waves challenge us all the way to the most northeastern island. To avoid concentrating on how hard we are working, I imagine that each of the Four Brothers should have a man's name. One could be Homer, another Harry. Apparently, the naming was more pragmatic. A man rowed out from Burlington Harbor to see these islands and called the first one he came to A, the second one B. You get the picture.

Ever so slowly the Four Brothers come closer. Vermont and the Green Mountains look far away behind us; New York and the Adirondacks seem equally distant. We paddle steadily, feeling vulnerable so far from shore. Finally reaching the lee of Island A, the waves give way to still water. Bird calls surround us, yet we are otherwise in the midst of profound silence, far from familiar things, the distant shores hidden beyond the other islands. For the first time in over an hour, our paddles still. I'm moved by the magic of these island mountain tips and curious about the raucous life around us.

▶ **The Four Brothers**

Four Brothers and the Changing Avian Population

The nesting bird population makes the Four Brothers a very important place. In the late 1970s, University of Vermont ornithologist Dr. David Capen began to monitor the islands, where he found a healthy and diverse population. Black ducks, mallards, gadwalls, and American widgeons nested here. More ring-billed gulls, but fewer herring gulls, and no greater black-back gulls could be found then. Great blue herons nested on one island, and black-crowned night herons on all four islands. Cattle egrets nested for a couple of years and then moved to Young Island off Grand Isle.

Times changed. The double-crested cormorant has made a huge impact on the Four Brothers. First identified on the Four Brothers in 1984 by Dr. Capen, by 2006 his team counted 3,499 cormorant nests, an increase of about 500 from the previous year. They have crowded out most other species and denuded these formerly wooded islands. Ducks have disappeared, and few egrets can be found. More predatory herring and black-backed gulls have increased. The Caspian tern, a new species here, proliferated to fifty nesting pairs in 2007, their population having doubled every year for the previous four. Deaths of Caspian Terns on Lake Ontario from botulism may be causing the survivors to move to Lake Champlain.

Islands A and B are covered with brush. Concerned about the waves on the trip back, we do not circumnavigate Island B, but later learn that it has the most diverse bird population. Dr. Capen counted 127 black-crowned night heron nests and two or three pairs of great egret nests here in 2006. In the past, cattle egrets have nested on the island, but none were found in 2007. Cormorants probably drive these other species out.

Island C. Cathy and I head toward Island C. The Capen team counted over 10,000 ring-billed gull nests on C in 2003, but cormorants and Caspian terns seem to be moving in. I think that I am far enough away from the island as I float, concentrating on the action on a spit of land. Suddenly, Caspian terns rise up from behind the top of the cliffs and circle above. Did I drift so close to shore that I frightened them? Two or three greater black-back gulls swoop in and disappear over the top of the cliff. Before I can wonder what is happening, a greater black-back gull swaggers to the edge of the cliff, grasping a tern chick in its beak. The chick's head, body, and legs dangle in a way that signals that any struggle is over. The gull swaggers in and out of my line of vision on the top of the cliff with that limp body hanging from its beak. I watch helplessly, wondering if the protective

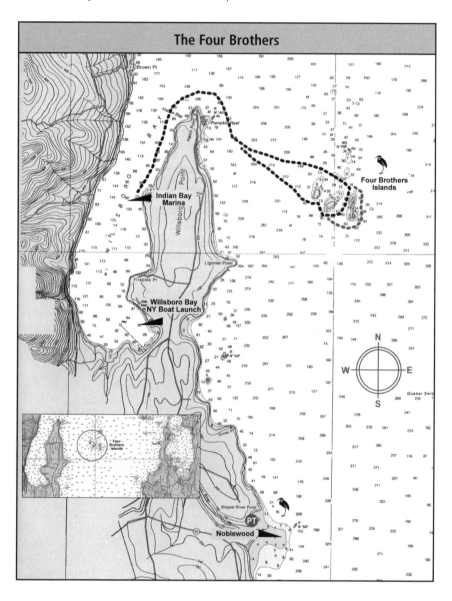

The Four Brothers

parents might have remained on the nest and the chick would have been safe had I stayed farther from shore. How simple it is to upset the delicate balance in the natural world. Scientists need to come close to the islands to collect data in order to help this ecosystem, but kayakers don't.

Island D. Not all of the inhabitants of western Island D are cormorants. A black-crowned night heron, unperturbed by our presence, watches from its safe haven on the cliff. Dr. Capen says that they fly here from Island B, where they nest, because they have learned that clumsy young cormorants will drop their fish, letting the faster black-crowned night herons steal them. The herring gulls prefer to nest on the other islands, where there is more space.

Island D looks like a crowded marina, because its leafless, almost branchless, bare tree trunks stick up like masts. These trees supported twenty-two great blue heron nests in 2006, but today cormorants occupy every other limb. The great blue herons will have to move on when the trees fall, but the adaptable cormorants have already begun to nest on the ground.

The wind and the waves hit us again as we leave the lee of Island D. Making slow progress back to shore, we pass Pumpkin Reef and look forward to the

Four Brothers cormorant colony.

peaceful lee inside Willsboro Point. We defensively keep an eye on the boat traffic, knowing we are hard to see in large wave troughs. Suddenly, a huge cigarette boat turns sharply, so close that his wake hits us from two sides. Luckily, we remain upright. Was that on purpose? Did he not see us? Or is he thoughtless?

The relative calm of Willsboro Bay is a welcome relief as we paddle the lee inside Willsboro Point to the Indian Bay Marina. Tired but hungry, we spontaneously decide to reward ourselves at the Marina restaurant. As women who take pride in healthy diets, we split French fries and fried onion rings. Enjoy now, suffer later. We've been to the Four Brothers!

Out in the middle—Four Brothers.

▶ The Four Brothers

by Margy Holden

■ **Launch site:** Willsboro Bay NY Boat Launch, Boat Launch Rd. off Rt. 27, east side of bay, Willsboro, New York
■ **Distance:** 16 miles (25.7 kilometers)
■ **Take out:** Beggs Park (PT day-use only, Lake St., ¼ mile south of ferry dock, Essex, New York)
■ **Alternative launch sites:** Noblewood (PT day-use only, south of Willsboro, off Rt. 22), Indian Bay Marina ($, snack bar, East Bay Rd., Willsboro, New York)
■ **Places to stop:** Above launch sites, and restaurants and shops in Essex that are a few steps from Beggs Park (on Rt. 22, Lake Shore Rd., Essex). The Old Dock Restaurant has docks.
■ **Highlights:** Significant architecture, mouth of Bouquet River, Noblewood Park beach and walking trails, wildlife, picturesque Essex with shops and restaurants
■ **Route:** After following the settled and shallow east shore of Willsboro Bay, this multifeatured route rounds Willsboro Point to follow the sparsely settled, pre-served but not public shore south to the sandy spit at the mouth of the Bouquet River and Noblewood Park. From there, it continues south along somewhat more settled shoreline to Essex. The only place to stop on this route, Noblewood, is 10 miles (16 kilometers) from Willsboro Bay. The well-protected Bouquet River offers an alternative route.
■ **Comments:** Much of this undeveloped shore has been privately conserved and is not accessible to the public. Most of the route is exposed to north and south winds. There is shallow water close to shore, but under the cliffs of Willsboro Bay it drops off quickly.

The Paddle:

On the east side of Willsboro Bay, small cottages nudge each other along a shore heavily populated in the summer. The Indian Bay Marina, a popular destination for boaters wanting an informal place to eat, is about halfway out on the point. I catch sight of a white-belted kingfisher, a kingbird, and a couple of great blue herons. In the clear water I occasionally see the flick of a fish tail as it darts away.

At the end of Willsboro Point, the open lake seems vast. Burlington is about 7 miles away (11.3 kilometers). Schuyler Island and Trembleau Point sit in the near view to the north, but beyond them the lake looks endless. The Champlain Islands are bumps on the northwest horizon. The lake is deep here, dropping quickly to over one hundred feet (30.5 meters). It isn't any deeper than Willsboro Bay (and who cares once it is over our head?), but it "feels" different paddling here. I take deep breaths, stay close to shore, and feel slightly giddy.

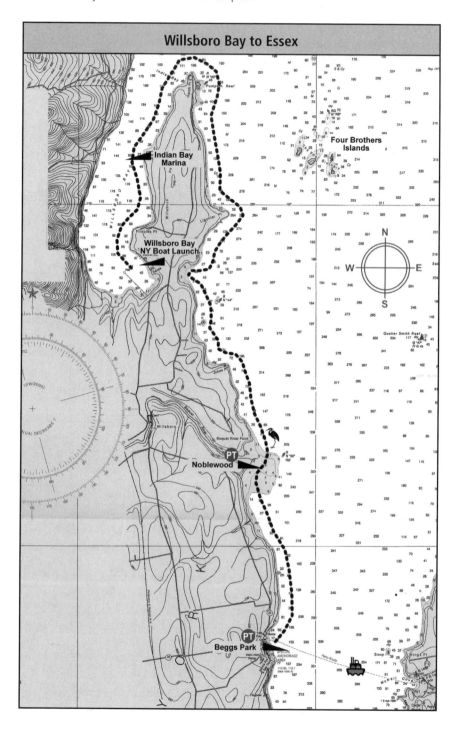

Willsboro Bay to Essex

Sitting just off the northeast side of Willsboro Point, a can marks Pumpkin Reef. We are tempted to return and paint a jack-o-lantern face on it. To the east, the Four Brothers Islands appear to float on the surface of the lake. Beyond them, Mt. Mansfield and Camel's Hump rise majestically. The scenery inspires us as we paddle steadily toward Ligonier Point.

Scragwood, the rambling nineteenth-century home built by Solomon and Rhoda Adsit Clark, stands out on Ligonier Point. Stone from the Clarks' Willsboro Point quarry was used for the Brooklyn Bridge, the Burlington breakwater, and several Lake Champlain lighthouses.

Flat Rock Camp, built by A. G. Paine in 1890 and the only Adirondack Great Camp left on Lake Champlain, graces Jones Point. It gets its name from its location on a huge mass of smooth rock that is so solid that it almost prevents any vegetation from growing. With its many rooms and chimneys, the camp is the very definition of "rambling." Paine bought the land in 1885 for $500, which was considered a deal by the seller, because there was so little soil that it wasn't good for farming. Today we pay for the view.

The Boquet River. The Paine family owned 1,000 acres (405 hectares) with 3 miles (5 kilometers) of shoreline that stretch from the southeastern part of Willsboro Point all the way to the Boquet River. The land has been conserved, which means it can never be developed, but it still remains in private hands and is posted, reserved for the use of the owners.

The mouth of the Bouquet River is the first place that is open to the public since leaving Willsboro Bay. A sun-warmed sand spit reaches far out into the lake. Ring-billed gulls, a few great black-backed gulls, and the cormorants squawk, but seem content to stay on one side of the spit while we relax on the other. The Boquet River flows lazily into Lake Champlain.

After lunch we paddle upstream. Huge cottonwood and sycamore trees overhang the river, making dappled shadows on the water. Painted turtles watch us from their sunning perches on fallen trees. In the fall, freshwater Atlantic salmon swim upstream to spawn. It is hard to believe that this slow-moving Boquet River can be a raging torrent in its 280-square-mile (72,520-hectares) watershed. Historians like to debate the origin of its name, which some believe was for a bouquet of flowers, while others assert that the name honors Charles Boquet, who was a benevolent guide for seventeenth-century French missionaries.

This land was first owned by William Gilliland, a New York City merchant who traveled north from New York in 1765 to establish a great estate. Attracted by the beauty of the Boquet River, he bought 12,000 acres (4,856 hectares) and recruited tenant settlers from New York. For a decade Willsboro, as his settlement was named, prospered. Unfortunately, the impending Revolutionary War caused the 100 settlers to flee for their safety. They returned, but Gilliland lost much of his land and fortune in the war and died a poor man in 1796, when he strayed from a trail in winter and froze to death.

Bouquet River delta.

Noblewood Park, with an inviting beach and bathhouse, adjoins the Boquet River on the south side. This is a stop on the Paddlers Trail. Hermit thrush and black-throated green warblers nest here. Close to the water we see great blue herons and belted kingfishers. Great egrets and Caspian terns also visit from the Four Brothers Islands. Rare migrants, including the black-headed gull, little gull, whimbrel, and red knot, also stop here.

It isn't far to Essex, arguably the most picturesque town on Lake Champlain. In the summer it is bustling with ice-cream stands, gift shops, and antique stores. In the winter the population drops to around 800 (one-third of what it was in 1850) and many of the stores close. In the early 1800s, Essex was a ship-building center, had a tannery, three "asheries" that made 300 tons of potash annually, and was a locus for lumber and iron shipments. Evidence of this early prosperity is still visible in the unique collection of Federal, Greek-revival, and Victorian buildings constructed of local stone from nearby quarries. Ancient fossils can be found in some of the building stone. Essex is on the National Register of historic places.

We pause to avoid the surge of the Essex/Charlotte ferry, which has run a regular route here since 1790. After admiring the waterfront, we take our kayaks out at the town landing.

Our paddle today has had something in common with the Shelburne shoreline directly east across the lake. We have seen fine buildings built by, and enjoyed the open space purchased by, prosperous people of the nineteenth century. The land and buildings have been preserved by other prosperous people in the twentieth century.

▶ **Willsboro Bay to Essex**

Westport to Essex
Steep and Deep

42

by Cathy Frank

■ **Launch site:** Westport NY Boat Launch, Rt. 22, north side of Westport, New York
■ **Distance:** 14.5 miles (23.3 kilometers)
■ **Take out:** Beggs Park (PT day-use only, Lake St., ¼ mile south of ferry dock, Essex, New York)
■ **Alternative launch sites:** Lee Park Playground and Nature Walk (Washington St., off Rt. 9—VERY STEEP road—Westport, New York)
■ **Places to stop:** Above launch sites and Partridge Harbor, Barn Rock Harbor (PT, called Barn Rock Cove, and another stop just north of it called Barn Rock North), Palisades (PT), Snake Den Harbor (PT), Ore Bed Harbor (PT day-use only), Wallon Bay (PT), Old Dock Restaurant, (off Rt. 22, Lake Shore Rd.), all in Essex
■ **Highlights:** All the harbors above, plus Barn Rock trails, old quarries, Palisades, Split Rock
■ **Route:** This linear route, arguably the most spectacular on Lake Champlain, follows an undeveloped shore that rises steeply to 1,000 feet. Beneath us, the depth plunges from 200 feet near shore to 400 feet farther out, one of the deepest points in the lake. Small, deepwater harbors are interspersed along the cliffs. Split Rock marks the end of the cliff area and, from there north to Essex, the shore is lined with camps and homes.
■ **Comments:** To fully enjoy its wonders and for safety reasons, this trip is best paddled in calm weather. Do not do this trip if N/NW or S/SW winds are moderate to strong, or storms are predicted. The lake narrows between Split Rock and Thompson's Point, funneling winds and waves to a higher pitch and, except for the harbors listed above, there is NO place to take out in an emergency.

The Paddle:
"Make sure you paddle Split Rock on a really good day," admonishes our good friend, Peter Espenshade, former Executive Director of the Lake Champlain Land Trust. So, on one near-perfect day in early July we undertake this much-anticipated paddle.

Glancing back, we can't help but appreciate how sweet Westport's location is, nestled at the end of a broad, protected bay with its buildings blending into the immediate landscape and under a mountainous Adirondack backdrop. We pass some unassuming vintage camps built close to shore. A sloping rock ledge continues down into the clear water, competing with the reflection of the evergreens to give the illusion that the trees are covered with zebra mussels.

A quick look at the chart confirms that we are rapidly approaching what can best be described as the "steep and deep" part of Lake Champlain, with water depths of over 300 feet (91 meters) near the shore. The almost solidly packed

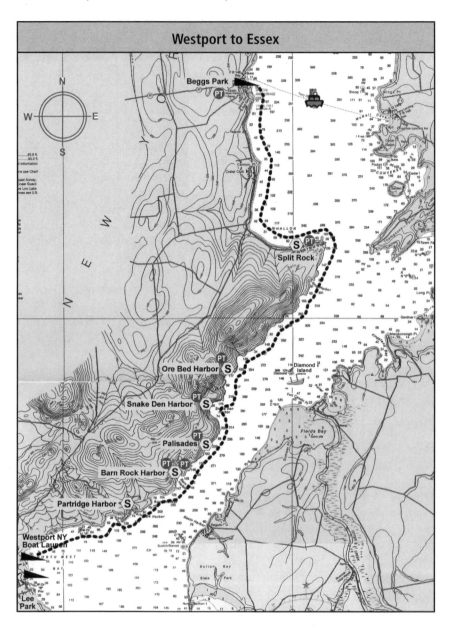

Westport to Essex

contour lines on the chart show a shoreline that quickly rises to over 800 feet (244 meters). Hunger Bay and then Partridge and Rock Harbors slip by as we pass a large sleeping turtle and several heron.

Just offshore the 75-foot-high (23-meter) rock on the north side of Barn Rock Harbor, a large yellow buoy marks the dive site for the passenger steam-

▶ **Westport to Essex**

boat *Champlain II*, which sank here in July 1875. With a jolting thud the ship ran smack into the rock shore. Fortunately no life was lost.

This steep shoreline with plunging water depths offers small, deep harbors scattered along an otherwise impenetrable shoreline. As we travel north, the rock cliffs rise higher. At the Palisades, I drop back to see if I can get a picture of the entire rock face as Margy paddles toward it for scale. I have to move so far back that she becomes too small to photograph. She cools herself under a narrow waterfall easily 100 feet high (30 meters) and gently trickling down a naturally creviced rock. Beneath us the water is crystal clear, but we have no way of knowing how far down we are looking because we cannot see rocks, or weeds, or anything indicating the bottom. A quick look at the chart indicates that the water here plunges to as much as 180 feet (55 meters). We reach our arms out and touch the wall to steady ourselves as we try to bend our necks back far enough to see the top of the cliff. It is almost impossible. This is a powerful place. Then we look down again into the water, trying to comprehend how high this cliff rises from lake bottom to mountaintop. Finally, slowly, silently, we resume paddling.

Moments later we are startled by the ear-shattering noise of two, large, four-engine planes racing up the lake at low altitude. We are both unnerved by the intrusion, but our immediate environment is too compelling to remain distracted.

We reach sinister-sounding Snake Den Harbor just in time for lunch. We pull our kayaks up on the small, steep, pebble beach, unable to avoid the sound of scraping plastic against rock. A good lunch, short swim, and no sightings (thankfully) of the harbor denizens (this is a natural habitat for the eastern rattlesnake), and then we are back on the water.

Ore Bed Harbor. The next harbor north, surprisingly unmarked on the navigational map, has much more history than is obvious today. Evidence of its short, intense, mining history between 1853 and 1888 remains buried beneath the water and covered by vegetation on the mountainside. In its day, Split Rock Mountain had one of the largest deposits of magnetic ore in New York. The iron ore could simply be blasted from the cliff, rolled down the mountainside, and put on large boats docked on the shore of this deepwater harbor.

It is hard to image several hundred miners and their families living and working here, not to mention the machinery needed for the mining operation. The mine and living quarters for the workers were 700 feet (213 meters) up the mountain, connected by a series of ladder-like stairs to the activities at the harbor. Imagine navigating those stairs in the dead of winter. The mine failed in 1888. In our wildest dreams we could not have concocted such a history for this pristine site.

Taking our eyes off this compelling shoreline for just a moment, we notice small Diamond Island off to our right. Its large beacon helps boaters navigate this part of the lake. Yellow dive buoys mark two shipwrecks available for divers to explore.

Nature's paintbrush—Split Rock.

Farther north, the cliff becomes less steep. A large bird flies above us, its white head highlighted against the dark green of the tree-covered mountainside. We eliminate it as an osprey or eagle, because of its coloring, size, and shape, although both eagles and ospreys nest in this area. When our white-headed bird reappears and lands on a top branch of a dead tree, it is easily identified as a peregrine falcon. Margy spots what could be a nest—a horizontal ledge on the cliff with lots of white streaks beneath it, not unlike what we saw on Cloak Island off Isle La Motte.

Farther north, more iron decorates the shoreline rock. We pass Grog Harbor, the last of these wonderfully pirate haven-like bays, and see the red, skeletal tower of Split Rock Light. Within minutes we are at the gap between Split Rock Point and the huge rock that sits no more than 10 to 15 feet (3 to 5 meters) from the shore, as if cleaved from its source by a giant bolt of lightning sent by an angry god. We can see the foothills of Essex through the gap. It looks like a small channel might be navigable during high water. The rock itself is 30 feet high (9 meters). The Abenaki called it *Tobapsqua*, "The pass through the rock." To Native Americans it was a boundary between the Mohawk and Algonquin tribes. Whenever someone from one nation crossed the boundary into the other nation's territory, he threw a food offering into the water as a gesture of peace.

▶ **Westport to Essex**

The trip around the rock brings even more surprises. The iron, for which this shore is so well known, looks as if a master sculptor has folded it into this large rock. On the northeast side, the dark iron streaks look like a huge Asian letter painted onto the rock. On the far side, thick swirls of rust-orange color contrast sharply with the grayish, light rock that makes up the core of this large structure, looking like the iron flowed into place.

Split Rock Mountain, including 2 miles (3.2 kilometers) of shoreline we have just paddled, was conserved in 1993, thanks to the efforts of the Open Space Institute, Lake Champlain Land Trust, Adirondack Nature Conservancy, and the Keene Valley Land Trust.

Surprisingly, what feels like a remote place to us, based on the distance we have traveled and the marvels we have seen, is only 3 miles (5 kilometers) from Essex, New York, and just one mile from Thompsons Point, Vermont.

Compared to this extraordinary shore, the rest of the trip to Essex is uneventful, but peaceful and pleasant. At some point we stop and look back at Split Rock Point and are surprised at how ordinary it looks from a distance.

Amazing. The entire day has been amazing.

Through Split Rock.

Port Henry to Westport
The Iron Shore

by Cathy Frank

- ◼ **Launch site:** Port Henry NY Boat Launch, off Rt. 9N just north of Port Henry, New York; if approaching from the north, the sign is after the launch site
- ◼ **Distance**: 12 miles (19 kilometers)
- ◼ **Take out:** Westport NY Boat Launch (Rt. 22, north side of Westport, New York)
- ◼ **Alternative launch sites:** None aside from launch sites
- ◼ **Places to stop:** Above launch sites and Cole Island
- ◼ **Highlights:** Iron Center Museum in Port Henry (Park Place off Rt. 22 by car), spectacular orange- and rust-colored iron-filled rock along the shore, wildlife at Stacey Brook and Cole Island
- ◼ **Route:** This linear route features a sharply rising shoreline from Westport to Stacey Brook, with tracks of the Delaware & Hudson following the shore. From Stacy Brook north, the topography becomes gentler and dotted with older Adirondack-style camps. Water depth along the shore averages 20–50 feet. There is only one stopping point—Cole Island, 4 miles (6.5 kilometers) from Westport and 7 miles (11 kilometers) from Port Henry. For a shorter loop trip, put in at Westport Boat Launch and paddle to Cole Island and Stacy Brook (9 miles/14.5 kilometers round-trip).
- ◼ **Comments:** This route is exposed to strong north and south wind and waves.

The Paddle:

The sleepy little village of Port Henry today is best known for its sightings of Champ and its outstanding ice fishing, but in the latter part of the nineteenth century it was a bustling port for the iron industry. Nestled into the foothills of the Adirondack Mountains with a direct view of the Champlain Bridge to the southeast, it marks the end of the broad lake, the last stop before the lake becomes narrow and river-like on the other side of the bridge.

With the slightest of breezes at our backs and a clear sky overhead, it feels good to be on the water as we head north, following our old friend the Delaware and Hudson Railroad. The riprap supporting the train track is occasionally punctuated with rocks mottled with rust and orange spots. One particular area of naturally occurring rock looks like a giant pallet of vivid brown, yellow, and orange oil paints mixed into a variety of exquisite colors by some larger-than-life artist. The entire rock surface is mirrored with such richness by the water that specks of yellow pollen on the water's surface are the only clue that it is a reflection.

As we progress north, the rock cliffs behind the tracks grow to 100 feet (30 meters) in height and then subside as the land starts to level off about 4 miles (6 kilometers) into our paddle. We pass several brooks (Mullen and Beaver), and once the railroad turns inland we begin to see camps again. Cedars firmly rooted

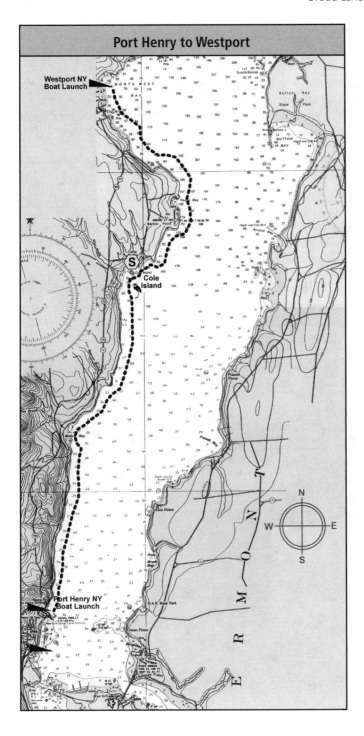

Port Henry to Westport

in the vertical face of a rock ledge grow through the deck of one camp. Which came first, the camp or the cedars?

Cole Bay and Cole Island. At Cole Bay at the mouth of Stacey Brook, the unusually high lake level has created a temporary lagoon that allows us to paddle among the usually land-bound trees and circumnavigate a large beaver dam. Some maples are already starting to turn color from the stress of their wet feet. This is a good area to spot wildlife. We are surprised by one, large, sleepy, map turtle, which shows no fear of us as we pass three feet from his temporary log perch.

Cole Island is a small, forested island about a quarter of a mile offshore, owned by the State of New York. It is the first really good place to stop since leaving Port Henry 7 miles (11 kilometers) back. Charmed by this island and delighted to be out of our kayaks, we linger over lunch. Historically this island was not always so peaceful, however. It is one of many places where the Mohawks tortured the Jesuit missionary Father Isaac Jogues (1607–1646). Amazingly, after fourteen months of captivity and torture, Father Jogues escaped and eventually returned to Canada—where he once again sought to convert the Mohawks to Christianity. When he was killed in 1646, he had failed to convert a single person.

Into the trees.

▶ **Port Henry to Westport**

Camp Dudley, the oldest continuously operating boys' camp in the country, established in 1885, is just to the north of Cole Island. With 2 miles (3 kilometers) of well-maintained and diverse shoreline, it is a treasure for the campers who have been fortunate enough to attend. One can only imagine how valuable the land must be, compared to how little it probably cost at the time it was purchased more than 120 years ago.

Farther north, the Westport shore is dotted with some old and newer Adirondack-style camps. Many are literally right on the water, and some don't even stop there. Westport was settled in 1804 and has a lumber and mining history, as well as now-defunct medicinal springs that purportedly had healing capacities. Today Westport is a picturesque and popular resort town.

Cole Island.

44 | **Crown Point, Bulwagga Bay, Port Henry**
Unique Places

by Margy Holden

- **Launch site/Take out:** Crown Point Campground Boat Launch ($), Bridge Rd., Crown Point, New York
- **Distance:** 11 miles (17.7 kilometers)
- **Alternative launch sites:** Chimney Point F&W Area (VT Rt. 17, Addison, Vermont), Port Henry NY Launch
- **Places to stop:** Above launch sites and Crown Point State Historic Site (Fort St. Frederic Museum), Port Henry Pier
- **Highlights:** Crown Point State Historic Site (Fort St. Frederic Museum), Iron Center Museum in Port Henry, wildlife, fossils in Bulwagga Bay, possible sighting of sunken drawboat, views of the Adirondacks, Green Mountains, Champlain Bridge and agricultural views, Champlain Memorial
- **Route:** From the launch site, this nature-filled route turns north and winds around Crown Point, offering dramatic views from beneath the bridge and the ruins of Fort St. Frederic, then rounds the long spit that was the old railroad bridge, circles Bulwagga Bay, and then heads north to the pier in Port Henry. From there, the choice is to return along the shallow shore or to cut diagonally through deep water back to the launch site.
- **Comments:** In a north wind the north side of Crown Point can have waves crashing against it, making it perilous for paddlers. The rest of the route is protected from most winds. In a south wind the return from Port Henry would best be done along the shore.

The Paddle:

Historic Crown Point, wild Bulwagga Bay, and the town of Port Henry each have something to offer. We launch our kayaks at the muddy parking lot, step over dead fish, push through the milfoil mire, and paddle out to clear water. The Champlain Bridge soars above us, with the view up the broad lake to the north framed by the cliffs of New York and the rolling fields of Vermont. The bridge, built in 1929, is a relative newcomer. Crown Point, on the New York side, and Chimney Point, on the Vermont side, together stand guard at the beginning of the narrow southern part of the lake. This has been a natural stopping point since man first traveled Lake Champlain.

Encounters. Many historians believe that Samuel de Champlain, his soldiers, and his Algonquin allies encountered the rival Iroquois here in 1609. After a night of feasting and dancing within sight of each other, the two forces engaged in a deadly battle. When a loud-sounding weapon instantly killed their chiefs, the remaining Iroquois, who had never seen a gun, fled.

▶ **Crown Point, Bulwagga Bay, Port Henry**

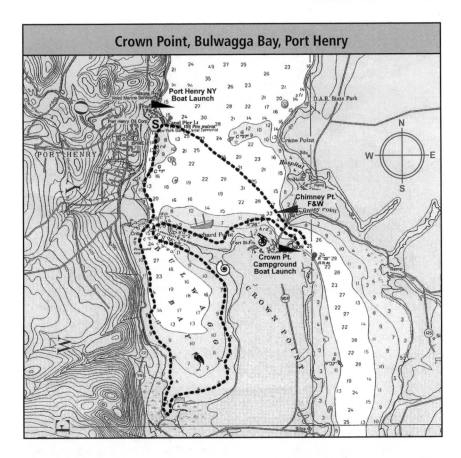

Crown Point's subsequent long history visibly lives on. We can see the extensive ruins of the redoubt of the British fort on the shore above us, while the distant fields remind us that this land provided a hospitable setting for French settlers close to their earlier fort. Quiet now, it incites our imaginations to remember that during much of the 1700s men from three countries fought to control this part of Lake Champlain. From canoes to sailing ships, expeditions of defense and offense set out from here.

There is a small but excellent museum on the grounds of Fort St. Frederic, accessible by both road and water. Today the soldiers and their families are gone, and Native Americans no longer arrive in their canoes, but it is still possible to wander about the ramparts and imagine this French community of the 1700s.

Leaving the ghosts of history behind, we paddle around Orchard Point to get our first glimpse of the long spit of land that almost cuts Bulwagga Bay off from the rest of the lake. We are intrigued by the word "Bulwagga." An investment company, an anchor, and a bookstore share its name, so we know that we're not alone in our affection for it.

Strategic Crown Point

The strategic importance of Crown Point cannot be missed. Jutting out into Lake Champlain, with Chimney Point a half mile away, it forms the door to the South Lake. Initially, the British established a trading post here, but the French, recognizing its key location, took over and built a simple wood stockade on Chimney Point in 1730. They began Fort St. Frederic on Crown Point three years later. With masonry walls eighteen feet high and a tower, or redoubt, with twenty cannon, it housed sixty soldiers, a blacksmith, a baker, a priest, and a laundrywoman. One entered the fort across a retractable drawbridge over a dry moat. A stone sawmill, fortified with four cannons, was later built nearby and ground locally grown grain for the soldiers.

The French were encouraged to settle near the fort and across the narrows at Chimney Point to buttress their claim to this area. Peter Kalm, a Swedish botanist who stopped at the fort in 1749, recorded that a house, three years of provisions, tools, and a cow were given to each soldier upon retirement. In addition, active soldiers were encouraged to grow kitchen gardens and to keep farm animals. With a priest in residence, Iroquois and Abenaki, as well as the French, came to worship here. The number of births, deaths, and baptisms recorded at Fort St. Frederic demonstrates how many gathered around Crown and Chimney points under the French flag. Evidence of roads and cellar holes that bordered Bulwagga Bay and stretched inland the length of the peninsula could still be seen a century later. Fort St. Frederic became a way station where settlers captured from English towns in southern New England were taken, but treated kindly, on the often-brutal forced marches to Quebec.

The French enjoyed this area for less than three decades. In 1759, Fort St. Frederic was abandoned and blown up, and the settlements and fields were burned as the French soldiers and settlers fled north to Quebec just in front of the advancing British. The victorious British, under Amherst, began immediately to build the largest fort in the Americas, which encompassed seven acres on Crown Point. Construction continued until it was almost finished but, since the British were now in firm control of Lake Champlain, the importance of this defensive location diminished except as a staging place for raids into Quebec. In 1773 a fire demolished much of the fort and it was never rebuilt. In 1775, Seth Warner of the Green Mountain Boys captured Fort St. Frederic shortly after the daring takeover of Fort

▶ **Crown Point, Bulwagga Bay, Port Henry**

Ticonderoga at the beginning of the Revolutionary War. But the days when Crown Point was the major defensive position ended when the rebellious Americans decided to move their main defensive position to Ticonderoga.

Today, remaining fortifications and a museum make it a worthwhile place to visit.

A Railroad Drawboat. The natural spit of land, obviously augmented by crushed rock and pilings, is the remains of an 1871 railroad bed that was built to move iron ore from mines above Port Henry to the smelters on Crown Point. Part of that railroad structure was a 250-foot-by-34-foot (76-meter-by-10-meter) drawboat. When a train needed to pass, the drawboat was aligned with the land-based tracks. The rest of the time the drawboat could be drawn away, allowing boats to pass. Winter ice destroyed the railroad four years later. For many years it was thought that the drawboat lay on the bottom, 25 feet (7.6 meters) beneath the surface of the water, almost completely intact, covered in zebra mussels. In 2009, however, it was discovered that the sunken craft is a barge that actually dates from a much later time and may have been sunk after having been used in the 1929 construction of the Champlain Bridge.

Bulwagga Bay.

Regardless of the barge's origin, divers in 2000 noticed sheepshead and yellow perch feeding on the zebra mussels that cover it. Encouraged that these fish might be part of a solution to the zebra-mussel problem, researchers at the School of Natural Resources at the University of Vermont have found zebra mussels in the stomachs of these and other species. This submerged barge, lying beneath our kayaks, is still useful, the site of research that could provide some answers to one of the serious problems on Lake Champlain.

Bulwagga Bay. Along the low, wooded, eastern shore of Bulwagga Bay, a flat rock surface just above the water's edge looks familiar. Scrambling onto land, we are rewarded by the sight of gastropods spread across the rocks under our feet. The area is small, but extraordinary. These 450-million-year-old fossils are clearly outlined in stone.

The shallow water of Bulwagga Bay provides a rich habitat for waterfowl and the plants and fish on which they feed. At the south end of the bay, great blue herons and egrets rise from hidden fishing spots. Aquatic plants are adapted to specific water depths, making this part of the bay look like a layered, aquatic garden. In the front row, we push carefully through lily pads, stopping to peer into an occasional creamy bloom. Behind, undulating clumps of pink knotweed with their tiny pink blooms mass into visible color. Low

Port Henry.

▶ **Crown Point, Bulwagga Bay, Port Henry**

bushes, too far away to identify, back the knotweed. At the innermost, inaccessible end of the bay are the tall trees. The water is opaque and appears to be filled with a combination of duckweed, algae, and possibly suspended mud. The west shore of Bulwagga Bay with its 600-foot cliffs stands in sharp contrast to the low-slung east shore.

A metallic taste and an irritating sulfur odor inject a literally sour note. Is this a reaction to output from the Ticonderoga paper mill, drifting our way in the light south wind? I don't want to think about what the impact is on the residents of Port Henry, who must experience this every time there is a southerly breeze.

Port Henry. We paddle straight north from Bulwagga Bay to Port Henry, where some of the old buildings reveal evidence of the more prosperous nineteenth century. Travelers in those days described Port Henry as a bustling city. Roughly 300,000 tons of iron ore a year were mined from the surrounding hills. Now, bats that summer in Vermont seek shelter in the deserted mines in the winter. The conical shapes of the slag heaps stand out as a reminder of the earlier activity.

We visited the small but excellent Iron Center Museum, accessible from Route 9 in Port Henry. Former mineworkers Les and Bill gave us a tour and told personal stories that clearly illustrated the history. Getting to work in the mines was literally a deep experience, accentuated even more if thought about from the point of view of a modern kayaker. Those miners, entering in the hills above Port Henry, traveled down the mine shaft for 1,050 feet to reach the same level of nearby Lake Champlain. From there, that mine shaft dove 2,250 farther down to the work site. This was accomplished with nineteenth-century technology!

Port Henry's population swells when the ice freezes. Fishermen tow shanties of all sizes and description out onto the ice, and instant villages sprout up—complete with street signs. It is rumored that possibly as many fish are caught as bottles of spirits are consumed. Port Henry has adopted Champ as its mascot, claiming that there are more sightings from its shores than from any other place on the lake. The Port Henry fishing pier, which must be one of the largest on Lake Champlain, makes a good viewing and stopping point.

It's calm enough to leave the shoreline and head directly back to the launch site at Crown Point. The water ripples gently under our kayaks. I turn to watch the whirlpools from my paddle float behind, torn between remaining in the present, a part of the water and the air, or imagining again that we are a part of a French or Native American party approaching Fort St. Frederic.

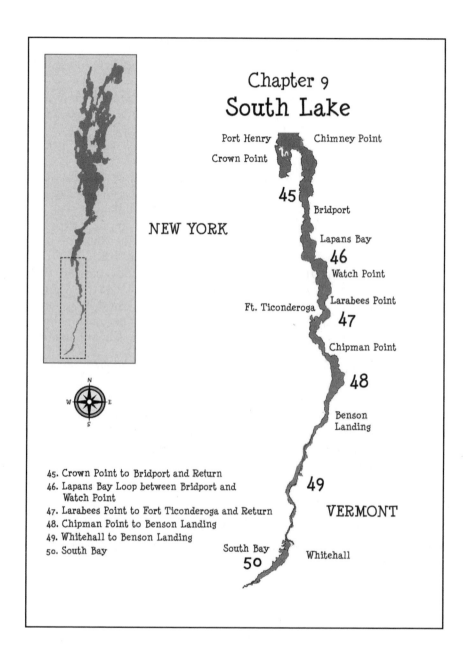

Chapter 9
South Lake

Port Henry   Chimney Point
Crown Point

45

NEW YORK

Bridport

Lapans Bay
46
Watch Point

Larabees Point
Ft. Ticonderoga
47

Chipman Point

48

Benson
Landing

49

VERMONT

South Bay
50   Whitehall

Chapter IX

South Lake

L ake Champlain continually narrows in its southernmost 30 miles (48 kilometers) until it looks more like a river than a lake. The lake between Crown and Chimney points and Benson Landing, 15 miles to the south, is never much more than a mile wide, and between points it cinches to half a mile. South of Benson Landing, the lake narrows even more. The sparsely populated west shore marks the beginning of the foothills of the Adirondack Mountains. Lush farms line the very northern end of the Vermont side of the South Lake, but cliffs and wetlands replaced the farms farther south. We make three circle trips north of Benson Landing, and one from Whitehall to Benson Landing.

South Bay.

Crown Point to Bridport and Return	45
Into the Narrows	

by Margy Holden

■ **Launch site/Take out:** Crown Point Campground Boat Launch ($), Bridge Rd., Crown Pt., New York
■ **Distance:** 14 miles (22.5 kilometers)
■ **Alternative launch site:** Chimney Point F&W Area (VT Rt. 17, Addison, Vermont), McCuen Slang F&W Area (Rt. 125, Addison, New York), Monitor Bay Park (Monitor Bay Rd. off Station Rd. off Rt. 9, Crown Point, New York), Bridport Town Boat Launch (Jones Dock Rd., Bridport, Vermont, down a steep gravel incline that looks like the private driveway to houses)
■ **Places to stop:** None aside from launch sites
■ **Highlights:** Crown Point, New York State Historic Site (Fort St. Frederic Museum), Chimney Point, Vermont State Historic Site, Champlain Memorial Lighthouse, agricultural views, Putnam Creek marsh
■ **Route:** The circle route turns south from the launch site, passes the Champlain Memorial Lighthouse and follows the shallow New York shore through some small bays to the large concrete abutments in the narrows. Crossing there to the Vermont side, the route goes north along an agricultural shallow shore to the Champlain Bridge, where there is a short, deepwater crossing to the launch site.
■ **Comments:** North and south winds can present a paddling workout, but high waves generally do not build here except in the deepwater crossing. Milfoil can make paddling challenging. There is no public land on the New York shore.

The Paddle:
Looking north from the launch site, Lake Champlain opens up into broad bays and cliffs stretching to the horizon, while Chimney Point looks a stone's throw away. Looking south, it is a different Lake Champlain. Launching from below the campsite in the historic park, we paddle our kayaks through a collection of milfoil, algae, duckweed, and a bit of jetsam. Luckily, we are immediately distracted.

The Champlain Monument. We've looked down at the Champlain Monument from the Champlain Point Bridge so many times and not really seen it. Today we learn that perspective is everything. Seen from the water, the monument soars above us, silhouetted against the sky. Back in 1858 the United States government built a 55-foot-high (17-meter), octagonal lighthouse here to guide ships around Crown Point. The lighthouse's metamorphosis into a work of art began in 1909 when local dignitaries decided to rebuild it to memorialize the 300-year anniversary of Samuel de Champlain's arrival on Lake Champlain.

Now, huge, granite, Doric columns and elaborate marble parapet and cornice look more like a monument to royalty that one would expect to find in a

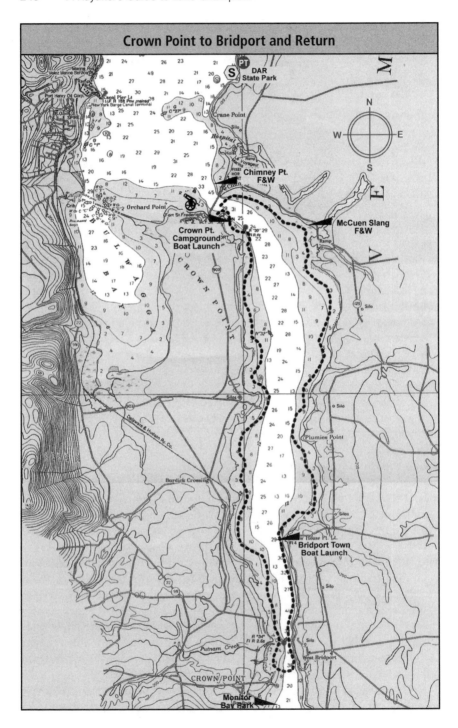

Crown Point to Bridport and Return

► **Crown Point to Bridport and Return**

major city. The French Renaissance design celebrates the style popular during Champlain's lifetime. A Carl Heber statue of the explorer stands tall in front of the columns. A crouching Native American flanks one side of Champlain, with an armored French soldier on the other. High above them the Crown Point light still shines.

Incredibly, under Heber's sculpture we see a work by Auguste Rodin, the famous French sculptor whose work usually graces museums. A gift of the French government in 1912, this work shows a bust of a woman and is entitled "La France." At the dedication, a French dignitary spoke about historic Franco-American connections. Ironically, most of the action here took place between the French and the British, and then between the British and the Americans. To closely see the monument and the sculptures, walk to it from the campground, combining the walk with a visit to the Crown Point Historic Site museum and grounds.

Leaving the protection of the pier below the monument, we encounter a stiff south breeze that far exceeds the "light and variable" wind forecast for the day. We hope the wind will be behind us on the way home, but this weather pattern resembles the one we encountered on another warm fall day around Cumberland Head. After struggling in the morning with an unexpected stiff wind, it dropped by afternoon. Meteorologist Chris Bouchard of the Fairbanks Museum suggests the process of "mixing" is a possible explanation for this phe-

Abutments.

nomenon. When following a cool night the sun penetrates the cool, dense air that has settled in the valley, warming the ground and the air just above it, warm air bubbles form. These bubbles rise, inviting fast, cool air from the winds aloft to move down, bringing with it speed energy that increases winds close to the ground. The higher the ground temperature, the higher the winds will be. When the temperature equalizes, the wind calms. The waves are small here because there is virtually no fetch, but we take advantage of each little point of land that provides a sheltered shore to get out of the wind.

Farms, the railroad bed, dwellings, and marshes line the shore as we head south. Milfoil-filled bays make paddling a challenge. We venture into an opening between the milfoil and the shoreline that appears a bit like a wandering back road, and we emerge on the other end of the bay. What a good way to get out of the waves while staying close to shore. We follow these protected, inside passages for most of the length of the New York shore.

Great blue herons, belted kingfishers, and mergansers like these secret passages too. We try not to disturb them, but wonder if the kingfisher is scolding us for intruding. The great blues move without complaining, seeming to disdain our presence, as if they had been planning to leave for a better fishing spot anyway.

Two men load a boat with gear and remind us that this is duck season and a prime duck hunting area. We heed the warning, as we don't want to be mistaken for ducks nor do we want to interfere with the hunters by spooking their sport. We have paddled for more than 8 miles (13 kilometers) into the wind and welcome the large cement abutments in the middle of the lake that mark the point where we cross to Vermont.

Up the Vermont Shore. Why are there four large concrete abutments in 40 feet (12 meters) of water in the middle of the lake? Margaret Sunderland of the Bridport Historical Society tells us that the abutments supported a power line that brought electricity from a generator in the village of Crown Point, New York, to the western part of Bridport until 1943, when Vermont finally provided power to Bridport. A ferry served this crossing from 1810 until roughly 1930, but in the winter cars drove across on the ice to the village of Crown Point.

We paddle amidst the abutments and then turn north. Of course, our brisk breeze of late morning dies. Phooey! We have to work to get back to Crown Point. The murky water that we have been paddling through all day stays with us. Milfoil winds around our paddles, challenging every stroke. We try new techniques to manage our paddles. Keeping the top of a paddle above the water so that the milfoil cannot wrap around it works, but we don't get much purchase. Drawing the paddle directly forward after each stroke, causing the milfoil to slide off, is awkward. We favor eradicating milfoil.

I celebrate the simple joys of being on the water. The hidden passage inside the milfoil, the curve and shadow of a reed, the chatter of a kingfisher, the reflec-

▶ **Crown Point to Bridport and Return**

tion of a cottonwood in the water, and the ring of small waves that slowly moves out from a passing boat are all part of the magic of being on the lake. The bright blue sky and the leaves that are beginning to turn add to my contentment. I like the feel of paddling, of pulling the paddle through the water, of wet hands and warm legs, of the breeze in my face, of my ability to make my kayak move, and the snug feeling of my life preserver. Mud flowing down a little gully into the lake, the persistence of the milfoil, duckweed and green algae obscuring what is below the surface, are also part of the reality of our time on the lake. These things that we would rather not see remind us that we all must take part of rescuing Lake Champlain.

Passing an inlet where a bridge provides a platform for a line of fishermen to cast from, we cannot miss Chimney Point just ahead. Neither could others from the time of the first settlements. Relics have been found here from the Archaic Period, more than 10,000 years ago, following the melting of the glaciers when fauna and man inhabited the area. The Champlain Bridge is silhouetted in the afternoon sun as we approach.

Champlain Bridge and Champlain Memorial.

46	**Lapans Bay Loop between Bridport and Watch Point** *Beauty and the Beast*

by Margy Holden

- **Launch site/Take out:** Lapham Bay F&W Area, off Lapham Bay Rd., Shoreham, Vermont (navigational charts call this location Lapans Bay; Vermont calls it Lapham Bay)
- **Distance:** 14.5 miles (23.3 kilometers)
- **Alternative launch sites:** Monitor Bay Park (Monitor Bay Rd. off Station Rd. off Rt. 9, Crown Point, New York)
- **Places to stop:** None aside from launch sites
- **Highlights:** Marsh at the mouth of Putnam Creek, wildlife (especially waterfowl during fall migration), agricultural views, International Paper Company (stark contrast between the mill and the nearby, understandably undeveloped, shore)
- **Route:** This interesting circle route turns north and follows the lightly developed, shallow, agricultural shore to the concrete abutments in the middle of the channel. Cross to the New York side through deeper water, pass the marsh and head south along the shallow New York shore, pass the paper mill towering above, cross over deeper water to the Vermont shore and head north again to the launch site.
- **Comments:** North and south winds can create a chop on the water, but generally this route is quite protected. About two-thirds of the route provides no place to stop. Milfoil can present a paddling challenge. While this is not the most beautiful paddle, the industrial/rural contrast is something to experience (and there are some nice views).

The Paddle:

Today we circle from Lapans Bay heading north and then crossing to the mouth of Putnam Creek. From there we paddle 6.5 miles (10.5 kilometers) south and cross back to Vermont at Watch Point to head back to our starting point. This constitutes a logical trip for us, because we are covering every inch of shoreline. We experience the visual impact of the International Paper Company and enjoy some lovely marshes.

The muddy Laphams Bay Fish & Wildlife Access features an impressive array of new-looking aquatic nuisance signs, which foreshadow what grows ahead. While the signs appear to be new, the issue is not. As we push off out of the access, we have an immediate decision to face about which way to circumnavigate a large mat of water chestnut. We know enough not to try to paddle through it; we would have better luck trying to walk on it. I look south, my jaw drops, and I gasp. Across the tranquil blue water, the huge International Paper Mill, spewing white from its chimneys, looms on the horizon. It continues to be a theme through most of the day.

▶ **Lapans Bay Loop between Bridport and Watch Point**

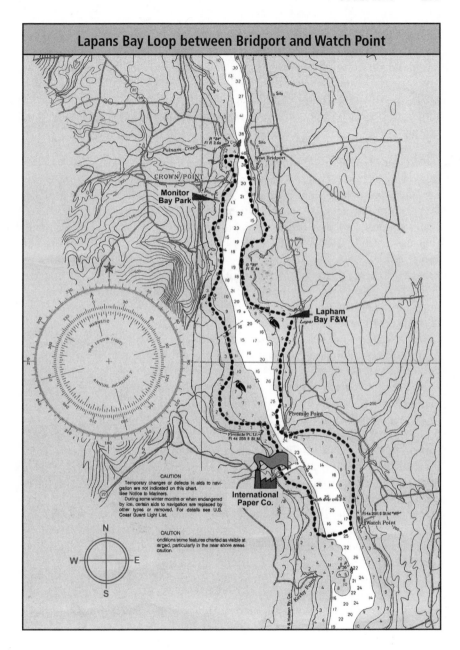

Lapans Bay Loop between Bridport and Watch Point

We cannot see our paddles in the water, nor can we see the lake bottom. The muddy water flowing from several streams suggests that yesterday's rain may be one culprit. We head north, passing a series of camps interspersed with farmland. When we reach West Bridport and cross to the New York side, we see the familiar concrete abutments that used to support a power line. In front of us, the mouth of Putnam Creek is obscured by seemingly endless reeds gently undulating in the water. No firm ground to be seen here. A few geese honk at the northern end of the bay, alerting us to flocks of geese and ducks floating among the reeds. This is such an inviting place to explore, but it is duck-hunting season, so we keep an eye out for blinds, not wanting ourselves to be the proverbial "sitting ducks."

The marshy shoreline south of Putnam Creek dictates that we eat a floating lunch. Fall leaves glow in the slanting afternoon sunlight. Do we explore this creek, or continue to cover the distance we have set out for ourselves? Cathy eats her lunch much faster than I do and keeps paddling. Well, I guess that makes *that* decision. Reluctantly leaving this reedy bay, we paddle south past Crown Point Monitor Park and occasional wetlands. On the Vermont side, farmland stretches down to the water's edge. Not here, where forest and railroad line the shoreline.

As the breeze picks up from the south, I detect a familiar acid taste and feel an acrid irritation in my nose and eyes. I believe that these physical reactions are in response to the paper mill's emissions. When we pass the tip of another point, the paper mill suddenly dominates our view. Close-up from the water, the mill looms over us, obtrusive with its huge buildings, eleven chimneys, pipes, big conduits, and unfamiliar machinery. The almost impenetrable milfoil beneath makes each stroke an effort. The clear outflow channel from the paper plant provides a brief respite, but within a few feet the milfoil returns.

We continue south beyond the plant for about a mile before crossing back to Vermont at Watch Point. Heading north along the Vermont shore for the next three miles, we have an uninterrupted view of the paper mill across the lake. Not surprisingly, we see little habitation along this Vermont shore. When describing the primitive camping site for the Lake Champlain Paddlers' Trail on Five-Mile Point, the guidebook comments, "Unfortunately, the view from this point is in stark contrast to most other LCPT sites, with International Paper's large mill just across the Lake (and in the Adirondack State Park!) One can only imagine the site before the mill was built. To avoid the sight and dampen the sounds of the mill, camp up slope on the old trail in the forest."

Turkey vultures riding the air currents above us complete my mood. I feel a bit like carrion myself. On the tip of Five-Mile Point, we get our first close-up view of these huge birds when three or four vultures strut and size each other up. A huge fish that has died in a contorted, upright position as if it could still swim has their complete attention. The carcass won't last long with this crowd around. Fascinated, we get too close to the vultures and they retreat, waiting just long enough for us to pass before going after their prize again. Spontaneously, a verse and dirge spew out of me and I croak, "I eat flesh," which expands into several verses and gestures. Cathy doesn't know whether to laugh or flee.

▶ Lapans Bay Loop between Bridport and Watch Point

The International Paper Mill

Effluent and toxic waste from a paper plant began flowing into Lake Champlain at the mouth of the La Chute River in the 1800s. It formed a sludge bed by the 1960s that measured 20 feet thick (6 meters) and covered 300 acres (121 hectares). The sludge bed stopped growing in 1973 when that plant closed. A new plant, 3.5 miles (5.6 kilometers) farther north and designed to be more eco-friendly, opened the same year. According to the November 1977 issue of the *Journal of Environmental Geology*, however, effluent from the new plant has "measurably affected the composition of suspended sediment and surficial bottom sediment despite construction and use of extensive facilities to reduce flow of pollutants into the Lake." During the 1980s, incidents were reported of fuel oil, dioxin-containing sludge, and waste leaking into Lake Champlain and nearby creeks and wetlands. In 1990 the Vermont Transportation Agency reported an 18-inch-deep (46-centimeter), football-sized field of sludge at the end of the effluent pipe. Documented incidents continue.

A proposed test burn of tires to fuel the plant operations highlights some of the more recent issues. Environmental groups protested the permit issue, but there was little public opposition in New York. Vermont citizens acted on their outrage. From the Vermont State House to the voters of Shoreham, petitions were drawn and demonstrations held. After three weeks the test burn was halted because of overwhelming particulate matter emitted during the burning.

In spite of emissions and effluent, strong support for the paper plant exists on the New York side of the lake, because employers of this size in this region are rare. Not only does this plant provide many jobs, but it also indirectly supports loggers and all the businesses that sell to plant employees. Many fear that the plant will move south, leaving the area further economically depressed. Others voice concern about the continuing degradation of Lake Champlain, as well as the eventual loss of tourism from a diminished lake. Nothing is simple when it comes to the economy, public health, and the health of our environment.

I feel pummeled by conflicting emotions. The colors and peace of the delta of Putnam Creek stand in stark relief to the industrial paper mill. How long can they coexist? We love this lake and understand how fragile it is. In a sober mood we leave Lapans Bay. How could the contrasts of this day be any greater?

International Paper Mill.

▶ Lapans Bay Loop between Bridport and Watch Point

Larrabees Point to Fort Ticonderoga and Return
The Historic Keyhole

47

by Cathy Frank

- ■ **Launch site/Take out:** Larrabees Point F&W Area, VT Rt. 73 off Rt. 74, Shoreham, Vermont
- ■ **Distance:** 15 miles (24 kilometers)
- ■ **Alternative launch sites:** Ticonderoga New York Boat Launch (adjacent to Ft. Ticonderoga Ferry dock, Rt. 74, Ticonderoga, New York)
- ■ **Places to stop:** None aside from launch sites
- ■ **Highlights:** Ft. Ticonderoga Ferry, Fort Ticonderoga, Mt. Independence, Mt. Defiance, La Chute River, East Creek, wildlife potential everywhere, including eagles and osprey, and schools of fish in the shallow waters south of the fort
- ■ **Route:** This feature-packed loop route is somewhat protected from the wind, mostly in shallow water and devoid of boat traffic except in the narrow channel that runs down the middle. Wildlife is abundant along the entire route, as is milfoil. The route passes the ferry dock and then crosses open water to the New York shore about 2 miles to the north. From there it turns south, past the ferry again, past Fort Ticonderoga high on the cliff, and past the mouth of the La Chute river and through marshes. It crosses open water again about 2 miles north of Chipman Point, heads north around Mt. Independence, and past the mouth of East Creek. It can be made as short or as long as you want, depending on where you turn around at either end. Detouring up East Creek is a wildlife-rich option.
- ■ **Comments:** It is a one-mile walk from the NY Boat Launch to Fort Ticonderoga (but no safe way to leave a kayak and gear unattended). Mt. Independence and Mt. Defiance can be reached easily by car. There is abundant milfoil along the shore, and the Ticonderoga paper mill looms at the north end of the loop.

The Paddle:

"Where's Fort Ticonderoga?" asks a kayaker, climbing out of his boat at the Larrabees Point Fish & Wildlife Boat Access. We wonder ourselves. Our chart reveals that, although unseen from here, the fort is less than a mile and a half as the crow flies, across the lake and around a bend to the south. Signage is minimal. We almost missed the Larrabees Point Fishing Access itself, ending up at the ferry landing on our first try.

Heading north, we carefully pick our way through the milfoil, water chestnut, and a pea-green, saturated, sponge-like growth along the shore. By now our paddling technique for growth-choked water is nearing perfection—keep it shallow, keep it short.

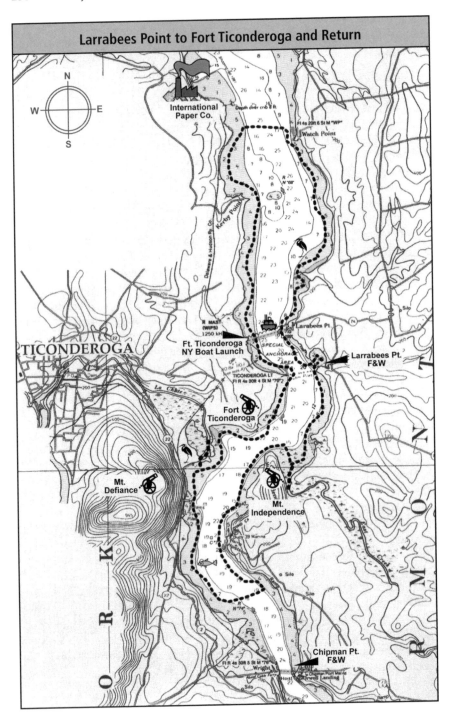

Larrabees Point to Fort Ticonderoga and Return

Ft. Ticonderoga Ferry. We look ahead with curiosity toward the Ft. Ticonderoga ferry moving back and forth across the lake. A barge, propelled by a small, double-ended tugboat attached to its side, is guided by cables that lie on the bottom of the lake when not being lifted by the ferry as it passes overhead. The constant stream of cars waiting on both sides is surprising for what feels like an out-of-the-way crossing. Then again, this oldest and smallest of Lake Champlain ferries has been in existence in one form or another since 1759.

Just past Larrabees Point, a bald eagle flies by. It is the first of four eagles we see in less than five minutes. At Watch Point, the southern tip of our last trip, we turn west and paddle across the lake, watching as the Ticonderoga paper mill to the north spews out a strong, steady stream of smoke. We both notice an irritation in our nose and throat and pick up our pace to get beyond this place as quickly as possible. Turning south, we are soon at the other ferry dock on the New York side, where we stop long enough to watch the ferry land. Perhaps because of its persistence over time, or maybe because of its unassuming nature despite its longevity, we feel a kinship with this little ferry.

There is a sizable public boat access here, a good place to stop for lunch or just to stretch. We opt for a floating lunch, as the light north wind moves us in the direction we want to go while we do nothing but eat, an arrangement that would do Tom Sawyer proud. A lone osprey flies high overhead. As we drift past the Ticonderoga light, historic Mount Independence rises sharply 250 feet (76 meters) above the water to the southwest. Thoughts of history are put on hold, however, when we spot yet another eagle. It flies into the tall trees along the shore, then suddenly reappears and flies no more than 15 feet (4.6 meters) directly above our heads. Spellbound, and feeling the power of this majestic bird, we stop and watch it fly ahead and alight at the top of a tall tree.

In no time we find ourselves around the bend and heading west. Pulling out from shore about 100 yards (91 meters), we finally get our first view of historic Fort Ticonderoga. Just then the sounds of drums and flutes carry clearly over the water as the Fort Ticonderoga Fife and Drum Corps starts to play. I confess to an attack of goose bumps. (Surely they have started to play just for us.) Cannons are evenly spaced along the south-facing stone wall, and the American flag flies high overhead.

The strategic position of this fort becomes obvious to us, as we sit exposed to a potential broadside should we have been British approaching from the south. Fort Ticonderoga sits at the confluence of the two routes available to travelers from the south in the 1700s. Mount Defiance, in New York, looms above us to the southwest and, on the Vermont side, Mt. Independence projects north, narrowing the passage between the two sides of the lake. If, as Ralph Nading Hill claims, Lake Champlain was the "Key to Liberty," surely this location was the most important keyhole. And here we sit in the middle of it all. (We highly recommend a visit by car to Fort Ticonderoga, Mt. Defiance, and Mt. Independence.)

Fort Ticonderoga

As early as 1666 the French built a simple fort at the mouth of the La Chute River to defend themselves against the Iroquois, but they soon made peace and the fort was abandoned. Less than one hundred years later (1755), at the beginning of the Seven Years War (French and Indian War), the French again built a fort here, this time to defend their hold on Lake Champlain against an anticipated British attack from the south. They named it Fort Carillon.

The two potential British invasion routes from the south converged on the Ticonderoga peninsula, making this a particularly strategic location for the French. One route involved sailing up Lake Champlain from Whitehall (then Skenesborough), the other, traveling north up Lake George and down the La Chute River.

The British Fort William Henry sat at the southern end of Lake George. Seizing the initiative, French General Marquis de Montcalm launched a successful attack from Fort Carillon on the British at Fort William Henry in 1757. In 1758 the British counterattacked, but failed to take Fort Carillon despite vastly outnumbering the French 15,000 to 3,200. Finally, in 1759, the British besieged Fort Carillon and defeated the much-weakened French force. In retreat, the French blew up the fort.

From then until the start of the American Revolution, the British controlled the renamed and rebuilt Fort Ticonderoga and maintained a small force there. In May of 1775, three weeks after the fighting at Lexington and Concord, in an act that is legendary to all Vermonters, Benedict Arnold, Ethan Allen, and the Green Mountain Boys captured Fort Ticonderoga from the surprised British garrison, which did not even know they were at war with the Americans. (Ethan Allen crossed the lake to New York at Hand's Cove, out of sight of the fort and just north of our launch site.) This gave the Americans not only a strategic location, but badly needed cannon, which they then dragged the following winter through snow and ice to Boston to help drive the British from Boston Harbor in the spring of 1776.

After a disastrous winter (1775–76), with a failed assault on Quebec City and Montreal and a retreat south on Lake Champlain, the weakened and demoralized Americans improved their defenses at Fort Ticonderoga. Unlike the French, who fortified themselves from an assault from the south, the Americans had to prepare for a British attack from the north. To do this they fortified Mt. Independence in Vermont, directly across from Fort Ticonderoga. Rising steeply, sur-

▶ **Larrabees Point to Fort Ticonderoga and Return**

Guarding the approach—Fort Ticonderoga.

rounded on three sides by water (north, west and south), and with a commanding view of the lake northward, fortifications on Mt. Independence significantly improved the American defensive position. Meanwhile, Benedict Arnold supervised the building of the fledgling American navy at Whitehall and sent the ships to Ticonderoga to be outfitted. This fleet sailed north and engaged General Sir Guy Carleton at the Battle of Valcour Island in October of 1776 (see "Battle of Valcour" sidebar in "Port Kent to Plattsburgh Bay" paddle).

After resoundingly defeating Arnold at Valcour, Carleton pursued what remained of the American fleet south to Ticonderoga, but he returned to Montreal without attacking, put off by the fortifications on Mt. Independence. During the ensuing winter (1776–77), the Americans built a bridge between Fort Ticonderoga and Mt. Independence. (Two timbers from this bridge can be seen at the Mt. Independence Museum, and a small model of the bridge is on display at Fort Ticonderoga.) To further block all traffic from traveling up and down the lake, the Americans placed a chain across the lake north of the bridge.

Unfortunately, defense of this critical location was short-lived. A superior British force returned in the summer of 1777 and dragged cannons to the top of 800-foot (244-meter) Mt. Defiance to the southwest of Fort Ticonderoga. This higher location gave the British the ability to fire down onto Fort Ticonderoga and across the lake onto Mt. Independence. When the American commander, who had unfortunately assumed that dragging cannons to the top of Mt. Defiance was impossible, realized his predicament, he ordered his troops to abandon the fort as well as Mt. Independence before the British commenced their attack. (It is well worth a drive up to the top of Mt. Defiance to appreciate this strategic location.)

The British then held the fort until Burgoyne's surrender at the Battle of Saratoga in October 1777. It's been America's ever since.

A little farther south, we paddle a short distance into the mouth of the La Chute River, the short, two-mile (3.2-kilometer), cascade-filled river that drains Lake George into Lake Champlain, dropping 200 feet (61 meters) in elevation in the process. White water lilies and tall rushes line both sides of the somewhat narrow entrance to the river, which is navigable as far as the dam in the town of Ticonderoga. The name Ticonderoga, "a land between two great waters," was given to this area by Native Americans who traveled and inhabited here thousands of years before Europeans arrived. Unfortunately, the beauty of this tranquil location is somewhat tempered by knowing we are sitting atop a 300-acre sludge bed created by the discharge from the International Paper Mill, which until 1973 was located less than a mile upstream. (See "The International Paper Mill" sidebar in "Lapans Bay Loop between Bridport and Watch Point" paddle.)

Back out on the lake, we pass a huge beaver dam as we weave in and out of milfoil-free channels. Forty-five minutes later we reach our turnaround point just north of Chipman Point, along with an energy low. The breeze has died, the sun is hot, and it feels like the milfoil and water chestnut have taken on personalities that purposely try to arrest our forward progress. But, suddenly, we find ourselves in the midst of a school of feeding fish, jumping around us like popcorn in hot oil. I put my camera away to keep it dry, but the excitement propels us through our mid-afternoon slump.

The breeze freshens as we cross back to Vermont and turn north. Mt. Independence is hard to see this close to shore. There is a steep hiking path that leads up to it on the north side of Catfish Bay. Around the northern tip of Mt. Independence, a turtle and a duck, amusingly sharing the same water-soaked log in the middle of the channel, guard the entrance to East Creek. Home to a stop on the Paddlers' Trail, as well as to an abundance of wildlife, evidence of human habitation has been found at this location dating back to the Woodland Period (400 to 3,000 years ago). The creek runs inland a little over 2 miles (3.2 kilometers).

▶ **Larrabees Point to Fort Ticonderoga and Return**

We are back at the boat access five hours after we started, hot and tired, but excited by our experience. Eagles and osprey, a cable ferry, an historic fort, two historic mountains, significant wetlands, and fish jumping everywhere—how could we have lived on the lake this long and never visited this remarkable place before?

Ticonderoga Cable Ferry.

by Margy Holden

- **Launch site/Take out:** Chipman Point F&W Area, adjacent to Chipman Point Marina ($) at the end of Chipman Point Rd., Orwell, Vermont. Use the small parking area beyond the marina parking area, marked by a Vermont bulletin board.
- **Distance:** 12.5 miles (20 kilometers)
- **Alternative launch sites:** Benson Landing F&W Area (West Lake Rd., Benson, Vermont), Singing Cedars F&W Area (Singing Cedars Rd., Orwell, Vermont)
- **Places to stop:** None aside from launch sites
- **Highlights:** Orwell Cliffs, Mills Bay, ruins of historic warehouses, Adirondack foothills, Mt. Defiance and Mt. Independence views, undeveloped shoreline, marshes, wildlife
- **Route:** Turn south (or north), pass the Orwell Cliffs and follow a shallow Vermont shore with little visible development except for historic ruins. At Benson Landing cross the narrow channel over deeper water and follow the shallow New York shore along the railroad bed past Putnam Station. Just to the north, it is possible to paddle under a railroad bridge to explore a marshy pond. Exiting the pond, the route turns north along an undeveloped, marshy New York shore to a point above the launch site, crosses the deeper water and returns south along the shallow Vermont shore to the launch site.
- **Comments:** This shoreline is relatively inaccessible from the New York side. High winds can create chop, but the route is protected from waves. The only ways to stop on the New York shore are to climb onto the railroad bed or stand in the often-murky water where the bottom is not visible. We were unable to find the ramp indicated on charts on the Vermont side just south of Mount Independence.

The Paddle:

The access road looks like a driveway serving the houses that line it, but it does end at the steep but paved Chipman Point F&W Access area next to the marina. We glance north through the moored boats of the marina to Mt. Defiance before heading south along the Vermont shore toward Benson Landing.

The shore takes us along pleasant farmland, in and out of shallow bays, through muddy water, and into liberal sprinklings of milfoil. We take note of the more direct route back along the straight New York shore. A freshly fallen large white pine demonstrates that erosion never ceases.

Two historic buildings hint of Chipman Point's past. Indeed, in the 1840s, after the completion of the Champlain Canal, Chipman Point thrived as a commercial center. Two historic warehouses, one built in 1810 by Walter Chipman and the other in 1824 by Joseph Sholes, attest to the extent of past activity. At one point a cable ferry crossed the lake here. After the railroads were

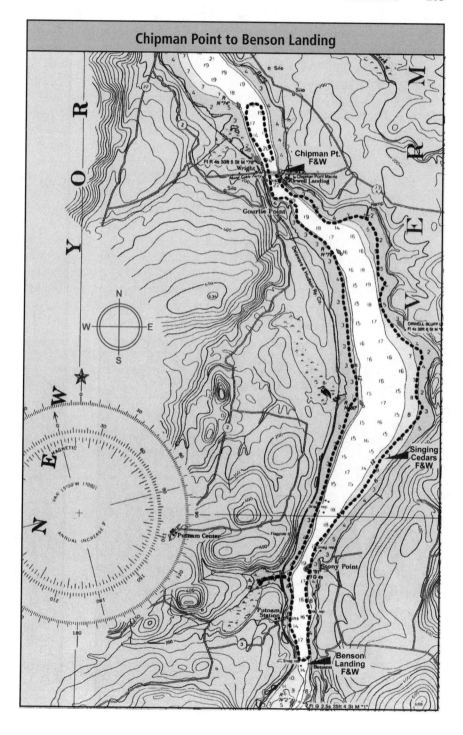

Chipman Point to Benson Landing

built, Chipman Point went into decline but, luckily, these beautiful old warehouses survive as testimony to an earlier time.

Beyond Chipman Point, Orwell Bluff stands as a real anomaly, like a mammoth geologic accidental left behind on this otherwise agricultural shore. Not without humor, the bluff sports a "no trespassing sign" about ten feet above the water—with no dry land below it. How did someone ever manage to affix a sign on that steep cliff, and why bother, since it's completely inaccessible from the water? We can only guess that when the rains cease, the lake level will recede and some kind of shoreline will appear.

Water lilies intermingle with the milfoil in some bays. We see one particularly chilling sight—a single bloom of water chestnut nestled among some particularly lovely lilies. The lilies won't last long if that water chestnut survives and multiplies.

Intriguing structures line the shore near Stony Point. It's hard to believe that the first house that we see started out as close to the water as it now sits. The front steps descend to a boulder that rests in the water, while three stories of stone rise above it. Elaborate twig grates cover openings at the water level, and the rest of this imposing structure appears equally fanciful. We wonder if it could have formerly been an inn. Close by, two huge chimneys mark the remnants of what

No trespassing.

▶ **Chipman Point to Benson Landing**

must have been another grand structure, and a two-story skeleton of beautifully crafted stone is all that remains of a warehouse built in 1810.

Benson Landing brings us back to present-day issues with a close-up view of a moored water chestnut harvester. No one is operating it today, and the business end is submerged, but the conveyor belt looks like it can carry a lot of water chestnuts. We sure hope so. Nearby, men overload a small houseboat with building material. There is a little too much action for a quiet lunch in Benson Landing. We retreat across the narrow ribbon of water to New York, defy the slippery rocks, pull our kayaks out, and perch on shoreline fill of the Delaware and Hudson track. Luckily, the train doesn't pass before we are on our way again.

We're entertained by the show in front of us. The boat overloaded with construction materials makes a wobbly start away from the Benson's Landing dock, listing dangerously to one side while we hold our breath wondering if it will capsize. Luckily, they quickly return to the dock to unload half of their cargo.

We head north along the New York shore and the Delaware and Hudson railroad bed. A few buildings indicate the location of Putnam Station just before the railroad bed crosses the outlet to Mill Bay. We scoot under the trestle to discover a reedy bay surrounded by hills—a quiet, pretty place. A bit farther north we encounter the formerly overloaded houseboat, the men unloading bags of concrete. Across the water we get a distant view of silos in Addison County. We see few other signs of activity on this New York shore or the treed hills behind it.

The railroad bed leaves the shore before Gourlie Point, where three canal boats lie beneath the surface, probably abandoned when they were no longer needed, rather than wrecked. We cross the narrow ribbon of water to Vermont at Chipman Point and continue north just far enough to determine that we really cannot find a ramp marked on the charts. From there we return south to the access area, still appreciating this attractive territory with a bit of history and humor thrown in.

Whitehall to Benson Landing
Both Sides Now

by Margy Holden

- **Launch site:** Lock 12 Marina ($), N. Williams St., Whitehall, New York
- **Distance:** 15 miles (24 kilometers)
- **Take out:** Benson Landing F&W Area (West Lake Rd., Benson, Vermont)
- **Alternative launch sites:** None
- **Places to stop:** None aside from launch sites
- **Highlights:** Skenesborough Museum, historic buildings, locks, old canal town, dramatic cliffs and marshes, wildlife, numerous channels to explore, Narrows of Dresden (can combine this paddle with "South Bay")
- **Route:** From Whitehall, this historic, river-like route heads north passing an island, the mouth of the Poultney River, the entrance to South Bay (a possible side trip), and eventually the Narrows of Dresden. The shoreline is mostly deserted, sometimes elusive in marshland, with cliffs rising sharply all the way to Benson Landing.
- **Comments:** Whitehall, New York, marks the southern tip of Lake Champlain, and from there, 17 miles (27 kilometers) north to Benson Landing, Lake Champlain looks like a slender, slinky river. We thought it was getting narrow south of Crown Point, but that was a highway compared to this back road.

  While the main channel can be as deep as 20 feet and the shore very shallow, water chestnut and milfoil fill many of the bays and can make paddling the shoreline impossible. Waves, except those created by passing boats, are not an issue in this protected route.

The Paddle:

We don't travel here often, and our choice of routes makes spotting a car and getting to the launch site an adventure. A selected shortcut turns into a winding track where overhanging trees threaten to shred our kayaks. When we finally find Benson Landing, the first thing we see is a large power boat plowing along, throwing off a tremendous wake. We vow to avoid close contact with the likes of that. We leave one car here and start out again, only to find that our shortcut to Whitehall turns into a swamp. Determined to forge ahead, we even construct a rock ford for the van. When finally forced to give up and reverse course, we find we are in a small section of New York that is actually east of Vermont and blank on our road map. With luck, we find Whitehall.

Whitehall, New York. Whitehall, originally founded in 1759 by British Captain Philip Skene, who modestly named the town Skenesborough, became the first permanent English-speaking settlement on Lake Champlain. Sixteen years later, the rebellious Americans captured Skenesborough along with Skene's ship,

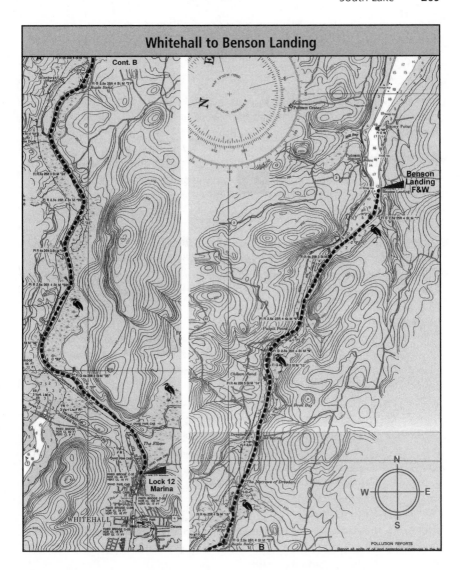

Whitehall to Benson Landing

which they appropriately renamed the *Liberty*, transforming it into the first vessel in the American Navy. Whitehall calls itself the birthplace of the American Navy for this and other good reasons. In 1776 the American rebels used Skene's saw-mills for timber to build thirteen ships that became part of Benedict Arnold's fleet at the Battle of Valcour.

After the 1814 Battle of Plattsburgh, remnants of both the American and British fleets were brought to Whitehall and moored near the mouth of the Poultney River. The remnants of the ship *Ticonderoga* were removed in 1958, preserved, and can be seen at the Skenesborough Museum, which is accessible from the water. Remnants of the American brig *Eagle* and the British brig *Linnet*, along with other boats, still lie beneath the water and have been the subject of considerable research.

The Champlain Canal. Early travelers recognized that Whitehall had the potential to be a trading and transportation hub, if only Lake Champlain could be connected to the Hudson River. Furs, flour, potash, and lumber from Canada and the Champlain Valley were already traded through Whitehall to the Hudson River and south from the days of the earliest settlement on Lake Champlain, but the trip required significant portages. A canal would create a major trade route, and everything would go through Whitehall.

Portages were eliminated in 1823 when New York completed the challenge of building the Champlain Canal. Part of this tremendous achievement is a 46-mile (74-kilometer) land-cut channel that roughly follows and sometimes incorporates a much-enlarged Wood Creek. The Champlain Canal changed everything. Easier access to southern markets stimulated shipbuilding and other industries from mining to milking throughout the Champlain Valley. Between 1823 and the development of sailing canal boats in 1841, most of the goods that traveled Lake Champlain by sail or steam had to be transferred to canal boats at Whitehall. Combine all these travelers, goods, sailors, and boats from the lake with the crews, mule skinners, passengers, and freight of the canal boats, and you have a Whitehall that Ralph Nading Hill characterizes as "the most boisterous canal town in the northeast."

The excitement and the prosperity lasted until 1874, when the railroad was completed from Albany to Ticonderoga. From then on, freight could be sent by rail between Ticonderoga and New York, bypassing Whitehall. Between 1870 and 1915 more than 1,500 canal boats still operated on Lake Champlain, but the railroads had taken much of their business. The Champlain Canal still carries traffic today, but the boats passing through Whitehall in the twenty-first century are interested in pleasure, not commerce.

Skene Manor looms over us and Whitehall. This huge, gothic revival castle, built in 1874, is on the National Historic Register. It has suffered through many uses, including a number of years as a restaurant, before a nonprofit corporation was formed to buy, repair and restore it.

A man doing yard work next to the marina boat ramp looks a bit surprised that we are setting out in kayaks and warns us to watch out for the wakes of large power boats. Good advice. When we begin paddling on opposite sides of the lake here, Cathy and I find it so narrow that we can easily call across to each other. We paddle along swampy shores lined with silver maples.

▶ Whitehall to Benson Landing

The Poultney River. Just ahead, the 40-milelong (64-kilometer) Poultney River empties into murky East Bay. Audubon Vermont designated 2,600 acres (1,052 hectares) here as an Important Bird Area, because it is the breeding location of peregrine falcons, golden-winged warblers, blue-gray gnatcatchers, and whip-poor-wills, which are all endangered species in Vermont. Most of these acres are owned by The Nature Conservancy, which means they will never be developed. Biologically diverse, it supports not only breeding birds, but also mammals, reptiles, and fish. Walleye and pike spawn in the Poultney River. More than twelve species of freshwater mussels with exotic names like pink heelsplitter and fragile papershell inhabit these waters. None of them is endangered, but it is an unusual variety for one place. We can only hope that the zebra mussels that already have destroyed much of the other mussel populations in Lake Champlain don't like it here.

In the 1990s the Vermont Department of Fish and Wildlife started using lampricides in the Poultney to control the lamprey eel population. These eels are the bane of sports fishermen and long distance swimmers, who find this parasite attached to their catches or their bodies. Using lampricides is controversial; while they are effective in limiting lamprey, the chemical impact on other species is unknown. As throughout the rest of Lake Champlain and its tributaries, those who treasure the Poultney are working to maintain its water and its habitat.

Approaching the Narrows of Dresden.

Water Chestnut

Water chestnut, found in slow-moving, nutrient-rich water, has no redeeming features. The stems can be as long as 16 feet (5 meters). The plants grow thickly enough to force out native species. They reduce the light penetration underwater, which in turn reduces oxygen and therefore is harmful to fish and other aquatic species. It interferes with boating and fishing. The only known controls for this pest are hand-pulling or machine-harvesting. Since the seeds can survive for up to twelve years, the harvesting has to be a continual process. The infestation on Lake Champlain extends 47 miles north from Whitehall to Little Otter Creek in Ferrisburg, where it has been contained.

We leave the mouth of the river and head north, where this narrow ribbon of Lake Champlain defines the New York and Vermont border. Cliffs dominate our view on the Vermont side of the water. The Delaware and Hudson Railroad bed follows the New York shore all the way to Benson Landing, backed by visibly deserted foothills of the Adirondacks. Marsh and swamp line both shores. Small bays are often filled with water chestnut. We see few buildings. About three miles north of Whitehall, we reach a railroad bridge on the New York shore, paddle under it, and get our first glimpse of South Bay. It is a special place, and we look forward to paddling it.

The water chestnut that fills the side bays is really hard for us to grasp, literally and conceptually. As we paddle north, clumps become huge mats, thick enough to support a bottle, Styrofoam cup, and dead fish. We couldn't paddle through it even if we tried. What looked pretty at first is one of Lake Champlain's nightmares. Uprooting one is like pulling up a heavy anchor line with the anchor stuck under a rock.

Great blue herons fishing in the shallows and belted kingfishers keep us company. Kingbirds swoop after insects, and red-winged blackbirds squawk at us from their perches on cattails. We pass five empty osprey platforms before reaching one that is occupied. The osprey on the nest keeps up a continuous angry chatter. Another osprey flies near, carrying something that looks smaller than a log and bigger than a stick. He tries to place the stick on the nest. We hold our breaths and groan when he misses, watching the stick fall into the marsh below.

At the Narrows of Dresden, cliffs rise sharply on both sides of the narrowed channel. The name conjures up dramatic Wagnerian music with the Valkyries flying above us. This dramatic view contrasts with the rest of this section of Lake Champlain. We continue winding our way through the channel, pass the last of many buoys that we have seen today, and head into Benson Landing, past a few swimmers, to the launch ramp.

▶ **Whitehall to Benson Landing**

In spite of our earlier concern about boat wakes, we survived. When two large power boats passed us, we instinctively turned into their wakes. We did see a number of bass boats at a distance; they caused no discernible wake. Still, the next time we will be careful as well. We have finally experienced this most southern, narrowest, and unique section of Lake Champlain.

Empty osprey nest platform.

50	**South Bay**
	Of Turtles, Thumps, and Cliffs

by Margy Holden

- **Launch site/Take out:** New York Boat Launch, Rt. 22 north of Whitehall, New York
- **Distance:** 9 miles (15 kilometers)
- **Alternative launch sites:** None
- **Places to stop:** None aside from launch site
- **Highlights:** Cliffs, undeveloped shores, views into Adirondack foothills, abundant wildlife, especially turtles
- **Route:** From the launch site, the route, filled with surprises, heads north away from the bridge into the smaller end of South Bay, through proven turtle habitat, passing the outlet to South Lake (a possible side trip) and extensive marshland, to the bridge. Passing under the bridge, the first set of cliffs opens to the left above a shore deserted except for a few rustic cabins. The shore continues deserted to the end of South Bay, which is marshy. The route returns along the other side under high cliffs followed by deserted farmland to the launch site.
- **Comments:** This route is very protected from wind. The shores are shallow, the water opaque. South Bay, a skinny southwesterly projection off the lower part of the Lake Champlain Narrows, looks a bit like Lake Champlain's appendix. Its placid water stretches between wild and wooded Adirondack foothills. South Bay gets as deep as 20 feet (6 meters), but along the shore rarely reaches 4 feet (1 meter) deep.

The Paddle:

We turn north from the launch site into the smaller end of South Bay and enter another world—turtle world. To paraphrase a Dr. Seuss rhyme, big ones, small ones, colorful ones, plain ones—all have come to a turtle party, a *big* turtle party. Turtles of all sizes and descriptions line up on logs and ledges as if waiting for some grand event. Some are in the balcony, having stacked themselves on top of another. Painted turtles flash a bit of red, while map turtles arch their striped necks and push off with striped legs. Could there be other varieties? Shadows, movement, and mud make it difficult to tell. The turtles allow us to glide within a few feet before they plop from their perch into the water. Would this be such a turtle world on another day? Yes, on warm, sunny days. Quiet, shallow water protected from the wind, and a good layer of mud on the bottom for winter protection, make this ideal turtle habitat. A muddy, sandy verge will emerge on which to lay eggs when the high water recedes.

Swinging east and then south past the Delaware and Hudson causeway that separates South Bay from Lake Champlain, we find ourselves under the Rt. 22 bridge ... and surrounded by swallows. Tiny heads peer from mud bowl-shaped

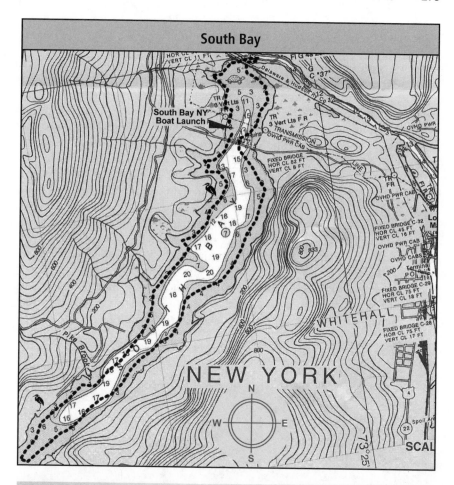

Turtle Sex and Sense

Sun-bathing not only matures the turtle eggs inside the mother, but helps rid turtles of parasitic leeches. Body temperature, influenced by sunning, even determines the sex of the next generation. Lower temperatures during incubation produce males; higher temperatures produce females—just one more example of women being hot stuff. With a 35–40-year anticipated lifespan, some of the larger turtles have seen many seasons in South Bay. Turtle sound perception is poor, but they do have a good sense of smell and color. We wasted our time being quiet; we should have dulled the bright shades of our kayaks and taken a bath. They feed on small fish, crustaceans, aquatic insects and, as they mature, plants.

nests that decorate most bridge supports. Swooping, calling barn swallows create a cacophony of sound. Are we causing all this excitement, or is it a part of normal feeding on the insects that collect under the bridge? Either way, we duck with each passing swoop and luckily emerge undecorated.

The larger section of South Bay stretches before us. Our paddles disappear below the surface and we declare the water opaque. In some places duckweed helps obliterate what lies below. We don't look far for another part of the explanation. Eroding banks and dangling tree roots visibly leach soil into the water. In this high water even more of the muddy cliff is exposed to waves.

Cliffs ahead! What a contrast to the low and swampy area we have just paddled through. Mud-covered shale rises straight out of the water. Fall lines crowd together on the chart, forming a solid mass that tops out at over 800 feet (244 meters). Under the water, the cliffs halt abruptly, reminding us of Missisquoi Bay. In the distance, at the far end of South Bay, the cliffs look even higher. Across the bay, old farm buildings and fields still hold their own before the hills take over.

Beyond the cliffs, a dozen rustic camps cling to ledges just above the water. When a far view opens up between two mountains, I can just make out a bird riding the wind currents in yet another valley. How big is it if I can see it from

Turtle territory.

▶ **South Bay**

so far away? By the time I wrestle my binoculars out of their waterproof case to check, it is gone.

South Bay has not always been this peaceful. In September 1755 these shores came alive with the sounds of men as General Baron de Dieskau led 1,800 French soldiers and 600 Native Americans to attack Sir William Johnson at Fort Edward and Fort George. The long battle between the French and British over who would control Lake Champlain reached even this remote place.

Paddling steadily, we reach the end of South Bay, only to be dwarfed by the majestic cliffs that tower over the head of the bay. With each stroke of our paddles, they loom larger. They rise, almost in steps, supporting a few teetering trees to almost 1,000 feet (305 meters). Beyond the cliffs the land slumps into swamp. Cattails, a huge beaver house, muskrat mounds, and clumps of reeds form islands to paddle between. We are startled when a bird that seems the size of an airplane glides over us. Is this what we saw soaring over the distant valley? At glide speed it disappears almost as suddenly as it appeared.

Curiosity definitely aroused but unsatisfied, we have to content ourselves with investigating the swamp. I don't know what causes me to look up at a sturdy branch above, but what an unmistakable sight. I am looking up at the rump of a very large, perching bird. The head and neck are golden, not white. The habitat is right—marsh for hunting, hills to create currents for soaring, and cliffs for nesting. Could I have really seen a golden eagle?

The return to the launch site could be an anticlimax, but the cliffs rivet our attention once again as we small beings paddle beneath. Beyond, a few old buildings, a dilapidated car, and evidence of earlier farming are scattered along this western shore. We're not paying much attention, when a huge thump jolts Cathy's kayak. Thumps and bumps and even splashes then pound both kayaks. In this opaque water, we can't see this mysterious pugilist, but it sure startles us each time. I suspect spawning carp, but Cathy gets other evidence. A particularly pesky muskrat resists having its picture taken, splashing Cathy and her camera when it surfaces next to her kayak. What a fitting farewell to South Bay.

The Last Trip

Our paddle from North Hero to Woods Island in the Inland Sea completed our circumnavigation of Lake Champlain and its major islands. We had paddled more than 750 miles (1,207 kilometers) over three summers, squeezed in-between all sorts of life events. We have come to know and have fallen in love with this lake, as we never had before. We have seen every inch of shoreline from Whitehall to Rouses Point, and The Gut to Snake Den Harbor. We may have looked down into the water, up at the cliffs, or across a marsh on any single day, but we have smelled, touched, felt, seen, and heard every point on Lake Champlain. In a few places we have even tasted it. We have rejoiced in the pristine parts of the lake, and felt diminished by the decline in parts of the lake that have experienced persistent invasive species and degraded water clarity. We have been surprised, challenged, rewarded, and always fulfilled by being able to paddle its shorelines.

On the day of our final paddle, Peter Espenshade invited us to a celebratory lunch at Hero's Welcome, paddled out to meet us, and arranged for Channel 5 News to interview us. Quite overcome, we said things like "wow, we did it" and "we don't want to stop paddling." Channel 5 saved us by focusing on Lake Champlain, its beauty, and its issues. In the evening we celebrated with husbands, houseguests, and a bottle of champagne.

By sharing our experience, we hope to encourage readers to paddle on Lake Champlain and discover its wonders. We also want to focus attention on this lake so that together we can better steward it for ourselves and for future generations. As for us, we are going to paddle all those tributaries that we passed, as well as continuing to rediscover Lake Champlain. Stay tuned.

Lake Organizations

- **Audubon Vermont.** 255 Sherman Hollow Road, Huntington, VT 05462, (802) 434-3068, www.vt.audubon.org.

- **ECHO Lake Aquarium and Science Center.** One College St., Burlington, VT 05401, 802.864.1848, www.echovermont.org.

- **Green Mountain Audubon Society.** www.greenmountainaudubon.org.

- **Isle La Motte Preservation Trust.** www.ilmpt.org.

- **Lake Champlain Basin Program.** 54 West Shore Road, Grand Isle, VT 05458, 800/468-5227 (NY & VT) or 802/372-3213, www.lcbp.org.

- **Lake Champlain Committee.** 106 Main Street, Suite 200, Burlington, Vermont 05401–8434, (802) 658–1414, www.lakechamplaincommittee.org.

- **Lake Champlain Land Trust.** One Main Street, Burlington, VT 05401, (802) 862-4150, www.lclt.org.

- **Lake Champlain Maritime Museum.** 4472 Basin Harbor Rd., Vergennes, VT 05491, (802) 475-2022, www.lcmm.org.

- **South Hero Land Trust.** P.O. Box 455, South Hero, VT, 05486, (802) 372-3786, www.shlt.org.

- **The Nature Conservancy, Adirondack Chapter.** www.nature.org/wherewework/ northamerica/states/newyork/preserves/art13582.html.

- **The Nature Conservancy of Vermont.** 27 State Street, Suite 4, Montpelier, VT 05602, (802) 229-4425, www.nature.org/wherewework/northamerica/states/ vermont/.

Champlain Islands	Miles	Kilometers	Circle trip	Places to stop	Historic site	Geologic site	Fossils
South Hero	10.5	17	●	●	●		●
Keeler Bay	7	11.2	●				
Grand Isle East	15	24		●			
Grand Isle West	8	13			●		
Grand Isle West to South Hero	8	13		●	●		
Drawbridge to North Hero Village	7	12	●	●			
Alburgh Dunes through The Gut	13	21					
North Half of North Hero	16	25		●			

▶ **Paddle Matrix**

Marshes	Cliffs	Exceptional Wildlife	Parks	Museum or Interpretive	Wind Exposure	Other places of interest	Restrooms	Food	PT
Champlain Islands									
					S/W/N/E	•			
•		•			MINI-MAL				
			•		N/S/E				•
•		•			N/W/S	•			•
					N/W/S	•	•	•	
•		•			N/S/E	•	•	•	•
									•
•			•		N/S		•	•	•

	Miles	Kilometers	Circle trip	Places to stop	Historic site	Geologic site	Fossils
Carry and Pelots Bays	8	13	●	●			
Isle La Motte	15	24	●	●			●
Inland Sea							
Missisquoi Bridge to East Alburgh Shore	7	11.2		●	●		
St. Albans to Missisquoi Bay Bridge	18.5	29.8		●			
St. Albans Bay to Milton	14	22.5		●			
Milton to Sandbar	6	9.6					
Cedar, Fishbladder & Savage Islands	11	17.7	●				
Burton Island	8	13	●	●			

▶ **Paddle Matrix**

Marshes	Cliffs	Exceptional Wildlife	Parks	Museum or Interpretive	Wind Exposure	Other places of interest	Restrooms	Food	PT
●		●			MINI-MAL	●			
●				●	N/S	●			
Inland Sea									
			●		S	●			●
●			●	●	N/W/S				●
●			●		N/W/S	●			●
●		●	●		N/W/S	●	●		●
					N/S	●			●
			●		S		●		●

	Miles	Kilometers	Circle trip	Places to stop	Historic site	Geologic site	Fossils
Knight and Butler Islands	12	19.3	●	●			
Woods Island	11	17.7	●	●			
Missisquoi Bay							
Missisquoi Wildlife Refuge to Highgate Springs	17.5	28.2	●				
Missisquoi Bay	23	37	●	●			
Broad Lake North							
Alburgh West Shore	13.5	21.7		●		●	
Rouses Point to Great Chazy River	10	16		●	●		●
Great Chazy River to Point au Roche	11.5	18.5		●			

▶ **Paddle Matrix**

Marshes	Cliffs	Exceptional Wildlife	Parks	Museum or Interpretive	Wind Exposure	Other places of interest	Restrooms	Food	PT
			●		N/S		●	●	●
					N/S		●	●	●
Missisquoi Bay									
●		●	●	●	N/W/S	●			
●	●		●		N/W/S	●	●	●	●
Broad Lake North									
●			●		N/W/S	●			
●					N/S				
●			●		N/S	●	●	●	

	Miles	Kilometers	Circle trip	Places to stop	Historic site	Geologic site	Fossils
Point au Roche to Cumberland Head	13	21		●	●	●	
Malletts Bay							
Outer Malletts Bay	20	32.2	●	●	●		
Inner Malletts Bay	12.5	20	●	●			
Broad Lake East							
Burlington Bay	5.5	8.8	●	●	●		
Burlington to South Hero	17.5	28		●	●	●	
Burlington/ Juniper/ Shelburne Bay	11	17.7		●			●
Shelburne Beach to Shelburne Bay	13.5	21.7		●	●	●	

▶ **Paddle Matrix**

Marshes	Cliffs	Exceptional Wildlife	Parks	Museum or Interpretive	Wind Exposure	Other places of interest	Restrooms	Food	PT
			•	•	N/S		•	•	•
Malletts Bay									
•	•		•		N/W/S/E	•			•
			•		N/W/S	•			•
Broad Lake East									
			•		W	•	•	•	•
			•		N/W/S	•	•	•	
	•				N/W S/E	•	•	•	•
	•		•		S/W/N/E				

	Miles	Kilometers	Circle trip	Places to stop	Historic site	Geologic site	Fossils
Converse Bay to Shelburne Beach	7.5	12			●		
Little Otter Creek to Converse Bay	10	16		●			
Arnold Bay to Little Otter Creek	15	24		●	●	●	●
Chimney Point to Arnold Bay	10	16		●	●	●	●
Broad Lake West							
Cumberland Head to Plattsburgh Bay	9	14.5	●	●	●	●	
Port Kent to Plattsburgh Bay	16	25.7		●	●		●
Valcour and Crab Islands	13.5	21.7	●	●	●		●
Port Kent to Willsboro	12	19		●	●		●

▶ **Paddle Matrix**

Marshes	Cliffs	Exceptional Wildlife	Parks	Museum or Interpretive	Wind Exposure	Other places of interest	Restrooms	Food	PT
					N/W/S				
	●	●			N/W/S	●			
●		●	●	●	S/W/N/E	●			●
●			●		S/W/N/E				●
Broad Lake West									
			●		S!!!		●		
●		●	●	●	N/S	●	●		●
		●		●	N/W/S/E				●
	●				N/S				●

	Miles	Kilometers	Circle trip	Places to stop	Historic site	Geologic site	Fossils
Schuyler Island	7	11		●	●		
The Four Brothers	10	16	●				
Willsboro Bay to Essex	16	25.7		●	●		
Westport to Essex (Split Rock)	14.5	23.3		●	●	●	
Port Henry to Westport	12	19		●			
Crown Point/ Bulwagga/ Port Henry	11	17.7	●	●	●	●	●
South Lake							
Chimney Point to Bridport	14	22.5	●	●	●		
Lapans Bay Loop	14.5	23.3	●	●			

▶ **Paddle Matrix**

Marshes	Cliffs	Exceptional Wildlife	Parks	Museum or Interpretive	Wind Exposure	Other places of interest	Restrooms	Food	PT
					N/W				●
		●			N/W/ S/E	●			
			●		S/W/ N/E	●	●	●	●
	●				N/S	●	●	●	●
●			●	●	N/S				
●	●	●	●	●	N	●	●	●	●
South Lake									
●			●	●	MINI-MAL				
●			●		MINI-MAL	●			

	Miles	Kilometers	Circle trip	Places to stop	Historic site	Geologic site	Fossils
Larrabees Point to Fort Ticonderoga	15	24	●	●	●		
Chipman Point to Benson Landing	12.5	20	●	●	●		
Whitehall to Benson Landing	15	124			●	●	
South Bay	9	15	●				

▶ **Paddle Matrix**

Marshes	Cliffs	Exceptional Wildlife	Parks	Museum or Interpretive	Wind Exposure	Other places of interest	Restrooms	Food	PT
●				●	MINI-MAL				
●	●				MINI-MAL				
●	●	●		●	MINI-MAL				
●	●				MINI-MAL				

Lake Champlain Public Launch Sites

These public launch sites on Lake Champlain are suitable for launching paddle boats. In areas where there are no convenient public launch sites, we have listed nearby marinas. Sites that require a fee are indicated with ($).

Champlain Islands
- Allen Point F&W Area (off Martin Rd., South Hero, VT)
- Whites Beach (West Shore Rd., South Hero, VT)
- Keeler Bay F&W Area (Rt. 2, Keeler Bay, South Hero, VT)
- Vantines F&W Area (West Shore Rd., Grand Isle, VT)
- Apple Island Marina ($, Rt. 2, South Hero, VT)
- Grand Isle State Park ($, State Park Rd. off Rt. 2, Grand Isle, VT)
- Grand Isle Town Beach (East Shore Rd. North in Pearl Bay, Grand Isle, VT)
- East side of Rt. 2 just north of drawbridge (unmarked, Rt. 2, North Hero, VT)
- Knight Point State Park ($, Rt. 2, North Hero, VT)
- Hero's Welcome ($, Rt. 2, North Hero village, VT)
- North Hero Marina ($, Pelots Point Rd., North Hero, VT)
- Kings Bay F&W Area, (Lake View Dr., North Hero, VT)
- Stoney Point F&W Area (also called Stephenson's Point, Lakeview Drive to North End Rd. East, North Hero, VT)
- North Hero State Park ($, 9 Lakeview Dr. to North Hero State Park Rd., North Hero)
- Horicon F&W Area (West Shore Rd., Alburgh, ½ mile north of Isle La Motte Bridge, Alburgh, VT)
- Alburgh Dunes State Park ($, Coon Point Rd., off Rt. 129, Alburgh, VT)

- Kelly Bay F&W Area (Rt. 2, adjacent to Rouses Point Bridge, Alburgh, VT)
- Alburgh Lakeshore Park (Trestle Rd., Alburgh, VT)
- Dillenbeck F&W Area (Rt. 2, Alburgh, VT east shore)
- Holcomb Bay–Labombard F&W Area (Access Rd. off Quarry Rd., Isle La Motte, VT)
- Stoney Point F&W Area (West Shore Rd., Isle La Motte, VT)

Inland Sea & Missisquoi Bay
- Philipsburg Public Wharf (Canadian Customs, Rt. 133 to Avenue Montgomery, Philipsburg, Quebec)
- Venise-en-Quebec Public Wharf (Rt. 202, Avenue de Venise, Venise-en-Quebec)
- Sedant Marine ($, Canadian Customs, Rt. 202, Avenue de Venise, Venise-en-Quebec)
- West Swanton F&W Area (Rt. 78 adjacent to Missisquoi Bridge, VT)
- Louie's Landing (Missisquoi Wildlife Refuge, on Rt. 78, Swanton, VT)
- Mac's Bend Missisquoi NWR Access (open September–mid-December, 1 mile on side road from Louie's Landing, off Route 78, Swanton, VT)
- Charcoal Creek F&W Area (car-top launch only, corner of Campbell Bay Rd. & VT 78, Swanton, VT)
- Tabor Point F&W Area (Tabor Rd. off VT Rt. 78, Swanton, VT)
- Swanton Beach (Rt. 36, corner of Lake Street, Maquam Shore Rd., Swanton, VT)

- Highgate Springs Town Park (Shipyard Rd. off Old Dock Rd., Highgate Springs, VT)
- Rock River F&W Area, (US Rt. 7, Spring St., Highgate, VT)
- Kill Kare State Park ($, Hathaway Point Rd. off Rt. 36, St. Albans, VT)
- Saint Albans Bay F&W Area (Hathaway Point Rd. off VT Rt. 36, St. Albans, VT)
- Georgia Municipal Recreation Park (Georgia Shore Rd., Georgia, VT)
- Van Everest F&W Area (Lake Rd., Milton, VT)
- Sandbar State Park ($, Rt. 2, Milton)
- Sandbar F&W Area (Rt. 2, Milton, serves both Inland Sea and Malletts Bay)

Malletts Bay

- Sandbar F&W Area (Rt. 2, Milton, VT)
- Malletts Bay F&W Area (Lakeshore Dr., Colchester, VT)
- Marble Island Resort and Marina ($, Marble Island Rd., Colchester, VT)
- Jake's Malletts Bay Marina ($, Lakeshore Drive, Colchester)
- Rossetti Natural Area (Junction of Rt. 127 and Holly Cross Rd., Colchester, VT; ¼ mile walk between parking area and beach)

Broad Lake East

- Colchester Point F&W Area (Windmere Way, on Winooski River, Colchester, VT)
- Auer Family Boat House ($, end of North Ave., Burlington, VT)
- Leddy Beach ($, Leddy Beach Rd. off North Ave., Burlington, VT)
- North Beach ($, Institute Rd., off North Ave., Burlington, VT)
- Burlington Community Sailing Center (Lake St., Burlington, VT)

- Perkins Pier ($ for nonresidents, Maple St., Burlington, VT)
- Burlington Waterfront Park Boat Launch (adjacent to Coast Guard Station, VT)
- Blanchard Beach (near Oakledge Park, Flynn Ave., Burlington, VT)
- Red Rocks Park Beach (Central Ave. off Queen City Park Rd., South Burlington, VT)
- Shelburne Bay F&W Area (Bay Rd., Shelburne, VT)
- Shelburne Town Beach (residents only in season, off Beach Rd., Shelburne, VT)
- Converse Bay F&W Area (Converse Bay Rd., Charlotte, VT)
- Ferrisburg Town Beach (Town Beach Rd., off Sand Rd., Ferrisburg, VT)
- South Slang F&W Area (Little Otter Creek, Hawkins Rd., Ferrisburg, VT)
- Lewis Creek F&W Area (off Lewis Creek Rd., Ferrisburg, VT)
- Fort Cassin F&W Area (Fort Cassin Rd., Ferrisburg, VT)
- Kingsland Bay Town Beach (Town Beach Rd. off Sand Rd., Ferrisburg, VT)
- Button Bay State Park ($, Webster Rd. to Button Bay Rd., Vergennes, VT)
- Arnold Bay Boat Launch (Adams Ferry Rd., Panton, VT)
- Chimney Point F&W Area (VT Rt. 17, Addison, VT)

Broad Lake North and West

- Rouses Point Boat Launch (Montgomery St. off Rt. 2, Rouses Point, NY)
- Stony Point Breakwater (Stony Point Rd., off Rt. 9B, Rouses Point, NY)
- Great Chazy River NY Boat Launch (off Rt. 9B, ¼ mile south of Coopersville, NY)
- Point au Roche NY Boat Launch at Chellis (Dickson Point Rd. off Point

au Roche Rd. off Rt. 9, NY)
- Point au Roche State Park ($, Point au Roche Rd. off Rt. 9, NY)
- Cumberland Head Ferry Landing (Rt. 314, NY)
- Cumberland Bay State Park, Plattsburgh Municipal Beach ($, Rt. 314, Plattsburgh, NY)
- Lung Healthy Trail and Wilcox Dock (Cumberland Ave., Plattsburgh, NY)
- Dock St. Landing & Waterfront Park (off Bridge St., Plattsburgh, NY)
- Peru NY Boat Launch (Rt. 9, Peru, NY)
- Ausable Point Public Campground and Day Use Area ($, Rt. 9 to Ausable Point Rd., NY)
- Port Kent Ferry Dock (Rt. 373, Port Kent, NY)
- Port Douglas NY Boat Launch (Rt. 16, Port Douglas, NY)
- Willsboro Bay NY Boat Launch (Boat Launch Rd. off Rt. 27 east side of bay, Willsboro, NY)
- Indian Bay Marina ($, East Bay Rd., Willsboro, NY)
- Noblewood ($, south of Willsboro on Rt. 22, NY)
- Beggs Park, (Lake St., ¼ mile south of ferry dock, Essex, NY)
- Westport NY Boat Launch (Rt. 22. north of Westport, NY)
- Lee Park Playground and Nature Walk (Washington St., off Rt. 9, VERY STEEP road, Westport, NY)
- Port Henry NY Launch (off Rt. 9N just north of Port Henry, NY; if approaching from the north, the sign is after the launch site.)

South Lake

- McCuen Slang F&W Area (Rt. 125, Addison, VT)
- Bridport Town Boat Launch (Jones Dock Rd., Bridport, VT, down a steep gravel incline that looks like the private driveway to houses)
- Lapham Bay F&W Area (off Lapham Bay Rd., Shoreham, VT—navigational maps call this Lapans Bay; Vermont calls it Lapham Bay)
- Larrabees Point F&W Area (VT Rt. 73 off Rt. 74, Shoreham, VT)
- Chipman Point Marina ($, at the end of Chipman Point Rd., Orwell, VT)
- Chipman Point F&W Area (at the end of Chipman Point Rd., Orwell, VT, small parking area beyond marina parking area, marked by Vermont bulletin board)
- Singing Cedars F&W Area (Singing Cedars Rd., Orwell, VT)
- Benson Landing F&W Area (West Lake Rd., Benson, VT)
- Monitor Bay Park (Monitor Bay Rd. off Station Rd. off Rt. 9, Crown Point)
- Ticonderoga NY Boat Launch (adjacent to Ft. Ticonderoga ferry dock, Rt. 74, Ticonderoga, NY)
- Lock 12 Marina ($, N. Williams St., Whitehall, NY)
- NY State Launch (Rt. 22 north of Whitehall, NY)

Places to Visit

Museums, Historic Places, Wildlife Areas, State Parks

New York
- **Adirondack Park locations on Lake Champlain.** visitadirondacks.com/home/park.cfm. Ausable Point—3346 Lake Shore Road, Peru, NY, 12972, www.dec.ny.gov/outdoor/24452.html
- **Cole Island, Crab Island, Schuyler Island, Valcour Island**
- **Fort Ticonderoga.** 30 Fort Ticonderoga Rd., Ticonderoga, NY 12883, (518) 585-2821, www.fort-ticonderoga.org.
- **Kent-DeLord House Museum.** 17 Cumberland Ave., Plattsburgh, NY, 12901, (518) 561-1035, www.kentdelordhouse.org/kdinfo.html.
- **Mt. Defiance.** Ticonderoga, NY. Dir: from NY Rt. 22, turn west onto Montcalm St., left onto River Rd., then immediate right on Cossey St., left on Defiance St., right at sign for Mt. Defiance.
- **New York State Parks on Lake Champlain.** nysparks.state.ny.us/parks/. Cumberland Bay, Point au Roche.
- **Noblewood Park.** On Bouquet River, Willsboro, NY, www.noblewoodpark.com/.
- **Port Henry Iron Center.** 16 Park Place, Port Henry, NY 12974, (518) 546-3587.
- **Crown Point State Historic Site.** 739 Bridge Road, Crown Point, NY 12928, (518) 597-4666, www.nysparks.com/sites/info.asp?siteID=8.
- **Skenesborough Museum.** Skenesborough Drive (off Route 4), Whitehall, New York.
- **Split Rock Mountain.** Westport, NY, www.lclt.org/guidesplitrock.htm.

Vermont
- **Chimney Point State Historic Site.** 7305 VT Route 125, Addison, VT 05491, (802) 759-2412, www.historicvermont.org/chimneypoint.
- **Ed Weed Fish Culture Station.** Rt. 314, Grand Isle.
- **Fisk Quarry.** Isle La Motte, www.ilmpt.org/preserves.html.
- **Goodsell Ridge Fossil Preserve.** Isle La Motte, www.ilmpt.org/preserves.html.
- **Missisquoi Wildlife Refuge and Visitor Center.** 29 Tabor Rd., Swanton, VT 05488, 802-868-4781, www.fws.gov/refuges/profiles/index.cfm?id=53520.
- **Mt. Independence State Historic Site.** 7305 VT Route 125, Addison, VT 05491, (802) 948-2000, www.historicvermont.org/mountindependence.
- **Shelburne Farms.** http://www.shelburnefarms.org, 1611 Harbor Rd., Shelburne, VT 05482
- **Vermont State Parks on Lake Champlain.** http://www.vtstateparks.com. Alburgh Dunes, Burton Island, Button Bay, DAR, Grand Isle, Kill Kare, Knight Island, Knight Point, Kingsland Bay, Niquette Bay, North Hero, Sandbar, Woods Island.
- **Winooski Park District.** Winooski Valley Park District, Ethan Allen Homestead, Burlington, VT 05408, (802) 863-5744, www.wvpd.org.

Glossary

ALGAE: A large group of primitive plants ranging from microscopic floating, single-cell, planktonic to some forms of what we call seaweed. They can be normal, essential elements of the food chain.

ALGAE BLOOM: A change in the algae as a result of temperature, light, nutrients, and other factors. Too much algae can deplete oxygen, affecting fish and other organisms.

ASHERY: A place where hardwood was burned and the ashes made into potash or lye.

DUCKWEED: This free-floating, smallest flowering plant grows in slow-moving or still water.

EFFLUENT: An outflow of water mixed with solid or liquid waste.

EUTROPHICATION: An increase of nutrients in the water, resulting in excessive plant growth, a lowering of water quality, and lack of oxygen.

FETCH: The length of water over which the wind blows. The length of the fetch affects the size of the waves that can build in wind.

FRESNEL: A lighter, thinner series of attached lens developed in the 1820s, which allowed more light to shine through and extended the distance over which lighthouse warnings could be seen.

GUNNEL: This shortened form of gunwale (the upper edge of a boat's side) is the rigid structure forming the top of the side of a boat.

LEE: The side or area that is sheltered from the wind.

INTERNAL SEICHE: Cyclic oscillations of subsurface water that result from gravitational force on water displaced by the wind. A subsurface wave action that continues to move after the cause, usually wind, ceases to exist.

JETSAM: Debris that is deliberately thrown overboard.

MILFOIL: An invasive submersed plant that grows upward, toward the water surface, and is characterized by whorled feathery leaves on long stems.

PADDLE FLOAT: A foam or inflatable device that, when attached to one paddle blade while the other blade is attached to the kayak, can be used as an outrigger.

PHRAGMYTES: A highly invasive, aggressive reed that can quickly take over marshland. This tall reed grows thickly and resists eradication.

REMEDIATE: Means to correct an issue or problem. In the case of Lake Champlain, often used when referring to cleaning up the lake and reversing undesirable conditions in the lake.

RIGHT OF WAY: Rules about passing and overtaking on the water. Paddle craft must avoid causing other boats to get into trouble. In narrow channels, kayaks or canoes should stay out of the main channel if they can safely operate in shallow water. When being overtaken from behind, the paddler should maintain speed and allow the overtaking boat to pass on the left. It is the responsibility of the overtaking boat to avoid the overtaken boat, but paddlers should never assume that this rule works with powerboats, because paddlers may be invisible to some of them. When meeting another boat, paddlers should move to the right to let the oncoming boat pass to the left, unless doing so puts one in danger. When the course of two boats will cross, the paddler on the right must give way. Above all, paddlers must assume that they will not be seen by other boats and must therefore behave defensively.

ROCK SNOT: (Didymosphenia geminata or didymo): Single-cell algae that in shallow and warmer water can form large mats on the bottom of streams and lakes. It may be damaging to fish habitat and food sources. Its appearance is as unattractive as its name implies.

SPONSONS: Inflatable, flexible cylinders that can be attached to both sides of the kayak for additional stability.

SPRAY SKIRTS: A barrier to prevent water from getting inside a kayak, made from a roughly doughnut-shaped waterproof fabric, trimmed to fit the opening of a kayak on the outside with a mechanism for snuggling to the waist of the wearer in the hole in the center.

SURFICIAL: Something that occurs on the surface.

WATER CHESTNUT: Rooted, floating, aquatic, invasive plant that forms mats of leaves on the surface of the water.

Bibliography

Books
- Albers, Jan. *Hands On the Land*. Cambridge, Mass.: MIT Press, 2000.
- Anderson, Fred. *Crucible of War*. New York: Vintage Books, 2001.
- Bassett, Elizabeth. *Nature Walks in Northern Vermont and the Champlain Valley*. Boston: Appalachian Mountain Club Books, 1998.
- Bellico, Russell P. *Chronicles of Lake Champlain: Journeys in War and Peace*. Fleischmanns, N.Y.: Purple Mountain Press, 1999.
- ———. *Sails and Steam in the Mountains*. Revised edition. Fleischmanns, N.Y.: Purple Mountain Press, 2001.
- Calloway, Colin G. *The Western Abenakis of Vermont, 1600–1800*. Norman, Okla.: University of Oklahoma Press, 1990.
- Carlough, Peter. *Bygone Burlington*. Burlington, Vt.: Printed by Queen City Printers, Inc., 1976.
- Chambers, Capt. William. *Atlas of Lake Champlain 1779–1780*. Bennington and Montpelier, Vt.: Vermont Heritage Press Inc. and Vermont Historical Society, 1984.
- Chittenden County Regional Planning Commission. *Explore Shelburne Bay, an Interpretive Water Trail*. Oct. 10, 2008. www.lcbp.org/PDFs/ShelburneBay-Brochure.pdf.
- Clark, Peg. *Memories of the Ups and Downs on the Island Line*. Burlington, Vt.: Printed by Hard Copy, 2003.
- Clifford, George. *Lake Champlain Lighthouses*. 2nd edition. Plattsburgh, N.Y.: Studley Printing & Publishing, Inc., 2005.
- Coffin, Howard, Will Curtis, and Jane Curtis. *Guns over the Champlain Valley, A Guide to Historic Military Sites and Battlefields*. Woodstock, Vt.: The Countryman Press, 2005.
- Cohn, Arthur B. *Lake Champlain's Sailing Canal Boats*. Basin Harbor, Vt.: Lake Champlain Maritime Museum, 2003.
- Consulting Archaeology Program, University of Vermont. *An Introduction to Vermont Archaeology*. Burlington, Vt.: 2003.
- Coolidge, Guy Omeron. *The French Occupation of the Champlain Valley from 1609 to 1759*. Fleischmanns, N.Y.: Purple Mountain Press, 1999.
- Dann, Kevin. *Lewis Creek Lost and Found*. Hanover and London: University Press of New England, 2001.
- Demarest, Amy B. *This Lake Alive*. Shelburne, Vt.: The Stewardship Institute of Shelburne Farms, 1997.
- Downs, Jack. *Kayak and Canoe Paddles in the New York Champlain Valley*. Trail-Marker Book, 2004.
- Everest, Allan S. *Point Au Fer on Lake Champlain*. Plattsburgh, N.Y.: Clinton County Historical Association, 1992.
- Fischer, David Hackett. *Champlain's Dream*. New York, London, Toronto, Sydney: Simon & Schuster, 2008.
- Fisher, Donald W. *Geology of the Plattsburgh and Rouses Point, New York–Vermont, Quadrangles*. Albany, N.Y.: The University of the State of New York, 1968.
- Fisher, Lori, Jeff Meyers, and Mike Winslow. *The Lake Champlain Paddlers' Trail, 2008 Guidebook & Stewardship Manual*. 10th edition. Burlington, Vt.: The Lake Champlain Committee, 2008.
- Hill, Ralph Nading. *Lake Champlain: Key to Liberty*. Woodstock, Vt.: Countryman Press, 1987.

- James, Henry. *Lake George to Burlington*. Burlington, Vt.: Rumble Press, 1991.
- Johnson, Charles W. *The Nature of Vermont*. Hanover, N.H.: University Press of New England, 1980, 1998.
- Johnson, Shelley. *The Complete Sea Kayaker's Handbook*. Camden, Me.: Ragged Mountain Press / McGraw-Hill, 2002.
- Jones, Robert C. *Railroads of Vermont Volume II*. Shelburne, Vt.: The New England Press, 1993.
- Lake Champlain Basin Program. *State of the Lake and Ecosystems Indicators Report, 2008*. Grand Isle, Vt.: 2008.
- Lake Champlain Land Trust. *A Portrait of the Lake Champlain Islands*. Burlington, Vt.: 1979.
- Lake Champlain Maritime Museum. *Canal Schooner Lois McClure, A Memento of the 2004 Inaugural Tour*. Burlington, Vt.: Queen City Printers Inc., 2004.
- Lipke, William, ed. Shelburne Farms: *The History of an Agricultural Estate*. Burlington, Vt.: Robert Hull Fleming Museum, University of Vermont, 1979.
- Matthews, Alex, and Ken Whiting. *Touring & Sea Kayaking*. Beachburg, Ontario: The Heliconia Press, 2006.
- McKibben, Alan, and Susan McKibben. *Cruising Guide to the Hudson River, Lake Champlain & the St. Lawrence River*. Burlington, Vt.: Lake Champlain Publishing Company, 2001.
- Meeks, Harold A. *Vermont's Land and Resources*. Shelburne, Vt.: The New England Press, 1986.
- Palmer, Peter. *History of Lake Champlain from Its First Exploration by the French in 1609 to the Close of the Year 1814*. New York: Frank F. Lovell & Company, n.d.
- Raymo, Chet, and Maureen E. Raymo. *Written in Stone, A Geological History of the Northeastern United States*. Hensonville, N.Y.: Black Dome Press Corp., 1989.
- Roberts, Kenneth. *Rabble in Arms*. Camden, Me.: Down East Books, 1933, 1947.
- Shaughnessy, Jim. *Delaware & Hudson*. Berkeley, Calif.: Howell-North Books, 1967.
- Stratton, Allen L. *History of the South Hero Island, Being the Towns of South Hero and Grand Isle Vermont, Vol. I*. Burlington, Vt.: Queen City Printers Inc., 1980.
- Swift, Ester Munroe. *Vermont Place Names, Footprints of History*. Camden, Me.: Picton Press, 1977, 1996.
- Thompson, Elizabeth, and Eric R. Sorenson. *Wetland, Woodland, Wildland, A Guide to the Natural Communities of Vermont*. Vermont Department of Fish and Wildlife and The Nature Conservancy: 2000.
- VanDiver, Bradford B. *Roadside Geology of Vermont and New Hampshire*. Missoula, Mont.: Mountain Press Publishing Company, 1987.
- Vogel, R. W. *Lake Champlain Atlas of Navigational Charts*. Burlington, Vt.: Lake Champlain Publishing Company, 2007.
- Warren, Susan. *A Key to Common Vermont Aquatic Plant Species*. Waterbury, Vt.: Lakes and Ponds Unity, Water Quality Division, Vermont Department of Environmental Conservation.
- Welby, Charles W. *Paleontology of the Champlain Basin in Vermont*. Montpelier, Vt.: Vermont Geological Survey and Vermont Development Department, 1962.

- Whitson, Peggy Hanford. *Once Upon a Rowboat: Adventures on Lake Champlain.* Burlington, Vt.: Whithaven Enterprises, 1986.
- Winslow, Mike. *Lake Champlain, A Natural History.* Burlington, Vt.: Lake Champlain Committee, 2008.

Maps
- *Lake Champlain, NY & VT — North.* Wareham, MA: Navionics Inc., 2006.
- *Lake Champlain, NY & VT — South.* Wareham, MA: Navionics Inc., 2006.
- *Lake Champlain.* Amesbury, MA: Maptech Inc., 2005.

Newspaper Articles
- Page, Candace. Numerous thoroughly researched and well-written articles. *Burlington Free Press.*

Web sites
- *Fossils of the Champlain Valley.* Article for VGS files, author unknown. 1990. http://www.anr.state.vt.us/DEC/GEO/foschamp.htm.
- *Grand Isle Lake House.* 20 Oct. 2008. www.grandislelakehouse.com.
- *Isle La Motte Preservation Trust.* 20 Oct. 2008. www.ilmpt.org.
- *Lake Champlain Basin Program.* 20 Oct. 2008. http://www.lcbp.org, http://www.lcbp.org/atlas/index.htm.
- *Lake Champlain Land Trust.* 20 Oct. 2008 http://www.lclt.org.

- *Lake Champlain Lighthouses. Lighthouse Friends.* 20 Oct. 2008. http://www.lighthousefriends.com.
- *Manchester, Lee. "Historic Willboro Point." Lake Placid News. 17 Sept. 2004.* http://aarch.org/archives/leeman/040917a%20VLP%20Willsboro%20Point.pdf.
- *Mason, D.L., D. W. Folger, R. S. Haupt, R. R. McGirr, W. H. Hoyt. Distribution of Pollutants from a new paper plant in southern Lake Champlain, Vermont and New York. pp. 341–347. Environmental Geology. Nov. 15, 1977. Heidelberg: Springer Berlin. 20 Oct. 2008.* http://www.springerlink.com/content/9u5x8p6746412x50/.
- *Millard, James. p. 20. Oct. 2008.* http://www.historiclakes.org.
- *Northern Forest Canoe Trail. 20 Oct. 2008.* http://www.northernforestcanoetrail.org.
- *Pine Street Barge Canal. 20 Oct. 2008.* http://www.lcbp.org/Wayside/PDFS/Pine_Street/Pine_Street.pdf.
- *Shipwrecks: War of 1812 Wrecks. 20 Oct. 2008.* http://www.lcmm.org/shipwrecks_history/shipwrecks_history.htm.
- *Split Rock Mountain Trails. 20 Oct. 2008.* http://www.lclt.org/guidesplitrock.htm.

About the Authors

Cathy Frank is a former, long-time instructor at the Community College of Vermont and currently is an independent computer consultant and Web site designer. She has been a member and chairperson of numerous nonprofit boards on the local and regional level. A long-time summer resident of the Champlain Islands, she is an avid biker, hiker, swimmer, and cross-country skier. She kayaks daily in the summer and has hiked the length of Vermont's Long Trail.

Margy Holden has worked for nonprofit and for-profit corporations, and as an organizational development and career consultant. She has chaired and participates in a number of nonprofit boards. She writes occasional articles and coauthored the *Women's Job Search Handbook*. Happiest when she is outdoors, Margy runs, hikes, bikes, paddles, and swims in the Champlain Islands in the summer and the Bahamas in the winter.

Margy's and Cathy's travels on Lake Champlain have been featured as presentation before numerous organizations, on television, and in the local press. Both women are committed to promoting a heightened awareness of Lake Champlain, its strengths, and its issues.

Cathy Frank and Margy Holden.

Index

Page numbers in italics indicate illustrations.